ARCO

MASTER THE

COURT OFFICER

EXAM

10th Edition

Jeffrey P. Rush, D.P.A.
Karen McGuffee, J.D.
William McGuffee

THOMSON
PETERSON'S

Australia • Canada • Mexico • Singapore • Spain • United Kingdom • United States

THOMSON

PETERSON'S

An ARCO Book

ARCO is a registered trademark of Thomson Learning, Inc., and is used herein under license by Thomson Peterson's.

About Thomson Peterson's

Thomson Peterson's (www.petersons.com) is a leading provider of education information and advice, with books and online resources focusing on education search, test preparation, and financial aid. Its Web site offers searchable databases and interactive tools for contacting educational institutions, online practice tests and instruction, and planning tools for securing financial aid. Thomson Peterson's serves 110 million education consumers annually.

Petersons.com/publishing

Check out our Web site at www.petersons.com/publishing to see if there is any new information regarding the test and any revisions or corrections to the content of this book. We've made sure the information in this book is accurate and up-to-date; however, the test format or content may have changed since the time of publication.

For more information, contact Thomson Peterson's, 2000 Lenox Drive, Lawrenceville, NJ 08648; 800-338-3282; or find us on the World Wide Web at www.petersons.com/about.

Editor: Joseph Krasowski; Production Editor: Susan W. Dilts; Manufacturing Manager: Ray Golaszewski; Composition Manager: Linda M. Williams

ISBN 0-7689-2234-8

Printed in the United States of America

10 9 8 7 6 5 4 3 2 1   08 07 06

Tenth Edition

Contents

Before You Begin. 1

How This Book Is Organized 1

Special Study Features 1

You're Well on Your Way to Success 2

Top 10 Ways to Raise Your Score 3

PART I: ALL ABOUT A CAREER AS A COURT OFFICER

1   Getting Started. **7**

A Career as a Court Officer 7

The Application Process 24

Summing It Up 35

2   Preparing for the Exams **37**

Written Exam 37

Promotion Exams 56

Medical Exam 56

Physical Ability Exam 56

Psychological Interview 57

Background Investigation 57

Summing It Up 58

PART II: FIVE PRACTICE TESTS

Practice Test 1 . . . . **63**

Answer Key and Explanations 77

Contents

Practice Test 2 . . . . **83**
 Answer Key and Explanations 98
Practice Test 3 . . . . **105**
 Answer Key and Explanations 123
Practice Test 4 . . . . **131**
 Answer Key and Explanations 152
Practice Test 5: Promotion Exam **161**
 Answer Key and Explanations 175

APPENDIXES

A **Civil Practice Law and Rules** **185**
 Selected Articles and Sections of the Civil
 Practice Law and Rules 186

B **Criminal Procedure Law** **191**
 Selected Articles and Sections of the
 Criminal Procedure Law 194
 Prosecution of Indictments 206
 Prosecution of Information 207

C **Judiciary Court Acts** **211**
 Selected Articles and Sections of the Family
 Court Act of the Judiciary Court Acts 213

D **Penal Law** **221**
 Selected Articles and Sections of the Penal Law 223

E **Glossary of Legal Terms** **229**

Before You Begin

HOW THIS BOOK IS ORGANIZED

You want to pass this test. That's why you bought this book. Used correctly, this self-tutor will show you what to expect and will give the most effective review of the subjects you can expect to see on the actual exam. *ARCO Master the Court Officer Exam* will provide you with the necessary tools to make the most of the study time you have, including:

- **Top 10 Ways to Raise Your Score** gives you a preview of some of the test-taking strategies you'll learn in the book.

- **Part I** provides career information about court officers, senior court officers, and court clerks, along with information about the application and examination processes.

- **Part II** includes five full-length practice tests followed by detailed answer explanations.

- The **Appendixes** contain reference materials, including Civil Practice Law and Rules, Criminal Procedure Law, the Family Court Act of the Judiciary Court Acts, Penal Law, and a Glossary of Legal Terms. It is impossible to include all necessary information in one book. You will find much that is very useful, but the complete laws are not included here. You will have to refer to some law books yourself. The listing of topics for each law that we have provided should help you plan your time in the library, so that you know what to look for and where to find it.

SPECIAL STUDY FEATURES

ARCO Master the Court Officer Exam is designed to be as user-friendly as it is complete. To this end, it includes several features to make your preparation much more efficient.

Overview

Each chapter begins with a bulleted overview listing the topics to be covered in the chapter. This will allow you to quickly target the areas in which you are most interested.

Summing It Up

Each chapter ends with a point-by-point summary that captures the most important points contained in the chapter. This is a convenient way to review key points.

Bonus Information

As you work your way through the book, keep your eye on the margins to find bonus information and advice. Information can be found in the following forms:

NOTE

Notes highlight critical information about a career as a court officer, senior court officer, or court clerk and the written exam.

TIP

Tips provide valuable advice for effectively handling the job-search process and the written exam.

ALERT!

Alerts do just what they say—alert you to common pitfalls or misconceptions.

YOU'RE WELL ON YOUR WAY TO SUCCESS

You have made the decision to pursue a career as a court officer. *ARCO Master the Court Officer Exam* will prepare you for the steps you'll need to take to achieve your goal—from understanding the nuances of the job to scoring high on the Court Officer Exam. Good luck!

Top 10 Ways to Raise Your Score

1. **Get to the test center early.** Make sure you give yourself plenty of extra time to get there, park your car, if necessary, and even grab a cup of coffee before the test.

2. **Listen to the test monitors and follow their instructions carefully.**

3. **Read every word of the instructions. Read every word of every question.**

4. **Mark your answers by completely darkening the answer space of your choice.**

5. **Mark only ONE answer for each question, even if you think that more than one answer is correct.** You must choose only one. If you mark more than one answer, the scoring machine will record your answer as wrong.

6. **If you change your mind, erase completely.** Leave no doubt as to which answer you mean.

7. **Check often to be sure that the question number matches the answer space—that you have not skipped a space by mistake.**

8. **Stay alert.** Be careful not to mark a wrong answer just because you were not concentrating.

9. **Do not panic.** If you cannot finish any part before time is up, do not worry. If you are accurate, you can do well even without finishing. It is even possible to earn a scaled score of 100 without entirely finishing an exam part if you are very accurate. At any rate, do not let your performance on any one part affect your performance on any other part.

10. **Check and recheck, time permitting.** If you finish any part before time is up, use the remaining time to check that each question is answered in the right space and that there is only one answer for each question. Return to the difficult questions and rethink them.

PART I

ALL ABOUT A CAREER AS A COURT OFFICER

CHAPTER 1   Getting Started

CHAPTER 2   Preparing for the Exams

Getting Started

OVERVIEW

- A career as a court officer
- The application process
- Summing it up

A CAREER AS A COURT OFFICER

There must be order in the court. Without order, witnesses cannot testify, attorneys cannot cross-examine, jurors cannot concentrate, and judges cannot deliberate. The title and additional duties of the person who keeps order in the court vary from system to system and from jurisdiction to jurisdiction. Whether the person is titled court officer, bailiff, court attendant, deputy sheriff, or U.S. marshal, it is their job to maintain order in the court. The judge orders it, the officer carries it out. These officers control the atmosphere and decorum of the courtroom, maintain the integrity of documents and exhibits, ensure the security of juries and see that they have optimum conditions under which to deliberate, and generally respond to the wishes of the judge.

Despite the importance of the court officer to the efficient running of a courtroom and a trial, like so many other positions in criminal justice, the pay is not commensurate with the duties and responsibilities. That said, it is one of the best jobs in criminal justice, and in larger court systems it is a career in itself. For those systems that require a test to be hired, to simply pass the test is not enough. A high score is essential to be appointed to the position of court officer. Likewise, high scores are necessary for the promotional exams for advancement in the position. This book is geared to help you earn those high scores.

If you are interested in entering this profession (or this part of the criminal justice profession), you must keep some things in mind. Not all systems have a separate career track known as court officer. The larger the system, the more likely will be the opportunity to specialize in this area. Smaller systems, and many in the South, use the local sheriff's office and/or appoint people to serve as court officers. In these situations, the court officer is almost always a sworn individual with arrest and other enforcement powers. It should be kept in mind, however, that in those systems in which the court officer is appointed by the presiding judge or by the judge for whom the individual works, the appointment is political. There is rarely, if ever, any kind of civil service protection afforded to these positions. Most judges serve in their position for many years and thus the court officer (should they so choose) will remain in service for the judge as well.

NOTE

In areas that use sheriff's deputies, often a deputy can choose to work as a court officer as part of his or her regular duties.

Few deputies like or appreciate the importance of court officer work, so the deputy who wants to do this will have little competition. The other benefit is that in these cases the deputy often rotates from courtroom to courtroom. This gives them the opportunity to be involved in a variety of different cases, work for a variety of judges, and receive a broader perspective than simply working years and years for the same judge or in the same kind of courtroom.

Being a court officer is an excellent job! It has varied duties, is often on the cutting edge of important cases, and is a relatively safe job (compared to other positions in criminal justice). It is worthy and deserving of the best possible candidates. This book is designed for those individuals.

Career Information Resources

Most federal, state, and municipal units have recruitment procedures for filling civil service positions. They have developed a number of methods to make job opportunities known. Places where such information may be obtained include:

1. **The offices of the State Employment Services.** There are almost 2,000 throughout the country. These offices are administered by the state in which they are located, with the financial assistance of the federal government. You will find the address of the one nearest you in your telephone book.

2. **Your state Civil Service Commission.** Address your inquiry to the capital city of your state.

3. **Your city Civil Service Commission.** It is sometimes called by another name, such as the Department of Personnel, but you will be able to identify it in your telephone directory under the listing of city departments.

4. **Your municipal building and your local library.**

5. **City and statewide publications devoted to civil service employees.** Many local newspapers run a section on regional civil service news.

6. **State and local agencies looking for competent employees.** They will contact schools, professional societies, veterans' organizations, unions, and trade associations.

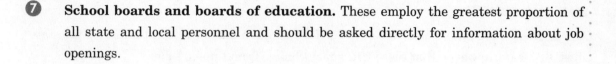

7   **School boards and boards of education.** These employ the greatest proportion of all state and local personnel and should be asked directly for information about job openings.

USEFUL WEB SITES

- *Career City* (www.careercity.com): A guide to federal and local government employment

- *Employment Index* (www.employmentindex.com/govjob.html): Links to Web sites of government agencies throughout the United States. Site lists both public- and private-sector jobs

- *Federal Job Search* (www.federaljobsearch.com): Listings for 40,000 U.S. jobs in the United States

- *FedWorld* (www.fedworld.gov): Provides searchable abstracts of federal government jobs

- *Government and Law Enforcement Jobs* (http://jobsearch.tqn.com/msubgov. htm): An annotated list of Web sites for jobs with federal, state, and local governments and law enforcement agencies

- *HRS Federal Job Search* (www.hrsjobs.com): A subscription job search and e-mail delivery service

- *The Internet Job Source* (www.statejobs.com): The federal jobs section of this site links users to job listings at a variety of federal agencies and also to online newspapers listing federal job opportunities

- *Public Services Employees Network* (www.pse-net.com): A guide to government employment, including job listings

- *USAJOBS* (www.usajobs.opm.gov): The official site for federal employment listings from the U.S. Office of Personnel Management

APPLICATIONS AND OTHER FORMS

- *Electronic forms* (www.opm.gov/forms): All forms and applications relating to federal employment from the Office of Personnel Management

- *The Federal Job Search and Application Form* (www.usajobs.opm.gov/forms): A description of the federal job search as a three-step process, including three downloadable versions of the OF-612 application

STATE EMPLOYMENT

Almost every state has its own Web site. The following is a list of the latest URLs for the state sites. Be aware, however, that these URLs may change from time to time.

Alabama: www.state.al.us

Alaska: www.state.ak.us

Arizona: http://az.gov/webapp/portal

Arkansas: www.state.ar.us

California: www.state.ca.us

Colorado: www.colorado.gov

Connecticut: www.ct.gov

Delaware: www.delaware.gov

District of Columbia:
www.dchomepage.net

Florida: www.myflorida.com

Georgia: www.georgia.gov

Hawaii: www.hawaii.gov/portal

Idaho: www.state.id.us

Illinois: www.illinois.gov

Indiana: www.state.in.us

Iowa: www.state.ia.us

Kansas: www.state.ks.us

Kentucky: http://kentucky.gov

Louisiana: www.louisiana.gov/wps/portal

Maine: www.state.me.us/

Maryland: www.maryland.gov

Massachusetts: www.mass.gov

Michigan: www.michigan.gov

Minnesota: www.state.mn.us/portal/mn/
jsp/home.do?agency=NorthStar

Mississippi: www.state.ms.us/index.jsp

Missouri: www.state.mo.us

Montana: www.mt.gov

Nebraska: www.nebraska.gov/index.phtml

Nevada: www.nv.gov

New Hampshire: www.state.nh.us

New Jersey: www.state.nj.us

New Mexico: www.state.nm.us

New York: www.state.ny.us

North Carolina: www.state.nc.us

North Dakota: www.nd.gov

Ohio: http://ohio.gov

Oklahoma: www.state.ok.us

Oregon: www.oregon.gov

Pennsylvania: www.state.pa.us

Rhode Island: www.state.ri.us

South Carolina: www.myscgov.com

South Dakota: www.state.sd.us

Tennessee: www.state.tn.us

Texas: www.state.tx.us

Utah: www.utah.gov

Vermont: http://vermont.gov

Virginia: www.virginia.gov/cmsportal

Washington: http://access.wa.gov

West Virginia: www.wv.gov

Wisconsin: www.wisconsin.gov

Wyoming: http://wyoming.gov

JOB DESCRIPTIONS

Court Officer (Bailiff, Court Attendant)

Court officers are responsible for maintaining courtroom security and protecting the judge, jury, and other participants during hearings and trials. Under the supervision of a judge or court administrator, court officers take charge of and escort juries, transfer prisoners, deliver case files, and perform various related services.

The work of a court officer involves providing general services in the operation of a court. It includes maintaining order, calling defendants and witnesses to the stand, and notifying attorneys and other interested parties during trial. Some of their time is spent in delivering court minutes, law books, supplies, forms, and similar items necessary for use by the judge and court staff. They also perform other errands inside and outside the courtroom. When not attending court sessions, they may perform incidental clerical tasks such as filling out forms and operating a copying machine to duplicate court calendars.

Court officers start the day by inspecting the courtroom for cleanliness, orderliness, and proper heat, light, and ventilation. Court sessions are opened by announcing the entrance of the judge. Order in the court is maintained, and jurors, witnesses, attorneys, news reporters, and spectators are seated in specific areas of the courtroom. Those who disturb the court's proceedings are ejected.

When necessary, food, lodging, and transportation are arranged for jurors, errands are run, and personal needs of jurors are taken care of when a jury is held overnight or longer. A court officer is responsible for the security of the jury during deliberations and, when those deliberations extend overnight, preventing jurors from having outside communication, thus avoiding a mistrial. Court officers escort jurors in and out of the courtroom before, during, and after trials; they not only accompany jurors to all meals but remain during the meal.

Job Requirements

To become a court officer, graduation from high school or the equivalent is required by the courts. In most states, appointment depends on passing a written and physical examination. The duties of these workers require the ability to understand and follow written instructions and to express themselves clearly and concisely, both orally and in writing. Tact and courtesy are also needed to deal effectively with the public, attorneys, witnesses, prisoners, and jurors. In addition, it is important to have knowledge of, or be experienced in, office practices, court procedures, and legal terminology and forms. In some courts, court officers are also expected to be skilled in the use of firearms.

Opportunities

Courts are expanding to keep pace with the need for their services, owing to the rising number of offenders and the desire of the courts and the public to speed up the handling of cases. The size

NOTE

Opportunities for court officers exist in the local, state, and federal courts, and employment is expected to increase as fast as the court system expands. Court officers employed in the larger courts may advance to supervisory positions, such as senior court officer or court clerk.

and number of courts have also increased over the past few years, and this growth is expected to continue.

Court Clerk

Court clerks serve as clerical assistants to circuit and other court judges, as supervisors of court clerks, and often as court administrators. They attend sessions of the court and enter information in the record about court proceedings, including witnesses' names, requests for rulings, verdicts reached, and other important facts. All documents brought to the court, including complaints, answers, attachments, executions, garnishments, orders to show cause, and restraining orders, are received by the court clerk, who makes sure that all requests affecting the progress of a case are properly handled.

The court clerk assists in preparation of the docket or calendar of cases to be called, depending on type of crime, priorities, or direction of the judge. All legal documents submitted to the court are examined for adherence to regulations. Case folders are prepared and legal documents concerned with the operation of the court are posted or filed or routed elsewhere. Other duties may include picking the names of prospective jurors, administering the oath to witnesses and jurors, and delivering subpoenas and court orders. The duties of court clerks also include explaining procedures about forms to parties in a case, contacting witnesses and attorneys to obtain information for the court, and instructing individuals about dates to appear in court. Case disposition, court orders, and judges' rulings are recorded and payment of fees arranged and sometimes collected.

Documents are checked not only for completeness of information but also to determine general case category and to assign a docket number. The need for signatures on documents is determined, action is taken to obtain signatures, and documents are stamped with the official court seal.

Other job duties include recording (by hand, typewriter, or computer) case-identification data and receipt of documents or court records. The clerks file cards, documents, and records according to date received or in alphabetical or numerical filing systems. In smaller courts, the court clerks type jury lists, prepare and mail jury notices, and assist in functions concerned with receipts and expenditures.

Job Requirements

High school graduation or the equivalent and two years of court officer or other court system experience are required. All court clerks must have knowledge of court procedures and policies, as well as of legal documents and laws. Some knowledge of court organization and its operations, functions, and scope of authority is also necessary. It is important that these workers have a good command of English and be able to deal effectively with legal personnel and the public.

Opportunities

Opportunities for court clerks exist in the local, state, and federal courts. Because of the rising number of offenders, courts are increasing both in number and size to keep pace not only with the need for services but to speed up handling of cases. This growth is expected to continue. Court clerks, especially in the larger courts, may advance to the position of chief court clerk.

Job Search

Now that you know where to look for a job, you need to understand the procedure. The procedure that you must follow to get a government job varies little from job to job and from one level of government to another. There are variations in details, of course, but certain steps are common to all.

NOTICE OF EXAMINATION OR ANNOUNCEMENT

When a position is open and a civil service examination is to be given, a job announcement is drawn up. This generally contains everything an applicant has to know about the job.

The announcement begins with the job title and salary. A typical announcement then describes the work, the location of the position, the education and experience requirements, the kind of examination to be given, and the system of rating. It may also have something to say about veteran preference and the age limit. It tells which application form is to be filled out, where to get the form, and where and when to file it.

Study the job announcement carefully. It will answer many of your questions and help you decide whether you like the position and are qualified for it. We have included sample job announcements later in this chapter.

There is no point in applying for a position and taking the examination if you do not want to work where the job is. The job may be in your community or hundreds of miles away at the other end of the state. If you are not willing to work where the job is, study other announcements that will give you an opportunity to work in a place of your choice.

The words **Optional Fields,** and sometimes just the word **Options,** may appear on the front page of the announcement. You then have a choice to apply for that particular position in which you are especially interested. This is because the duties of various positions are quite different even though they bear the same broad title. A public relations clerk, for example, does work that is different from a payroll clerk, although they are considered broadly in the same general area.

Not every announcement has options. But whether or not it has them, the precise duties are described in detail, usually under the heading, **Description of Work.** Make sure that these duties come within the range of your experience and ability.

TIP

A civil service job close to your home has an additional advantage, since local residents usually receive preference in appointments.

Most job requirements give a **deadline for filing** an application. Others bear the words, **No Closing Date** at the top of the first page; this means that applications will be accepted until the needs of the agency are met. In some cases a public notice is issued when a certain number of applications have been received. No application mailed past the deadline date will be considered.

Every announcement has a detailed section on **education and experience requirements** for the particular job and for the optional fields. Make sure that in both education and experience you meet the minimum qualifications. If you do not meet the given standards for one job, there may be others open where you stand a better chance of making the grade.

If the job announcement does not mention **veteran preference,** it would be wise to inquire if there is such a provision in your state or municipality. There may be none or it may be limited to disabled veterans. In some jurisdictions, surviving spouses of deceased veterans are given preference. All such information can be obtained through the agency that issues the job announcement.

Applicants may be denied examinations and eligible candidates may be denied appointments for any of the following reasons:

- intentional false statements
- deception or fraud in examination or appointment
- use of intoxicating beverages to the extent that ability to perform the duties of the position is impaired
- criminal, infamous, dishonest, immoral, or notoriously disgraceful conduct

The announcement describes the **kind of test** given for the particular position. Please pay special attention to this section. It tells what areas are to be covered in the written test and lists the specific subjects on which questions will be asked. Sometimes sample questions are given.

Usually the announcement states whether the examination is to be **assembled** or **unassembled.** In an assembled examination, applicants assemble in the same place at the same time to take a written or performance test. The unassembled examination is one where an applicant does not take a test; instead, he or she is rated on his or her education and experience and whatever records of past achievement the applicant is asked to provide.

In the competitive examination, all applicants for a position compete with each other; the better the mark, the better the chance of being appointed. Also, competitive examinations are given to determine desirability for promotion among employees. Civil service written tests are rated on a scale of 100, with 70 usually as the passing mark.

Sample Announcements

Career Opportunities in the New York State Unified Court System

Court Officer

THE OFFICE OF COURT ADMINISTRATION ANNOUNCES AN OPEN-COMPETITIVE EXAMINATION

TITLE

Court Officer Exam Number: 45-6:L2

Applicants Please Note: At the present time, there are approximately 950 court officer positions. All these positions are currently filled on a permanent basis. We expect to appoint approximately 150 court officers per year during the anticipated four-year life of the eligible list.

LOCATION OF POSITIONS
The Court Officer title exists in the Civil, Criminal, Family, and Surrogate's Courts in New York City and the District, Family, and Surrogate's Courts in Nassau, Suffolk, and Westchester Counties.

LOCATION OF TEST CENTERS
This examination will be held exclusively in New York City, Albany, Binghamton, Brentwood, Buffalo, Hicksville, Riverhead, Rochester, Syracuse, and White Plains.

STARTING SALARY
This title is graded at JG-16. Appointees may receive additional annual location pay.

MINIMUM QUALIFICATIONS
At the time of appointment, a court officer candidate must be at least 18 years old and possess a high school diploma or its equivalent. Candidates must be legally eligible to carry firearms. An unpardoned felon is ineligible to carry firearms under federal law 18 U.S.C. section 1202 (A) (1). No candidate will be eligible for appointment if he or she has ever been convicted of a felony.

APPLICATION FEE
A $10 money order filing fee must accompany your application.

CITIZENSHIP
Candidates must be citizens of the United States at the time of appointment.

RESIDENCE
Candidates must be residents of New York State for one year prior to the date of the examination as well as at the time of appointment.

DISTINGUISHING FEATURES OF WORK
Court Officers are responsible for maintaining order and providing security in court facilities. They work under the direct supervision of security supervisors and court clerks. Court Officers are peace officers, are required to wear uniforms, and may be authorized to carry firearms. They perform clerical duties while handling court documents and forms, and may coordinate the activities of other court-related duties.

SCOPE OF WRITTEN, MEDICAL, PHYSICAL ABILITY, AND PSYCHOLOGICAL EXAMINATIONS

Candidates who are successful on the written portion of the examination will be called, in order of their rank on the eligible list, to qualify on the medical, physical ability, and psychological examinations and undergo a background investigation.

WRITTEN EXAMINATION

The written examination will be multiple-choice and will assess a candidate's ability to:

1. *Read, Understand, and Interpret Written Material*—Candidates will be presented with brief reading selections followed by questions relating to the selections. All of the information required to answer the questions will be provided in the selections; candidates will not be required to have any special knowledge relating to the content area covered in the selections.

2. *Remember Facts and Information*—Candidates will be provided with a series of pictures and/or a description of an event or incident. After a brief period of time to review and study the description and/or pictures, the description and/or pictures will be removed from the candidates. Candidates will later be asked questions about the facts involved in the event or incident.

3. *Apply Facts and Information to Given Situations*—Candidates will be provided with facts and information and will be asked questions that require the application of these facts and information to specific actions that should be taken in a given situation.

4. *Recognize and Size Up Written Information*—Candidates will be presented with written information designed to assess skills and abilities necessary to quickly and accurately recognize and size up verbal and numerical materials, to perceive differences in small details, and to classify and code information presented under timed conditions. Candidates will not be required to have any special knowledge of the content of the material presented.

MEDICAL EXAMINATION

Each candidate is required to be free of any medical impairment that would jeopardize his or her safety, health, or ability to carry out effectively the duties of the position. Candidates are required to meet the medical requirements both at the time of the medical examination and at the time of appointment. A partial list of the medical standards is shown below:

1. *Hearing*—Each candidate must be able to pass an audiometric test of hearing acuity in both ears. The average hearing loss in the voice frequency ranges of 500, 1,000, 2,000, and 3,000 Hz should not be greater than 30 decibels. Also, for the frequency ranges of 4,000, 6,000, and 8,000 Hz, the average hearing loss should not be greater than 35 decibels.

2. *Vision*—Each candidate must have at least 20/40 vision in each eye and have at least 20/30 vision using both eyes (corrective lenses or glasses are permitted). However, each candidate must have at least 20/70 vision using both eyes without correction. The visual fields must not be less than 145, and color vision is also required. Both near and far vision are tested. Vision will be tested with and without corrective lenses, including contacts.

3. *Cardiovascular System*—Candidates must be free of impairment due to organic heart disease resulting from failure of myocardial function and impairment of coronary circulatory function. Candidates are examined for hypertensive vascular disease and for vascular diseases affecting the extremities. Blood pressure should not exceed 146/90.

Candidates will be evaluated on an individual basis relevant to the physical demands of the job.

4. *Alcohol or Drug Abuse*—Candidates must not be dependent on or abuse alcohol or drugs. Candidates are required to submit to a comprehensive drug screening evaluation.

PHYSICAL EXAMINATION

Each candidate will be required to qualify on a series of physical tests designed to assess a candidate's ability to perform the physically demanding tasks required by the job. Minimum qualifying scores are required for each of the following five categories: strength/muscular endurance, coordination/equilibrium, arm-hand steadiness, flexibility, and stamina/aerobic fitness.

PSYCHOLOGICAL EXAMINATION

Each candidate will be required to undergo a psychological assessment designed to test for emotional or psychological problems that might interfere with effectively carrying out the duties of the position.

BACKGROUND INVESTIGATION

Each candidate will be investigated with respect to employment history, educational qualifications, military service record, arrest and summons record, and other pertinent factors deemed important to the performance of required job duties.

Important Information to All Candidates

APPLICATION FORMS

How to File for the Examination

An application fee is being charged to file for this examination. The application must be accompanied by a money order made payable to N.Y.S. Office of Court Administration. Neither checks nor cash will be accepted. The applications must be postmarked no later than the close of filing and mailed to:

State of New York, Unified Court System
Office of Court Administration
P.O. Box 1879
Albany, New York 12201

Applications and fees not submitted in accordance with the above requirements will be returned unprocessed.

HOW TO OBTAIN AN APPLICATION PACKAGE

By Mail—To obtain an application by mail, you must submit a self-addressed, 9-inch by 12-inch envelope with sufficient postage to:

State of New York
Office of Court Administration
P.O. Box 2951 Church Street Station
New York, New York 10008

Only one application package will be sent for each self-addressed stamped envelope received. Requests for application packages that do not have the correct amount of postage and/or are received less than ten days before the close of filing cannot be processed.

EEO DATA COLLECTION FORM

Please complete the buff-color EEO data collection sheet in addition to the special Court Officer application form.

ADMISSION TO EXAMINATION

All candidates will receive a notice to appear for the examination. Contact the Office of Court Administration if you have not received your notice three days before the examination. You may not be admitted to the examination room without an official notice. Notice to appear for the test constitutes only conditional approval of your application. Your eligibility for a Court Officer position will be determined at the time you are considered for appointment. If you have not received your admission card three days before the examination, contact the Office of Court Administration at 212-417-5891 or the Department of Civil Service at 518-457-7020.

VETERANS

Disabled and nondisabled veterans who are eligible for extra credit will have 10 or 5 points, respectively, added to their scores if they are otherwise successful in the examination. They should claim these credits when they file their application. If granted, candidates will have an option to waive the veteran's credits any time prior to appointment. If veteran's credits are claimed, the Office of Court Administration will send forms to establish eligibility for such credits after the written examination. Veteran's credits will not be granted if they have previously been used for permanent or contingent permanent appointment from an eligible list in New York State or any of its political subdivisions since January 1, 1951.

RATINGS

The passing score for this examination will be determined at a date following the administration of the examination.

VERIFICATION OF QUALIFICATIONS

Candidates will be investigated or called for an interview to determine whether they are qualified for appointment. In addition to meeting specific requirements, candidates must be of good moral character.

RELIGIOUS OBSERVANCE

If, because of religious belief, you are unable to attend and take the examination on its scheduled date, special arrangements can be made to permit you to take this examination on another day without fee or penalty. Please indicate your needs on the application form.

DISABLED INDIVIDUALS

Arrangements will be made for disabled individuals who require special assistance on the date of the written examination. Please indicate your needs on the application form.

FINGERPRINTING FEE

A fingerprinting fee will be charged to all candidates who are successful on the written portion of the examination and whose ranks are reached for further medical, physical, and other screening tests.

PROBATIONARY PERIOD

All appointees will be required to successfully complete a probationary period subsequent to their appointment. They will also be required to complete a training program during their probationary period.

SENIOR COURT OFFICER

THE OFFICE OF COURT ADMINISTRATION ANNOUNCES A PROMOTION EXAMINATION

TITLE

Senior Court Officer Exam Number: 55-570

The promotion examination for Senior Court Officer is limited to qualified employees of the unified court system. There will be no open-competitive Senior Court Officer examination held in conjunction with this examination.

LOCATION OF POSITIONS
The Senior Court Officer title exists in the Supreme and Surrogate's Courts in New York City and the County, Supreme, and Surrogate's Courts in Nassau, Suffolk, and Westchester Counties.

LOCATION OF TEST CENTERS
This examination will be held exclusively in New York City, Brentwood, and White Plains.

STARTING SALARY
This title is graded at JG-18. Appointees may receive additional annual location pay.

MINIMUM QUALIFICATIONS FOR TAKING EXAMINATION
To be eligible *to compete* in this examination, candidates must, by the examination date, have current, permanent competitive class status in the title of Court Officer. (Applicants please note: All individuals with permanent competitive class status in the title of Court Officer as of the date of the examination will be prefiled by this office. Therefore, they need not submit an application for this examination. Prior to the examination date, all permanent Court Officers will receive admission cards to examination sites based upon their work location.)

MINIMUM QUALIFICATIONS FOR APPOINTMENT
To be eligible for *appointment* from the resultant eligible list, candidates must have, at the time of appointment, one year of current, permanent competitive class service in the title of Court Officer.

CITIZENSHIP
Candidates must be citizens of the United States at the time of appointment.

DISTINGUISHING FEATURES OF WORK
Senior Court Officers are responsible for maintaining order and providing security in court facilities. They work under the direct supervision of security supervisors and court clerks. Senior Court Officers are peace officers, are required to wear uniforms, and may be authorized to carry firearms. They are responsible for jury escort and security, perform clerical duties while handling court documents and forms, may coordinate the activities of other court security personnel, and perform related duties.

SCOPE OF EXAMINATION
The written examination will be multiple-choice and will assess a candidate's knowledge of the laws, rules, regulations, procedures, techniques, and practices relating to the duties and responsibilities of a Senior Court Officer, including, but not necessarily limited to, knowledge of the following topical areas shown below (in alphabetical order):

- Arrest
- Bail
- Courthouse/courtroom security
- Court terminology, documents, and forms
- Crowd control and evacuation
- Evidence
- Firearms and firearms licensing
- Firstaid and CPR
- Handling emergencies
- Handling prisoners
- Hostage situations
- Jury sequestration and tampering
- Operation and use of security equipment
- Search
- Self-defense
- Use of physical force
- Warrants

Sources for these knowledge questions will be the Criminal Procedure Law, the Penal Law, and the various documents given to Court Officers during formal training and on the job.

Important Information to Senior Court Officer Promotion Candidates

ADMISSION TO EXAMINATION

All individuals with permanent status in the title of Court Officer as of the examination date will be prefiled and will receive a notice to appear for the examination. They are to contact the Office of Court Administration if they have not received their notice five days before the examination. They may not be admitted to the examination room without an official notice.

VETERANS

Disabled and nondisabled veterans who are eligible for extra credit will have 5 or 2.5 points, respectively, added to their scores if they are otherwise successful in the examination. Forms for claiming these credits will be available on the day of the examination. If granted, candidates will have an option to waive the veteran's credits any time prior to appointment. If veteran's credits are claimed, the Office of Court Administration will send forms to establish eligibility for such credits after the written examination. Veteran's credits will not be granted if they have previously been used for permanent or contingent permanent appointment from an eligible list in New York State or any of its political subdivisions since January 1, 1951.

RATINGS

The passing score for this examination will be determined at a date following the administration of the examination.

RELIGIOUS OBSERVANCE

If, because of religious belief, candidates are unable to attend and take the examination on its scheduled date, special arrangements can be made to permit them to take this examination on another day. They are to indicate their needs in a letter to the Examination Unit, Office of Court Administration, at least twelve weeks before the date of the examination.

Court Clerk

THE OFFICE OF COURT ADMINISTRATION ANNOUNCES A PROMOTION EXAMINATION

TITLE

Court Clerk Exam Number: 55-581

THIS PROMOTION EXAMINATION IS LIMITED TO QUALIFIED EMPLOYEES OF THE UNIFIED COURT SYSTEM. An examination for the title of Senior Court Clerk (55-582) will also be held on the same date. Candidates may apply for both examinations through the filing of separate applications. Please refer to the announcement for the Senior Court Clerk examination for further information.

STARTING SALARY

The title of Court Clerk is graded at JG-18. In addition, employees in Rockland County may receive additional annual location pay.

ELIGIBLE LISTS

The eligible lists established as a result of this examination will be used to fill appropriate positions in the Unified Court System in New York State.

At present, the title of Court Clerk exists throughout most of New York State, with the exception of New York City, Nassau, Suffolk, and Westchester Counties.

Separate promotion unit eligible lists will be established for the Third through Ninth (except for Westchester County) Judicial Districts. If appropriate, separate promotion unit eligible lists may be established for other promotion units as well. In addition, a statewide general promotion list will be established but will not be used until the appropriate promotion unit list is exhausted.

MINIMUM QUALIFICATIONS TO COMPETE
To be eligible to compete in this examination, candidates must, by the close of filing, have current, permanent competitive class status in any competitive title in the Unified Court System. (Under Section 25.15(h) of the Rules of the Chief Judge, includes: (1) employees of the Unified Court System who are holding or who have held positions in the Noncompetitive, Exempt, or Labor Class if said employees in the past have held qualifying competitive class positions on a permanent basis, and (2) employees with Noncompetitive status in qualifying titles by virtue of the Handicapped Set Aside Program (HSAP).)

MINIMUM QUALIFICATIONS FOR APPOINTMENT
To be eligible for appointment from the resultant eligible list, successful candidates must have at the time of appointment two years of current, permanent competitive class status in any competitive title in the Unified Court System.

CITIZENSHIP
Candidates must be citizens of the United States at the time of appointment.

DISTINGUISHING FEATURES OF WORK
Court Clerks work in the Court of Claims; Supreme and County Courts in counties with two or more full-time County Court Judges or one full-time County Court Judge and combined annual filings of indictments and Supreme Court civil actions exceeding 650; Family Courts with two or more full-time Judges; and city and district-level courts with six or more full-time Judges. Court Clerks serve as part-time clerks swearing witnesses, polling jurors, maintaining custody of exhibits, and keeping court minutes in the individual assignment system and other parts. Court Clerks also work in court offices where they supervise Court Assistants and other court personnel engaged in processing prisoner correspondence, reviewing calendaring decisions, motions for sufficiency and preference, and orders for conformance with decisions. Court Clerks may also supervise a full-time branch office of a court staffed by Court Assistants and may be designated to act in the absence of the Chief Clerk or Commissioner of Jurors and perform other related duties.

SUBJECT OF EXAMINATION
The written examination will be multiple-choice and designed to assess the following:

1. *Knowledge of Court Procedures and Legal Terminology:*

   Shall include, but not be limited to, topical areas such as jurisdiction, venue, service of process, service of papers, parties, motions, subpoenas, oaths, affirmations, calendar practice, trials in general, trials by jury, judgments, warrants, indictments, and pleas, as set forth in:

   (a) Civil Practice Laws and Rules, including but not limited to Articles 1, 3, 4, 5, 6, 10, 12, 21, 22, 23, 26, 30, 34, 40, 41, 42, 44, and 63.

   (b) Criminal Procedure Law, including but not limited to Articles 1, 10, 30, 120, 180, 190, 195, 200, 210, 220, 255, 260, 270, 300, 310, 320, 330, 350, 360, 380, 390, 410, 420, 430, 500, 720, 725, 730.

   (c) Family Court Act, including but not limited to Articles 1 (Parts 1, 5, 7), 3 (Parts 1,

2, 4, 5, 6), 4, 5, 6 (Parts 1, 3, 4, 5), 7 (Parts 2, 3, 4, 5, 7), 8, 10 (Parts 2, 3, 5), and 11.

2. *Ability to Understand, Interpret, and Apply Written Material (Reading Comprehension):*

Candidates will be presented with brief reading selections followed by questions that require the interpretation and/or application of the information presented in the reading selections to given situations. All of the information required to answer the questions will be provided in the selections. Candidates will not be required to have any special knowledge relating to the content area covered in the selections.

NOTES

Disabled persons seeking special arrangements for testing are required to indicate their needs on the application form.

Please complete the beige EEO data collection sheet in addition to the green application form.

The passing score for this exam will be determined at a date following the administration of the examination.

INFORMATION FOR CANDIDATES (PROMOTION)—PLEASE READ CAREFULLY

ELIGIBILITY FOR EXAMINATION: To be eligible to compete in this examination, you must be presently employed in the competitive class in a court or court agency of the Unified Court System specified on this announcement and must have been continuously employed on a permanent (or contingent permanent) basis in specified title(s) and/or grade(s) for the required length of time. You may not compete in a test for a title if you are permanently employed in that title or in a higher title in the direct promotion line. In the following instances you may take the examination if you meet the requirements detailed in this announcement:

(a) You have been separated from service and permanently reemployed within one year or reinstated in the same or a higher grade position.

(b) Your name is on a preferred eligible list.

APPLICATION FORMS: These forms may be obtained from your administrative office. If you want to submit additional information or make any change in your application after it has been filed, write to the Office of Court Administration.

VETERANS: Disabled and nondisabled veterans who are eligible for extra credit will have 5 and 2.5 points, respectively, added to their earned scores if they are otherwise successful in the examination. You should claim these credits when you file your application and, if they are granted, you have an option to waive them any time prior to appointment. If you claim additional credits as a veteran, the Office of Court Administration will send forms to you for establishing your eligibility for such credits. If you do not receive these forms by the examination date, write to the Office of Court Administration (see mailing instructions below). Veteran's credits will not be granted if they have previously been used for permanent or contingent permanent appointment from an eligible list in New York State or any of its political subdivisions since January 1, 1951.

ADMISSION TO EXAMINATION: Notice to appear for the test does not constitute approval of your application by the Office of Court Administration. Review of application for minimum requirements may be made after the written test. CONTACT THE OFFICE OF COURT ADMINISTRATION IF YOU HAVE NOT RECEIVED YOUR NOTICE THREE DAYS BEFORE THE EXAMINATION.

TIME REQUIRED FOR WRITTEN TEST: The written tests usually will not exceed one session of 4 hours unless otherwise indicated on your admission notice.

RATINGS REQUIRED: Tests usually are rated on a scale of 100, with the passing mark at 70. Test instructions may further divide the tests into parts and set minimum standards for each part.

SENIORITY: Rating of seniority is based upon the length of your continuous permanent competitive service in the Unified Court System or predecessor courts or court agencies. Rating of seniority for this test shall be for service up to twenty years, with 0.2 credits added per year of service for persons who are otherwise successful on the examination.

VERIFICATION OF QUALIFICATIONS: Candidates may be investigated or called for an interview to determine whether they are qualified for appointment. In addition to meeting specific requirements, candidates must be of good moral character and habits.

MEDICAL EXAMINATION: You may be required to take a medical examination as part of the qualifying process for the position(s) in the announcement.

RELIGIOUS OBSERVANCE: If, because of religious belief, you are unable to attend and take this examination on its scheduled date, special arrangements can be made to permit you to take the examination on another day without any additional fee or penalty. Please indicate your needs on the application form.

When writing to the Office of Court Administration concerning an examination, enter: ***Attention: EXAMINATION*** directly above the address. Include in your correspondence the number and title of the examination you are applying for.

**IF YOU FILE AN APPLICATION FOR THIS EXAMINATION,
RETAIN A COPY OF THIS ANNOUNCEMENT.**

THE APPLICATION PROCESS

Once you have read the job announcement and understand the requirements for the position, it's time to apply for the position. In doing so, you must concentrate on the following:

- **Education and experience requirements.** If you cannot meet these requirements, do not bother to apply. Government service can be very competitive. The government has more than enough applicants from which to choose. It will not waive its requirements for you.

- **Age requirements.** Discrimination on the basis of age is illegal, but a number of jobs demand so much sustained physical effort that they require retirement at an early age. For these positions, there is an entry age limit. If you are already beyond that age, do not apply. If you are still too young, inquire about the time lag until hiring. It may be that you will reach the minimum age by the time the position is to be filled.

- **Citizenship requirements.** Many jobs are open to all people who are eligible to work in the United States, but all law enforcement jobs and most federal jobs are limited to U.S. citizens. If you are well along the way toward citizenship and expect to be naturalized soon, inquire as to your exact status with respect to the job.

- **Residency requirements.** If there is a residency requirement, you must live within the prescribed limits or be willing to move. If you are not willing to live in the area, do not waste time applying.

- **Required forms.** The announcement of the position for which you are applying will specify the form of application requested. For most federal jobs, you may submit either the Optional Application for Federal Employment (OF 612) or a resume that fulfills the requirements set forth in the pamphlet, Applying for a Federal Job (OF 510). For other than federal jobs, the Notice of Examination may tell you where you must go or write to get the necessary form or forms. Be sure you secure them all. The application might be a simple form asking nothing more than name, address, citizenship, and social security number, or it may be a complex Experience Paper. An Experience Paper, as its title implies, asks a great deal about education, job training, job experience, and life experience. Typically, the Experience Paper permits no identification by name, sex, or race; the only identifying mark is your social security number. The purpose of this procedure is to avoid permitting bias of any sort to enter into the weighting of responses. The Experience Paper generally follows a short form of application that does include a name. When the rating process is completed, the forms are coordinated by means of the social security number.

- **Filing date, place, and fee.** There is great variation in this area. For some positions, you can file your application at any time. Others have a first day and last day for filing. If you file too early or too late, your application will not be considered. Sometimes it is sufficient to have your application postmarked by the last day for filing. More often, your application must be received by the last date. If you are mailing your application, allow five full business days for it to get there on time. Place of filing will be stated right on the notice. Most applications may be filed by mail, but occasionally in-person filing is specified. Follow directions. Federal and postal positions require no filing fee. Most other government jobs do charge a fee for processing your application. The fee is not always the same. Be sure to check this out. If the notice specifies "money order only," plan to purchase a money order. If you send or present a personal check, your application will be rejected without consideration. Of course, you should never mail cash; but if the announcement specifies "money order only," you cannot submit cash, even in person.

- **How to qualify.** This portion of the notice will tell you the basis on which the candidate will be chosen. Some examination scores consist of a sum of weighted education and experience factors. (This type of examination is called an "unassembled exam," because you do not come to one place to take an exam.) Obviously, these must be complete for you to get full credit for all you have learned and accomplished. The notice may tell you of a qualifying exam, an exam that you must pass in addition to scoring high on an unassembled, written, or performance test. In addition, the notice may tell you of a written, performance, or combined competitive exam. The competitive exam may be described in very general terms or may be described in detail. It is even possible that a few sample questions will be attached. If the date of the exam has been set, that date will appear on the notice. Write it down.

The Application Form

Having studied the job announcement and having decided that you want the position and are qualified for it, your next step is to get an application form. The job announcement tells you where to send for it.

On the whole, civil service application forms differ little from state to state and locality to locality. The questions that have been worked out after years of experimentation are simple and direct, designed to elicit a maximal amount of information about you.

Give the application serious attention, for it is the first important step toward getting the job you want.

Here, along with some helpful comments, are the questions usually asked on the average application form, although not necessarily in this order.

ALERT!

Many prospective civil service employees have failed to get a job because of slipshod, erroneous, incomplete, misleading, or untruthful answers.

- **Name of examination or kind of position applied for.** This information appears in large type on the first page of the job announcement.

- **Optional job** (if mentioned in the announcement). If you wish to apply for an option, simply copy the title from the announcement. If you are not interested in an option, write *None.*

- **Primary place of employment applied for.** The location of the position was probably contained in the announcement. You must consider whether you want to work there. The announcement may list more than one location where the job is open. If you would accept employment in any of the places, list them all; otherwise list the specific place or places where you would be willing to work.

- **Name and address.** Give in full, including your middle name if you have one, and your maiden name as well if you are a married woman.

- **Home and office phones.** If none, write *None.*

- **Legal or voting residence.** The state in which you vote is the one you list here.

- **Height without shoes, weight, sex.** Answer accurately.

- **Date of birth.** Give the exact day, month, and year.

- **Lowest grade or pay you will accept.** Although the salary is clearly stated in the job announcement, there may be a quicker opening in the same occupation but carrying less responsibility and thus a lower basic entrance salary. You will not be considered for a job paying less than the amount you give in answer to this question.

- **Will you accept temporary employment if offered you for (a) one month or less, (b) one to four months, (c) four to twelve months?** Temporary positions come up frequently and it is important to know whether you are available.

- **Will you accept less than full-time employment?** Part-time work comes up now and then. Consider whether you want to accept such a position while waiting for a full-time appointment.

- **Were you in active military service in the Armed Forces of the United States?** Veterans' preference, if given, is usually limited to active service during the following periods: 12/7/41-12/31/46; 6/27/50-1/31/55; 6/1/63-5/7/75; 6/1/83-12/1/87; 10/23/83-11/21/83; 12/20/89-1/3/90; 8/2/90 to current hostilities.

- **Do you claim disabled veterans credit?** If you do, you have to show proof of a war-incurred disability compensable by at least 10 percent. This is done through certification by the Veterans Administration.

- **Special qualifications and skills.** Even though not directly related to the position for which you are applying, information about licenses and certificates obtained for teacher, pilot, registered nurse, and so on, is requested. List your experience in the use of machines and equipment and whatever other skills you have acquired. Also list published writings, public speaking experience, membership in professional societies, and honors and fellowships received.

- **Education.** List your entire educational history, including all diplomas, degrees, and special courses taken in any accredited or armed forces school. Also give your credits toward a college or a graduate degree.

- **References.** The names of people who can give information about you, with their occupations and business and home address, are often requested.

- **Your health.** Questions are asked concerning your medical record. You are expected to have the physical and psychological capacity to perform the job for which you are applying. Standards vary, of course, depending on the requirements of the position. A physical handicap usually will not bar an applicant from a job he or she can perform adequately unless the safety of the public is involved.

- **Work history.** Considerable space is allotted on the form for you to tell about all your past employment. Examiners check all such answers closely. Do not embellish or falsify your record. If you were ever fired, say so. It is better for you to state this openly than for the examiners to find out the truth from your former employer.

FILLING IT OUT

Make a copy of the application when you get it so you can practice filling it out and make any changes you wish. When you are satisfied with your draft, copy the information onto the original form(s). Be sure to include any backup material that is requested; by the same token, do not send more "evidence" than is truly needed to support your claims of qualification. Your application must be complete according to the requirements of the announcement but should not be overwhelming. You want to command hiring attention by exactly conforming to requirements.

Check over all forms for neatness and completeness. Sign wherever indicated. Attach the fee, if required. Then mail or personally file the application on time.

When the civil service commission or personnel office to which you submitted your application receives it, the office will date, stamp, log, and open your file. The office may acknowledge receipt with more forms, with sample exam questions, or with a simple receipt slip. You may not hear anything from the office for months.

Eventually, you will receive a testing date or an interview appointment. Write these on your calendar so that you don't let the dates slip by. If you receive an admission ticket for an exam, be sure to put it in a safe place, but keep it in sight so that you will not forget to take it with you to the exam. Begin to study and prepare right away if you have not already done so.

Following are samples of a New York City Application for Examination and a state application from Louisiana.

New York City Application for Examination

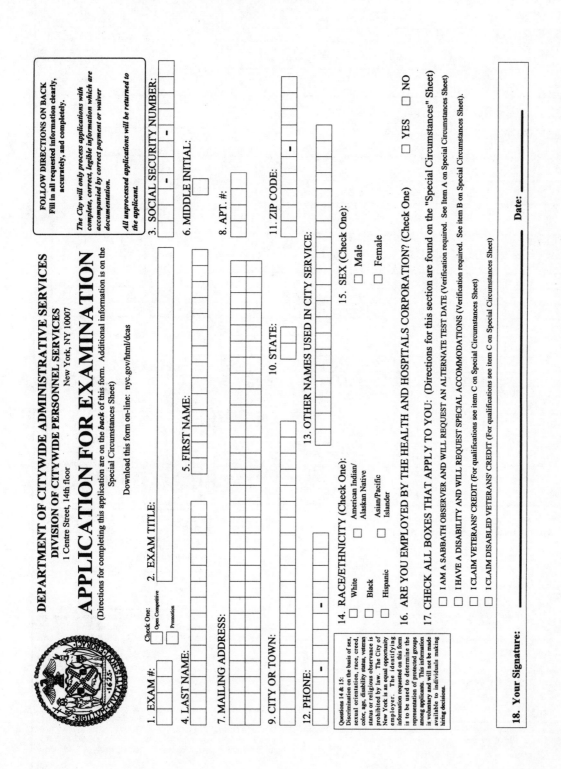

State of Louisiana Application—page 1

SF10
(Page 1)
REV. 1/97

STATE PRE-EMPLOYMENT APPLICATION

STATE OF LOUISIANA
DEPARTMENT OF CIVIL SERVICE
P.O. Box 94111, Capitol Station
Baton Rouge, Louisiana 70804-9111

AN EQUAL OPPORTUNITY EMPLOYER

FOR OFFICE USE

Special _____
Promo _____
Action(s) _____

Session _____

Data Entry Completed _____

1. TEST LOCATION-Check only one.

| Baton Rouge (3) (Weekday) ☐ | New Orleans (6) (Weekday) ☐ | Lafayette (4) (Sat. only) ☐ | Shreveport (7) (Sat. only) ☐ |
| | New Orleans (12) (Saturday) ☐ | Lake Charles (5) (Sat. only) ☐ | West Monroe (8) (Sat. only) ☐ |

2. Enter Name and Complete Address below.

3. Parish of Residence

4. Are you 18 or older? ☐ Yes ☐ No

5. Other names ever used on SF-10

NAME - First   Middle   Last

Mailing Address

City   State   Zip Code

6. Social Security Number (For identification purpose)

Work Telephone No.

Home Telephone No.

L A S T → P R I N T → F I R S T N A M E → M I D D L E

7. REGISTER TITLE(S) APPLIED FOR

	FOR OFFICE USE					ADDITIONAL TITLES	FOR OFFICE USE				
	SER	CD	REJ	GRD	TR		SER	CD	REJ	GRD	TR

JS No.

V.P.

S.R.

ALL TITLES LISTED ABOVE MUST HAVE THE SAME SERIES NO.

8. JOB LOCATION AVAILABILITY - IMPORTANT: Read Item 9 on the Instruction Page before completing this item. Mark at least one (1), but no more than twenty (20) parishes.

01 Acadia	09 Caddo	17 E. Baton Rouge	25 Jackson	33 Madison	41 Red River	49 St. Landry	57 Vermillion
02 Allen	10 Calcasieu	18 E. Carroll	26 Jefferson	34 Morehouse	42 Richland	50 St. Martin	58 Vernon
03 Ascension	11 Caldwell	19 E. Feliciana	27 Jeff Davis	35 Natchitoches	43 Sabine	51 St. Mary	59 Washington
04	12 Cameron	20 Evangeline	28 Lafayette	36 Orleans	44 St. Bernard	52 St. Tammany	60 Webster
05 Avoyelles	13 Catahoula	21 Franklin	29 Lafourche	37 Ouachita	45 St. Charles	53 Tangipahoa	61 W. Baton Rouge
06 Beauregard	14 Claiborne	22 Grant	30 LaSalle	38 Plaquemines	46 St. Helena	54 Tensas	62 W. Carroll
07 Bienville	15 Concordia	23 Iberia	31 Lincoln	39 Pte. Coupee	47 St. James	55 Terrebonne	63 W. Feliciana
08 Bossier	16 DeSoto	24 Iberville	32 Livingston	40 Rapides	48 St. John	56 Union	64 Winn

9. ☐ Permanent ☐ Temporary—Type of employment you will accept

NOTE: Most Temporary Appointments are 3 - 12 months

10. ☐ YES ☐ NO Do you possess a valid driver's license?

11. ☐ YES ☐ NO Do you possess a valid commercial driver's license?

12. ☐ YES ☐ NO Are you currently holding or running for an elective public office?

13. ☐ YES ☐ NO Have you ever been on probation or sentenced to jail/prison as a result of a felony conviction or guilty plea?

14. ☐ YES ☐ NO Have you ever been fired from a job or resigned to avoid dismissal?

NOTE: If answers to Items 13 and/or 14 are "YES", you MUST complete Item 24 on Page 2 of this application

15. ☐ YES ☐ NO Are you claiming Veteran's Preference points on this application? (If "YES", see Item 20 on Page 2.)

The following information is collected to complete Equal Opportunity Reports required by law. You ARE NOT LEGALLY OBLIGATED to provide this information.

16. RACIAL/ETHNIC GROUP   **16A. DATE OF BIRTH**   **17. SEX** ☐ Male ☐ Female

_____   _____

I HAVE READ THE FOLLOWING STATEMENTS CAREFULLY BEFORE SIGNING THIS APPLICATION:

18. Date | Social Security No. (for verification)

19. Signature of Applicant

AUTHORITY TO RELEASE INFORMATION: I consent to the release of information concerning my capacity and/or all aspects of prior job performance by employers, educational institutions, law enforcement agencies, and other individuals and agencies to duly accredited investigators, personnel technicians, and other authorized employees of the state government for the purpose of determining my eligibility and suitability for employment.

I certify that all statements made on this application and any attached papers are true and complete to the best of my knowledge. I understand that information on this application may be subject to investigation and verification and that any misrepresentation or material omission may cause my application to be rejected, my name to be removed from the eligible register and/or subject me to dismissal from state service.

State of Louisiana Application—page 2

20. ACTIVE MILITARY SERVICE/VETERAN'S PREFERENCE

See Item 10 on the Instruction Page to determine your eligibility for Veteran's Preference. If you are a first-time applicant or if you are claiming Veteran's Preference for the first time, required PROOF MUST BE ATTACHED to this application to have preference points added to your score.

List the dates (month and year) and branch for all ACTIVE DUTY military service. Was this service performed on an active, full-time basis with full pay and allowances? (Check YES or NO for each period of service.)

FROM	TO	BRANCH OF SERVICE	YES	NO

List all GRADES held and dates of each grade. Begin with the highest grade. IMPORTANT: Use E-, O-, or WO-grade.

FROM	TO	GRADE HELD	FROM	TO	GRADE HELD

21. TRAINING AND EDUCATION

☐ YES   Date received _____

Have you received a high school diploma or equivalency certificate?

☐ NO   Highest grade completed _____

A. LIST BUSINESS OR TECHNICAL COLLEGES ATTENDED	NAME/LOCATION OF SCHOOL	Dates Attended (Month & Year) FROM TO	Did You Graduate? YES NO	TITLE OF PROGRAM	CLOCK HOURS PER WEEK

List any accounting practice sets completed:

B. LIST COLLEGES OR UNIVERSITIES ATTENDED (Include graduate or professional schools)	NAME OF COLLEGE OR UNIVERSITY/ CITY AND STATE	Dates Attended (Month & Year) FROM TO	Total Credit Hours Earned Semester Quarter	Type of Degree Earned	Major Field of Study	Date Degree Received (Month & Yr.)

C. MAJOR SUBJECTS	CHIEF UNDERGRADUATE SUBJECTS (Show Major on Line 1.)	Total Credit Hours Earned Semester Quarter	CHIEF GRADUATE SUBJECTS (Show Major on Line 1.)	Total Credit Hours Earned Semester or Qtr.
1				
2				
3				

22. LICENSES AND CERTIFICATION   **23. TYPING SPEED**

List any job-related licenses or certificates that you have (CPA, lawyer, registered nurse, etc.)

	TYPE OF LICENSE OR CERTIFICATE (Specify Which One)	DATE ORIGINALLY LICENSED/ CERTIFIED	EXPIRATION DATE	NAME AND ADDRESS OF LICENSING OR CERTIFYING AGENCY	TYPING SPEED
1					_____ WPM
2					DICTATION SPEED _____ WPM

24. Explain a "YES" answer to Items 13 and/or 14 here. A "YES" ANSWER WILL NOT NECESSARILY BAR YOU FROM STATE EMPLOYMENT. WE WILL CONSIDER THE DATE, FACTS, AND CIRCUMSTANCES OF EACH INDIVIDUAL CASE. For Item 13, give the law enforcement authority (city police, sherrif, FBI, etc.), the offense, date of offense, place, and disposition of case.

_____

_____

Name   _____

State of Louisiana Application—page 3

Name _____

25. WORK EXPERIENCE — IMPORTANT: Read Item 11 of Instruction Page carefully before completing these items. List all jobs and activities including military service, part-time employment, self-employment, and volunteer work. BEGIN with your FIRST job in Block A; END with your MOST RECENT or PRESENT job.

A

EMPLOYER/COMPANY NAME	KIND OF BUSINESS

STREET ADDRESS	YOUR OFFICIAL JOB TITLE

CITY AND STATE	BEGINNING SALARY	ENDING SALARY

DATES OF EMPLOYMENT (MO/DA/YR)	AVERAGE HOURS WORKED PER WEEK	REASON FOR LEAVING	NO. OF EMPLOYEES YOU DIRECTLY SUPERVISED
FROM	TO		

NAME/TITLE OF YOUR SUPERVISOR)	LIST JOB TITLES OF EMPLOYEES YOU DIRECTLY SUPERVISED
NAME/TITLE OF PERSON WHO CAN VERIFY THIS EMPLOYMENT (IF OTHER THAN SUPERVISOR)	

DUTIES: List the major duties involved with job and give an approximate percentage of time spent on each duty.

% OF TIME	MAJOR DUTIES
100%	

B

EMPLOYER/COMPANY NAME	KIND OF BUSINESS

STREET ADDRESS	YOUR OFFICIAL JOB TITLE

CITY AND STATE	BEGINNING SALARY	ENDING SALARY

DATES OF EMPLOYMENT (MO/DA/YR)	AVERAGE HOURS WORKED PER WEEK	REASON FOR LEAVING	NO. OF EMPLOYEES YOU DIRECTLY SUPERVISED
FROM	TO		

NAME/TITLE OF YOUR SUPERVISOR)	LIST JOB TITLES OF EMPLOYEES YOU DIRECTLY SUPERVISED
NAME/TITLE OF PERSON WHO CAN VERIFY THIS EMPLOYMENT (IF OTHER THAN SUPERVISOR)	

DUTIES: List the major duties involved with job and give an approximate percentage of time spent on each duty.

% OF TIME	MAJOR DUTIES

State of Louisiana Application—page 4

100%

USE REVERSE SIDE OF THIS PAGE IF ADDITIONAL SPACE REQUIRED FOR WORK EXPERIENCE

Name _____

25. WORK EXPERIENCE (Continued)

C

EMPLOYER/COMPANY NAME	KIND OF BUSINESS	
STREET ADDRESS	YOUR OFFICIAL JOB TITLE	
CITY AND STATE	BEGINNING SALARY	ENDING SALARY
DATES OF EMPLOYMENT (MO/DA/YR) / AVERAGE HOURS WORKED PER WEEK	REASON FOR LEAVING	NO. OF EMPLOYEES YOU DIRECTLY SUPERVISED
FROM / TO		
NAME/TITLE OF YOUR SUPERVISOR	LIST JOB TITLES OF EMPLOYEES YOU DIRECTLY SUPERVISED	
NAME/TITLE OF PERSON WHO CAN VERIFY THIS EMPLOYMENT (IF OTHER THAN SUPERVISOR)		

DUTIES: List the major duties involved with job and give an approximate percentage of time spent on each duty.

% OF TIME	MAJOR DUTIES

100%

D

EMPLOYER/COMPANY NAME	KIND OF BUSINESS	
STREET ADDRESS	YOUR OFFICIAL JOB TITLE	
CITY AND STATE	BEGINNING SALARY	ENDING SALARY
DATES OF EMPLOYMENT (MO/DA/YR) / AVERAGE HOURS WORKED PER WEEK	REASON FOR LEAVING	NO. OF EMPLOYEES YOU DIRECTLY SUPERVISED
FROM / TO		
NAME/TITLE OF YOUR SUPERVISOR)	LIST JOB TITLES OF EMPLOYEES YOU DIRECTLY SUPERVISED	
NAME/TITLE OF PERSON WHO CAN VERIFY THIS EMPLOYMENT (IF OTHER THAN SUPERVISOR)		

DUTIES: List the major duties involved with job and give an approximate percentage of time spent on each duty.

% OF TIME	MAJOR DUTIES

The Interview

If there is no exam and you are called directly to an interview, what you wear is more important. Take special care to look businesslike and professional. A neat dress, slacks and blouse, or skirted suit is fine for women; men should wear a suit or slacks, a jacket, shirt, and tie.

If you are called for an interview, you are most likely under serious consideration. There may still be competition for the job—someone else may be more suited than you—but you are qualified, and your skills and background have appealed to someone in the hiring office. The interview may be aimed at getting information about the following.

- **Your knowledge.** The interviewer wants to know what you know about the area in which you will work. You may also be asked questions probing your knowledge of the agency for which you are interviewing. Do you care enough to have educated yourself about the functions and role of the agency?

- **Your judgment.** You may be faced with hypothetical situations—job-related or interpersonal—and be asked questions like, "What would you do if..." Think carefully before answering. Be decisive and diplomatic. There are no "right answers." The interviewer is aware that you are being put on the spot. How well you can handle this type of question is an indication of your flexibility and maturity.

- **Your personality.** You will have to be trained and supervised. You will have to work with others. What is your attitude? How will you fit in? The interviewer will make judgments in these areas on the basis of general conversation with you and from your responses to specific lines of questioning. Be pleasant, polite, and open with your answers, but do not volunteer a great deal of extra information. Stick to the subjects introduced by the interviewer. Answer fully, but resist the temptation to ramble on.

- **Your attitude toward work conditions.** These are practical concerns. The interviewer also wants to know how you will react to overtime or irregular shifts.

SUMMING IT UP

- Most federal, state, and municipal units have recruitment procedures for filling civil service positions. They have developed a number of methods to make job opportunities known, including newspapers, online job searches, and state Web sites.

- Job announcements are designed to give you a good idea of what will be required of you on the job, whether you are considering a position as a court officer, senior court officer, or court clerk.

- When you have your application forms in hand, photocopy them and complete the photocopies first. This way you can correct mistakes or make changes before transferring the information to the original form.

Preparing for the Exams

chapter 2

OVERVIEW

- Written exam
- Promotion exams
- Medical exam
- Physical ability exam
- Psychological interview
- Background investigation
- Summing it up

WRITTEN EXAM

The Court Officer exams are primarily multiple-choice tests and involve a variety of different types of questions. They include clerical checking questions, observation and memory questions, reading comprehension, and subject-oriented questions. The questions in this book are similar to those you may encounter on the actual tests. In some test locations, it is possible that you will receive reference materials prior to the test. It is important that you read and memorize as much as possible, since some of it may actually appear on your examination.

Video Tests

In some instances, the entrance-level exams may be part of your test. The test will involve watching a video and then you will be asked questions about what you saw and heard. This test will measure your ability to observe, listen, and memorize—similar to the paper-pencil portion of the test. You may also be asked to write an overview of what you saw.

How to Answer Clerical Checking Questions

The court officer handles many forms and documents during the course of each working day. It is imperative that the information on each piece of paper be read accurately and that the information be processed correctly. The court officer must be able to read quickly and note errors or discrepancies. Clerical checking questions are designed to measure these skills.

Each clerical checking question presents three sets of essentially the same information in three columns. Sometimes the items are in the same order and sometimes in a different order in each set. There may or may not be some slight variations in the information from one set to another. The directions tell the test taker to:

Mark (**A**) if *ALL THREE* sets are exactly alike.

Mark (**B**) if only the *FIRST* and *THIRD* sets are exactly alike.

Mark (**C**) if only the *FIRST* and *SECOND* sets are exactly alike.

Mark (**D**) if *NONE* of the sets is exactly like any other.

These directions are very specific. They refer to the slightest of differences—even variations in spacing after colons, spelling of abbreviations, capitalization of prepositions in titles—as well as to the more obvious, real differences. Furthermore, any difference in presentation in any single item of information from one set to the next constitutes a difference between the sets. This narrows your task considerably.

TIP

Once you have found any difference in any item from one set to the next, you need not compare any further items in those two sets.

In general, you should begin with the "easy" comparisons. If names have first or middle initials, check these first. Then go on to Jr., Sr., II, M.D., and the like, noting the presence or absence of punctuation as well as its placement. Another common area of easy-to-see difference is in prefixes like Mc, Mac, Van, von, de, D', etc. If there are no differences among the easy comparisons, you must focus on the names themselves. Be on the lookout for added or dropped *e's* or *s's* in particular. Look for the true identity of people's names. (Marie and Maria are two different people.) Check for spelling, double letters, letter reversals, and letters dropped into the middle of names. For numbers, check actual number of digits, groupings, spacing, and punctuation as well as digit reversals and digit substitutions.

There is a strategy for making comparisons quickly and accurately. It is more efficient to work through one item at a time rather than one set at a time. So, start with the first item in the first set. Compare it with the same item in the second set. If the two items are on the same line, this is quite easy. If they are not on the same line, you must engage in some visual gymnastics. If the item is identical in the first and second sets, compare the item in the second set with its counterpart in the third set. If the first and second are alike and the second and third are alike, then all three are alike. You do not need to compare the first with the third. If the first and second are alike, but the second and third are different, then the first and third are different and you do not need to compare the first with the third. If, on the other hand, the first and second are different, then you must make the visual leap and compare the item in the first and third sets. Each time you find an item that differs in any way from the item in the first set, draw a line through that item. Any set with any line drawn through it drops out of the comparisons for that question. The following simple comparisons illustrate this principle and the economy it represents.

1. Cyriac Aleyamma   Cyriac Aleyamma   Cyriac Aleyamma

    Eric O. Hartman   Eric O. Hartman   ~~Eric O. Harpman~~

    4726840   ~~4728640~~   4726840

-- STOP HERE --

    Jaime Chiquimia   Jaime Chiquimia   Jaime Chiquimia

    7621489   7624189   7621849

The first item is identical in all three sets, so you must move to the second item. The second item is identical in the first two sets, but in the third set, the last name is spelled differently. Draw a line through the item that shows a difference and move on to the third item in the first set. Comparing the third item in the first set with its counterpart in the second set, we find a digit reversal in the second set. Draw a line through that item and stop. We already know that the correct answer is (D). None of the three sets is exactly like any other. There is no need to look at any further items in question 1. Mark (D) and move on immediately.

2. Roy L. Gildesgame   ~~Roy L. Gildegame~~   Roy L. Gildesgame

    4243275   4243275   4243275

    3245270   3245270   3245270

    Susan B. Vizoski   Susan B. Vizoski   Susan B. Vizoski

    M.R. von Weisenseel   M.R. von Weisensteel   M.R. von Weisenseel

With the very first item, the second set is eliminated from further comparisons. Draw a line through the entry that differs. Then X out the remainder of the second set. The correct answer to question 2 cannot be (A) or (C), but you must continue comparing the first and third sets to determine whether the answer is (B) or (D). Since the first and third sets are exactly alike, the correct answer is (B).

The procedure is similar, though somewhat more difficult, when the items are not on the same lines in each set.

3.

Cornelius Detwiler	Rose T. Waldhofer	1768232
1768232	1065407	9673035
9673035	Cornelius Detwiler	~~Rose T. Walderhofer~~
Rose T. Waldhofer	1768232	1065047
1065407	9673035	Cornelius Detwiler

Our system is of limited usefulness in this question. The first three items are exactly the same in all three sets. The fourth item is the same in the first two sets, but different in the third. Cross it out. You must still consider the fifth item because it might introduce a difference into the second set. In this instance it does not. The first and second sets are exactly alike, and the answer is (C). There is already a difference in the third set, so the last item need not be compared there.

4.

2312793	Frima V. Spiner, MD	6219354
Stricklund Kanedy	7692138	2312793
6219354	2312793	Frima V. Spiner, MD
Frima V. Spiner, MD	Stricklund Kanedy	7692138
7692138	6219354	Stricklund Kanedy

This is perhaps the most difficult type of question of all. Since you have found no differences, you must make all of the comparisons. This is time consuming. Then, you must trust yourself. Do NOT go back and check again for differences. If you have found no differences in one round of comparison, mark (A) and go on. There are questions in which all three sets are exactly alike.

How to Answer Observation and Memory Questions

Memory is a very individualized skill. Some people remember details of what they see and hear; others remember only the most obvious facts. Some people memorize easily, others find memorizing very difficult. Some people remember forever, others remember for just a short time. Some people memorize in a systematic manner, others are haphazard in their methods or have no method at all.

We really cannot tell you how to memorize. We can, however, teach you how to observe, show you how to look at photographs, and point out the details on which you should concentrate. The systematic observation of photographs transfers very readily to the systematic study of narrative description of events. The memory questions on your court officer exam may be based on pictures, narrative, or both.

Car Repair

Begin by looking at the photograph "Car Repair."

START WITH THE PEOPLE

1. How many people are in the photograph?

2. How many men? How many women?

3. What do the people appear to be doing?

4. What is the man holding in his hands?

5. Note the clothing. Both are wearing light colored shirts, the man is wearing shorts. Are any shoes visible in the photograph? Is the woman wearing any jewelry?

6. Note hair. Does the woman have light or dark hair? How would you describe her hairstyle? Does the man have a mustache or beard?

7. Note the expressions: Is the woman looking at the man? What is she looking at? How would you describe her expression?

OBSERVE THE ACTION

8. What part of the car is visible?

9. What does the man have in his right hand? What is he probably doing? What does he hold in his left hand?

10. What might be the relationship of the man to the woman?

11. Are both people under the hood of the car, or is just the man?

NOTE THE BACKGROUND

12. What time of day is it?

13. What season could it be?

14. Is there anything visible in the background? Can you remember every detail of this setting?

In looking at a photograph, focus first on the people. Notice their clothing, physical features, and activities. Count, but also make note of which person or persons is wearing what, doing what, interacting with whom, and so on. Then notice the prominent objects. Next, turn your attention to the background, any visible activity or action. Finally, start at the left side of the photograph and move your eyes very slowly to the right, noticing special details such as hairstyles, expression, and any unidentified objects. If you work very hard at noticing, you are likely to remember what you noticed, at least for the duration of the exam.

Refreshments

Look at the photograph "Refreshments."

1. The people in the picture are . . . number, gender, and age.

2. The people are wearing . . . notice the pattern of the man's shirt and the woman's sweater. (Also notice that she is wearing layered clothing.) What are the girls wearing?

3. Notice hair color, type (curly or straight), and length and style.

4. Note that no shoes are visible. Is anyone wearing glasses, a watch, or a hat? Does the woman wear a necklace or ring?

5. What is the woman holding in her hands?

6. Who is standing? Who is sitting? On what?

7. What is the design of the tablecloth?

8. What else is on the table? Notice beverages, bread, condiments, and other items.

9. What is on the ground? Snow? Sand? Gravel? Lawn? Rocks? Flowers? Wild grasses?

10. The day is . . . cold? warm? rainy? cloudy? sunny? Where is the sun in the picture?

11. In the background are . . . mountains? trees? water? boats? tents? more grass? other people? animals?

12. Is the sky visible? What else is there on the land?

13. What is the shape of the table? Squared off? Rounded? Other?

14. Is the family likely sitting on chairs or a bench?

15. How many beverage cans or bottles?

16. Is there any activity in the background?

17. Describe the food on the table. Is anyone eating? Who is interacting with whom?

How did you do with this photograph? Are you developing skill at noticing everything?

Narrative Description

On October 30, the Belton First National Bank discovered that the $3,000 it had received that morning from the Greenville First National Bank was in counterfeit $10, $20, and $50 bills. The genuine $3,000 had been counted by Greenville First National Bank clerk, Iris Stewart, the preceding afternoon. It was packed in eight black leather satchels and stored in the bank vault overnight. Greenville First National clerk, Brian Caruthers, accompanied armor carriers James Clark and Howard O'Keefe to Belton in an armored truck. Belton First National clerk, Cynthia Randall, discovered the counterfeit bills when she examined the serial numbers of the bills.

During the course of the investigation, the following statements were made.

1. Gerald Hathaway, clerk of the Greenville bank, told investigators that he had found the bank office open when he arrived at work on the morning of October 30. The only articles that appeared to be missing were eight black leather satchels of the type used to transport large sums of money.

2. Jon Perkins, head teller, told investigators that he did not check the contents of the black leather satchels after locking them in the vault around 4:30 p.m. on October 29.

3. Henry Green, janitor, said that he noticed Jon Perkins leaving the bank office around 5:30 p.m., one-half hour after the bank closed on October 29. He said that Perkins locked the door.

4. A scrap of cloth identical to the material of the armor carriers' uniforms was found caught in the seal of one of the black leather satchels delivered to Belton.

5. Brian Caruthers, clerk, said he saw James Clark and Howard O'Keefe talking in a secretive manner in the armored truck.

6. Thomas Stillman, bank executive, identified the eight black leather satchels containing the counterfeit money that arrived at the Belton First National Bank as the eight satchels that had disappeared from the bank office. He had noticed a slight difference in the linings of the satchels.

Approach the story in the same way that you approached the photographs.

WHO ARE THE PEOPLE?

Iris Stewart—clerk, Greenville First National Bank

Brian Caruthers—clerk, Greenville First National Bank

James Clark—armor carrier

Howard O'Keefe—armor carrier

Cynthia Randall—clerk, Belton First National Bank

Gerald Hathaway—clerk, Greenville First National Bank

Jon Perkins—head teller, Greenville First National Bank

Henry Green—janitor, Greenville First National Bank

Thomas Stillman—bank executive, Greenville First National Bank

WHAT IS THE CHRONOLOGY?

Money counted and packed afternoon of October 29

Satchels locked into vault at 4:30 p.m., October 29

Bank closed at 5:00 p.m.

Jon Perkins left and locked bank office 5:30 p.m., October 29

Satchels delivered morning of October 30

Counterfeit discovered October 30

OTHER DETAILS?

The total sum was $3000

Money was in $10, $20, and $50 bills

Money was packed in eight black leather satchels

Counterfeit discovered by Cynthia Randall examining serial numbers of bills

Apparent theft and switching of black satchels

Scrap of armor carrier uniform cloth caught in seal on one satchel

Money transported from Greenville First National Bank to Belton First National Bank

WHO DID WHAT?

Iris Stewart counted the genuine $3,000.

Jon Perkins locked the vault.

Henry Green saw Jon Perkins lock the bank.

James Clark and Howard O'Keefe delivered the satchels.

Brian Caruthers accompanied the armor carriers in the armored truck and noticed them whispering.

Gerald Hathaway found the Greenville bank open in the morning and noticed that eight satchels were missing. Cynthia Randall discovered that the money was counterfeit.

Thomas Stillman noticed a slight difference in linings of satchels and was able to identify the ones that had arrived at Belton as the ones missing from Greenville.

Obviously, there are a great many details on which you might be questioned. Read the passage carefully. Organize people, events, and facts in some logical order. Remember as much as you can in the best way you know how. The questions immediately follow the memorizing time, so you will not need to remember for long.

How to Answer Reading Comprehension Questions

TIP

The key to success with reading questions is comprehension, not speed.

Civil service exams are not, as a rule, fast-paced. There is ample time in which to complete the exam, provided that you do not spend excessive time struggling with one or two "impossible" questions. If you are reading with comprehension, your mind will not wander and your speed will be adequate.

Between now and the test day, you must work to improve your reading concentration and comprehension. Your daily newspaper provides excellent material to improve your reading. Make a point of reading all the way through any article that you begin. Do not be satisfied with the first paragraph or two. Read with a pencil in hand. Underscore details and ideas that seem to be crucial to the meaning of the article. Notice points of view, arguments, and supporting information. When you have finished the article, summarize it for yourself. Do you know the purpose of the article? The main idea presented? The attitude of the writer? The points over which there is controversy? Did you find certain information lacking? As you answer these questions, skim back over your underlinings. Did you focus on important words and ideas? Did you read with comprehension?

As you repeat this process day after day, you will find that your reading will become more efficient. You will read with greater understanding and will "get more" from your newspaper.

One aspect of your daily reading that deserves special attention is vocabulary building. The most effective reader has a rich, extensive vocabulary. As you read, make a list of unfamiliar words. Include in your list words that you understand within the context of the article but that you cannot really define. In addition, mark words that you do not understand at all. When you put aside your newspaper, go to the dictionary and look up every new and unfamiliar word. Write the word and its definition in a special notebook. Writing the words and their definitions helps seal them in your memory far better than just reading them, and the notebook serves as a handy reference for your own use. A sensitivity to the meanings of words and an understanding of more words will make reading easier and more enjoyable even if none of the words you learn in this way crops up on your exam. In fact, the habit of vocabulary building is a good lifetime habit to develop.

Strange as it may seem, it's a good idea to approach reading comprehension questions by reading the questions—not the answer choices, just the questions themselves—before you read the selection. The questions will alert you to look for certain details, ideas, and points of view. Use your pencil. Underscore key words in the questions. These will help you direct your attention as you read.

Next skim the selection very rapidly to get an idea of its subject matter and its organization. If key words or ideas pop out at you, underline them, but do not consciously search out details in the preliminary skimming.

Now read the selection carefully, with comprehension as your main goal. Underscore the important words as you have been doing in your newspaper reading.

Finally, return to the questions. Read each question carefully. Be sure you know what it asks. Misreading of questions is a major cause of error on reading comprehension questions. Read all the answer choices. Eliminate the obviously incorrect answers. You may be left with only one possible answer. If you find yourself with more than one possible answer, reread the question. Then skim the passage once more, focusing on the underlined segments. By now you should be able to conclude which answer is best.

Reading comprehension questions may take a number of different forms. In general, some of the most common forms are as follows:

❶ *Question of fact or detail.* You may have to mentally rephrase or rearrange, but you should find the answer stated in the body of the selection.

❷ *Best title or main idea.* The answer may be obvious, but the incorrect choices to the "main idea" question are often half-truths that are easily confused with the main idea. They may misstate the idea, omit part of the idea, or even offer a supporting idea quoted directly from the text. The correct answer is the one that covers the largest part of the selection.

❸ *Interpretation.* This type of question asks you what the passage means, not just what it says.

TIP

Success with reading questions depends on more than reading comprehension. You must also know how to draw the answers from the reading selection and be able to distinguish the *best* answer from a number of answers that all seem to be correct or from a number of answers that all seem to be wrong.

4 *Inference.* This is the most difficult type of reading comprehension question. It asks you to go beyond what the selection says and to predict what might happen next. Your answer must be based upon the information in the selection and your own common sense, not upon any other information you may have about the subject. A variation of the inference question might be stated as, "The author would expect that ..." To answer this question, you must understand the author's point of view and then make an inference from that viewpoint based upon the information in the selection.

5 *Vocabulary.* Some civil service reading sections, directly or indirectly, ask the meanings of certain words as used in the selection.

Before you begin the practice tests, review this list of hints for scoring high on reading comprehension tests.

1 Read the questions and underline key words.

2 Skim the selection to get a general idea of the subject matter, the point that is being made, and organization of the material.

3 Reread the selection, giving attention to details and point of view. Underscore key words and phrases.

4 If the author has quoted material from another source, be sure that you understand the purpose of the quote. Does the author agree or disagree?

5 Carefully read each question or incomplete statement. Determine exactly what is being asked. Watch for negatives or all-inclusive words, such as *always, never, all, only, every, absolutely, completely, none, entirely, no.*

6 Read all the answer choices. Eliminate those choices that are obviously incorrect. Reread the remaining choices and refer to the selection, if necessary, to determine the best answer.

7 Avoid inserting your own judgments into your answers. Even if you disagree with the author or even if you spot a factual error in the selection, you must answer on the basis of what is stated or implied in the selection.

8 Do not allow yourself to spend too much time on any one question. If looking back at the selection does not help you to find or figure out the answer, choose from among the answers, mark the question in the test booklet, and go on. If you have time at the end of the exam or exam portion, reread the selection and the question. Often a fresh look provides new insights.

Test-Taking Techniques

MULTIPLE-CHOICE QUESTIONS

Almost all of the tests given on civil service exams are in a multiple-choice format. This means that you have four or five answer choices from which to select the correct answer. It's not something that should be overwhelming. There is a basic technique to answering these types of questions. Once you understand this technique, your test-taking will be far less stressful.

First, there should only be one correct answer. Since these tests have been given time and again, and the test-developers have a sense of which questions work and which questions don't work, it is rare that your choices will be ambiguous. They may be complex and somewhat confusing, but there will still be only one right answer.

The first step is to look at the question, without looking at the answer choices. Now select the correct answer. That may sound somewhat simplistic, but it's usually the case that your first choice is the correct one. If you go back and change it, redo it again and again, it's more likely that you'll end up with the wrong answer. Thus, follow your instinct. Once you have come up with the answer, look at the answer choices. If your answer is one of the choices, you're probably correct. It's not 100 percent infallible, but it's a strong possibility that you've selected the right answer.

With math questions you should first solve the problem. If your answer is among the choices, you're probably correct. Don't ignore things like the proper function signs (adding, subtracting, multiplying, and dividing), negative and positive numbers, and so on.

But suppose you don't know the correct answer. You then use the "process of elimination." It's a time-honored technique for test-takers. There is always one correct answer. There is usually one answer choice that is totally incorrect—a "distracter." If you look at that choice and it seems highly unlikely, then eliminate it. Depending on the number of choices (four or five), you've just cut down the number of choices to make. Now weigh the other choices. They may seem incorrect, or they may seem correct. If they seem incorrect, eliminate them. You've now increased your odds at getting the correct answer.

In the end, you may be left with only two choices. At that point, it's just a matter of guessing. But with only two choices left, you now have a 50 percent chance of getting it right. With four choices, you only have a 25 percent chance, and with five choices, only a 20 percent chance at guessing correctly. That's why the process of elimination is important.

"TESTWISENESS"

Many factors enter into a test score. The most important factor should be the ability to answer the questions, which in turn indicates the ability to learn and perform the duties of the job. Assuming that you have this ability, knowing what to expect on the exam and familiarity with techniques of effective test taking should give you the confidence you need to do your best on the exam.

There is no quick substitute for long-term study and development of your skills and abilities to prepare you for doing well on tests. However, there are some steps you can take to help you do the very best that you can. Some of these steps are done before the test, and some are followed when you are taking the test. Knowing these steps is often called being "test-wise." Following these steps may help you feel more confident as you take the actual test.

"Testwiseness" is a general term that simply means being familiar with some good procedures to follow when getting ready for and taking a test. The procedures fall into four major areas: (1) being prepared, (2) avoiding careless errors, (3) managing your time, and (4) guessing.

Being Prepared

Don't make the test harder than it has to be by not preparing yourself. You are taking a very important step in preparation by reading this book and taking the practice tests that are included. This will help you to become familiar with the tests and the kinds of questions you will have to answer.

As you use this book, carefully read the sample questions and directions for taking the test. Then, when you take the practice tests, time yourself as you will be timed in the real test.

As you are working on the sample questions, don't look at the correct answers before you try to answer them on your own. This can fool you into thinking you understand a question when you really don't. Try it on your own first, and then compare your answer with the one given. Remember, in a practice test, you are your own grader; you don't gain anything by pretending to understand something you really don't.

ALERT!

If you do not understand any of the examiner's instructions, ASK QUESTIONS. It would be ridiculous to score less than your best because of poor communication.

On the examination day assigned to you, allow the test itself to be the main attraction of the day. Do not squeeze it in between other activities. Be sure to bring admission card, identification, and pencils, as instructed. Prepare these the night before so that you are not flustered by a last-minute search. Arrive rested, relaxed, and on time. In fact, plan to arrive a little bit early. Leave plenty of time for traffic tie-ups or other complications that might upset you and interfere with your test performance.

In the test room, the examiner will hand out forms for you to fill out. He or she will give you the instructions that you must follow in taking the examination. The examiner will tell you how to fill in the grids on the forms. Time limits and timing signals will be explained.

At the examination, you must follow instructions exactly. Fill in the grids on the forms carefully and accurately. Misgridding may lead to loss of veteran's credits to which you may be entitled or misaddressing of your test results. Do not begin until you are told to begin. Stop as soon as the examiner tells you to stop. Do not turn pages until you are told to do so. Do not go back to parts you have already completed.

The answer sheet for most multiple-choice exams is machine scored. You cannot give any explanations to the machine, so you must fill out the answer sheet clearly and correctly.

Marking Your Answer Sheet

❶ **Blacken your answer space firmly and completely.**

❷ **Mark only one answer for each question.** If you mark more than one answer, you will be considered wrong, even if one of the answers is correct.

❸ **If you change your mind, you must erase your mark.** Attempting to cross out an incorrect answer will not work. You must erase any incorrect answer completely. An incomplete erasure might be read as a second answer.

❹ **All of your answering should be in the form of blackened spaces.** The machine cannot read English. Do not write any notes in the margins.

❺ **Answer each question in the right place.** Question 1 must be answered in space 1; question 52 in space 52. If you should skip an answer space and mark a series of answers in the wrong places, you must erase all those answers and do the questions over, marking your answers in the proper places. You cannot afford to use the limited time in this way. Therefore, as you answer each question, look at its number and check that you are marking your answer in the space with the same number.

Avoiding Careless Errors

Don't reduce your score by making careless mistakes. Always read the instructions for each test section carefully, even when you think you already know what the directions are. It's why we stress throughout this book that it's important to fully understand the directions for these different question-types before you go into the actual exam. It will not only reduce errors, but it will save you time—time you will need for the questions.

What if you don't understand the directions? You will have risked getting the answers wrong for a whole test section. As an example, vocabulary questions can sometimes test synonyms (words that have similar meanings) and sometimes test antonyms (words with opposite meanings). You can easily see how a mistake in understanding in this case could make a whole set of answers incorrect.

If you have time, reread any complicated instructions after you do the first few questions to check that you really do understand them. Of course, whenever you are allowed to, ask the examiner to clarify anything you don't understand.

Other careless mistakes affect only the response to particular questions. This often happens with arithmetic questions, but can happen with other questions as well. This type of error, called a "response error," usually stems from a momentary lapse of concentration.

ALERT!

Any infraction of the rules is considered cheating. If you cheat, your test paper will not be scored, and you will not be eligible for appointment.

A common error in reading interpretation questions is bringing your own information into the subject. For example, you may encounter a passage that discusses a subject you know something about. While this can make the passage easier to read, it can also tempt you to rely on your own knowledge about the subject. You must rely on information within the passage for your answers. In fact, sometimes the "wrong answers" to the questions are based on true information about the subject not given in the passage.

Managing Your Time

Before you begin, take a moment to plan your progress through the test. Although you are usually not expected to finish all of the questions given on a test, you should at least get an idea of how much time you should spend on each question in order to answer them all. For example, if there are 60 questions to answer and you have 30 minutes, you will have about one-half minute to spend on each question.

Keep track of the time on your watch or the room clock, but do not fixate on the time remaining. Your task is to answer questions. Do not spend too much time on any one question. If you find yourself stuck, do not take the puzzler as a personal challenge. Either guess and mark the question in the question booklet or skip the question entirely, marking the question as a skip and taking care to skip the answer space on the answer sheet. If there is time at the end of the exam or exam part, you can return and give marked questions another try.

Guessing

You may be wondering whether or not it is wise to guess when you are not sure of an answer (even if you've reduced the odds to 50 percent) or whether it is better to skip the question when you are not certain. The wisdom of guessing depends on the scoring method for the particular examination part. If the scoring is "rights only," that is, one point for each correct answer and no subtraction for wrong answers, then by all means you should guess. Read the question and all of the answer choices carefully. Eliminate those answer choices that you are certain are wrong. Then guess from among the remaining choices. You cannot gain a point if you leave the answer space blank; you may gain a point with an educated guess or even with a lucky guess. In fact, it is foolish to leave any spaces blank on a test that counts "rights only." If it appears that you are about to run out of time before completing such an exam, mark all the remaining blanks with the same letter. According to the law of averages, you should get some portion of those questions right.

A wrong answer counts heavily against you. On this type of test, do not rush to fill answer spaces randomly at the end. Work as quickly as possible while concentrating on accuracy. Keep working carefully until time is called. Then stop and leave the remaining answer spaces blank.

For those tests that are scored by subtracting a fraction of a point for each wrong answer, the decision as to whether or not to guess is really up to you. A correct answer gives you one point;

a skipped space gives you nothing at all, but costs you nothing except the chance of getting the answer right; a wrong answer costs you 1/4 point. If you are really uncomfortable with guessing, you may skip a question, BUT you must then remember to skip its answer space as well. The risk of losing your place if you skip questions is so great that we advise you to guess even if you are not sure of the answer. Our suggestion is that you answer every question in order, even if you have to guess. It is better to lose a few 1/4 points for wrong guesses than to lose valuable seconds figuring where you started marking answers in the wrong place, erasing, and re-marking answers. On the other hand, do not mark random answers at the end. Work steadily until time is up.

One of the questions you should ask in the testing room is what scoring method will be used on your particular exam. You can then guide your guessing procedure accordingly.

Scoring

If your exam is a short-answer exam such as those often used by companies in the private sector, your answers will be graded by a personnel officer trained in grading test questions. If you blackened spaces on the separate answer sheet accompanying a multiple-choice exam, your answer sheet will be machine scanned or will be hand scored using a punched card stencil. Then a raw score will be calculated using the scoring formula that applies to that test or test portion—rights only, rights minus wrongs, or rights minus a fraction of wrongs. Raw scores on test parts are then added together for a total raw score.

A raw score is not a final score. The raw score is not the score that finds its way onto an eligibility list. The civil service testing authority converts raw scores to a scaled score according to an unpublicized formula of its own. The scaling formula allows for slight differences in difficulty of questions from one form of the exam to another and allows for equating the scores of all candidates. Regardless of the number of questions and possible different weights of different parts of the exam, most civil service clerical test scores are reported on a scale of 1 to 10. The entire process of conversion from raw to scaled score is confidential information. The score you receive is not your number right, is not your raw score, and, despite being on a scale of 1 to 100, is not a percentage. It is a scaled score. If you are entitled to veterans' service points, these are added to your passing scaled score to boost your rank on the eligibility list. Veterans' points are added only to passing scores. A failing score cannot be brought to passing level by adding veterans' points. The score earned plus veterans' service points, if any, is the score that finds its place on the rank order eligibility list.

PROMOTION EXAMS

Examinations for the positions of senior court officer and court clerk are very different from the open competitive examination for the entry position of court officer. While the entry examination is geared to measure the applicant's ability to learn the duties of the job quickly and thoroughly and to perform effectively on the job, the promotional exam asks, "What do you know? What have you learned?" Aside from a reading comprehension section on the court clerk exam, all the questions on the promotional exams are based on knowledge of the functioning of the courts, of the law itself, and about the actual duties of court officers.

Applicants for the position of senior court officer must have served for at least one year in the position of court officer. Those who seek to become court clerks must have served for at least two years as court officers or in similar responsible positions within the court system. These years of exposure should have led to familiarity with the vocabulary of the court system, to an understanding of the responsibilities of, and limitations on, the court officer, and to an appreciation of emergencies that may arise and how to handle them.

The knowledge for answering questions on the promotional exams comes from three sources: experience; the training, instruction, and handouts given to court officers and responsible employees of the court; and study of the laws themselves. Part of your preparation for the exam must involve going back to training materials and handouts and rereading the contents in light of your own experiences. Part of your preparation should consist of going into the law library and browsing through articles and sections that seem applicable to the exam as enumerated on the announcement. The rest of your preparation is right here in this book.

MEDICAL EXAM

A medical exam is self-explanatory. Passing or failing this exam does not necessarily have any bearing upon your passing or failing other exams. However, if there are eyesight and/or hearing requirements for the specific position, these must be checked against agency standards. If the job requires standing, lifting, or running, you must be medically able to withstand the rigors. Drug testing may be included and is legal if applied routinely and equally to all applicants and if notice is given beforehand.

PHYSICAL ABILITY EXAM

Physical ability testing is limited to applicants for physically demanding jobs. Police officers, firefighters, and correction officers, for example, must be able to run, climb, and carry, often under stress of personal danger as well as under the pressures of the immediate situation. Normally, a court officer's responsibilities are less physically stressful. Usually, the physical ability test is a qualifying test—either you can do it or you can't. Again, like the medical examination, passing or failing this test may have little bearing upon passing the exams—only your suitability for a specific job.

PSYCHOLOGICAL INTERVIEW

Finally, there may be a psychological interview. It is not a prerequisite for passing the exams, but instead, may be used to determine your suitability for a specific job. This interview differs from the general information interview or the final hiring and placement interview in that it tries to assess your behavior under stress.

BACKGROUND INVESTIGATION

Because of the sensitive nature of the court officer's functions, candidates will be investigated with respect to employment history, educational qualifications, military service record, arrest and summons record, and other pertinent factors deemed important to the performance of required job duties.

Reading all the applications and weeding out the unqualified ones takes time. Weighing education and experience factors takes time. Administering and scoring of exams takes time. Interviews, medical exams, and physical ability tests take time. Verifying references takes time. And, finally, the vacancies must occur, and the government agency must have the funds to fill the vacancies.

All of this clarifies why you must not leave a job or a job search at any step along the way. Wait until you are offered your government job before you cut other ties. But when you finally do get that job, you will have a good income, many benefits, and job security.

SUMMING IT UP

- The written exam is a key component of the court officer screening process and tests a variety of subject areas, including clerical checking, observation and memory, and reading comprehension.

- The court officer screening process is extensive and includes a written exam, interview, medical examination, physical ability examination, psychological interview, and background investigation.

PART II

FIVE PRACTICE TESTS

PRACTICE TEST 1

PRACTICE TEST 2

PRACTICE TEST 3

PRACTICE TEST 4

PRACTICE TEST 5: Promotion Exam

ANSWER SHEET PRACTICE TEST 1

1. Ⓐ Ⓑ Ⓒ Ⓓ	19. Ⓐ Ⓑ Ⓒ Ⓓ	37. Ⓐ Ⓑ Ⓒ Ⓓ	54. Ⓐ Ⓑ Ⓒ Ⓓ	71. Ⓐ Ⓑ Ⓒ Ⓓ
2. Ⓐ Ⓑ Ⓒ Ⓓ	20. Ⓐ Ⓑ Ⓒ Ⓓ	38. Ⓐ Ⓑ Ⓒ Ⓓ	55. Ⓐ Ⓑ Ⓒ Ⓓ	72. Ⓐ Ⓑ Ⓒ Ⓓ
3. Ⓐ Ⓑ Ⓒ Ⓓ	21. Ⓐ Ⓑ Ⓒ Ⓓ	39. Ⓐ Ⓑ Ⓒ Ⓓ	56. Ⓐ Ⓑ Ⓒ Ⓓ	73. Ⓐ Ⓑ Ⓒ Ⓓ
4. Ⓐ Ⓑ Ⓒ Ⓓ	22. Ⓐ Ⓑ Ⓒ Ⓓ	40. Ⓐ Ⓑ Ⓒ Ⓓ	57. Ⓐ Ⓑ Ⓒ Ⓓ	74. Ⓐ Ⓑ Ⓒ Ⓓ
5. Ⓐ Ⓑ Ⓒ Ⓓ	23. Ⓐ Ⓑ Ⓒ Ⓓ	41. Ⓐ Ⓑ Ⓒ Ⓓ	58. Ⓐ Ⓑ Ⓒ Ⓓ	75. Ⓐ Ⓑ Ⓒ Ⓓ
6. Ⓐ Ⓑ Ⓒ Ⓓ	24. Ⓐ Ⓑ Ⓒ Ⓓ	42. Ⓐ Ⓑ Ⓒ Ⓓ	59. Ⓐ Ⓑ Ⓒ Ⓓ	76. Ⓐ Ⓑ Ⓒ Ⓓ
7. Ⓐ Ⓑ Ⓒ Ⓓ	25. Ⓐ Ⓑ Ⓒ Ⓓ	43. Ⓐ Ⓑ Ⓒ Ⓓ	60. Ⓐ Ⓑ Ⓒ Ⓓ	77. Ⓐ Ⓑ Ⓒ Ⓓ
8. Ⓐ Ⓑ Ⓒ Ⓓ	26. Ⓐ Ⓑ Ⓒ Ⓓ	44. Ⓐ Ⓑ Ⓒ Ⓓ	61. Ⓐ Ⓑ Ⓒ Ⓓ	78. Ⓐ Ⓑ Ⓒ Ⓓ
9. Ⓐ Ⓑ Ⓒ Ⓓ	27. Ⓐ Ⓑ Ⓒ Ⓓ	45. Ⓐ Ⓑ Ⓒ Ⓓ	62. Ⓐ Ⓑ Ⓒ Ⓓ	79. Ⓐ Ⓑ Ⓒ Ⓓ
10. Ⓐ Ⓑ Ⓒ Ⓓ	28. Ⓐ Ⓑ Ⓒ Ⓓ	46. Ⓐ Ⓑ Ⓒ Ⓓ	63. Ⓐ Ⓑ Ⓒ Ⓓ	80. Ⓐ Ⓑ Ⓒ Ⓓ
11. Ⓐ Ⓑ Ⓒ Ⓓ	29. Ⓐ Ⓑ Ⓒ Ⓓ	47. Ⓐ Ⓑ Ⓒ Ⓓ	64. Ⓐ Ⓑ Ⓒ Ⓓ	81. Ⓐ Ⓑ Ⓒ Ⓓ
12. Ⓐ Ⓑ Ⓒ Ⓓ	30. Ⓐ Ⓑ Ⓒ Ⓓ	48. Ⓐ Ⓑ Ⓒ Ⓓ	65. Ⓐ Ⓑ Ⓒ Ⓓ	82. Ⓐ Ⓑ Ⓒ Ⓓ
13. Ⓐ Ⓑ Ⓒ Ⓓ	31. Ⓐ Ⓑ Ⓒ Ⓓ	49. Ⓐ Ⓑ Ⓒ Ⓓ	66. Ⓐ Ⓑ Ⓒ Ⓓ	83. Ⓐ Ⓑ Ⓒ Ⓓ
14. Ⓐ Ⓑ Ⓒ Ⓓ	32. Ⓐ Ⓑ Ⓒ Ⓓ	50. Ⓐ Ⓑ Ⓒ Ⓓ	67. Ⓐ Ⓑ Ⓒ Ⓓ	84. Ⓐ Ⓑ Ⓒ Ⓓ
15. Ⓐ Ⓑ Ⓒ Ⓓ	33. Ⓐ Ⓑ Ⓒ Ⓓ	51. Ⓐ Ⓑ Ⓒ Ⓓ	68. Ⓐ Ⓑ Ⓒ Ⓓ	85. Ⓐ Ⓑ Ⓒ Ⓓ
16. Ⓐ Ⓑ Ⓒ Ⓓ	34. Ⓐ Ⓑ Ⓒ Ⓓ	52. Ⓐ Ⓑ Ⓒ Ⓓ	69. Ⓐ Ⓑ Ⓒ Ⓓ	86. Ⓐ Ⓑ Ⓒ Ⓓ
17. Ⓐ Ⓑ Ⓒ Ⓓ	35. Ⓐ Ⓑ Ⓒ Ⓓ	53. Ⓐ Ⓑ Ⓒ Ⓓ	70. Ⓐ Ⓑ Ⓒ Ⓓ	87. Ⓐ Ⓑ Ⓒ Ⓓ
18. Ⓐ Ⓑ Ⓒ Ⓓ	36. Ⓐ Ⓑ Ⓒ Ⓓ			

answer sheet

Practice Test 1

Directions: Answer questions 1–15 based on the incident described below. You will have 10 minutes to read and study the description of the incident. Then you will have to answer the 15 questions about the incident without referring back to the description of the incident.

Police Officers Brown and Reid are on patrol in a radio car on a Saturday afternoon in the fall. They receive a radio message that a burglary is in progress on the fifth floor of a seven-floor building on the corner of 7th Street and Main. They immediately proceed to that location to investigate and take appropriate action.

The police officers are familiar with the location, and they know that the Fine Jewelry Company occupies the entire fifth floor of the building. They are also aware that the owner, who is not in the office on weekends, often leaves large amounts of gold in his office safe. Upon arrival at the scene, the officers lock their radio car and proceed to look for the building superintendent in order to get into the building. The superintendent states that he has not heard or seen anything unusual, although admitting he did leave the premises for approximately 1 hour to have lunch. The officers start for the fifth floor, using the main elevator. As they reach that floor and open the door, they hear noises followed by the sound of the freight elevator door in the rear of the building closing and the elevator descending. They quickly run through the open door of the Fine Jewelry Company and observe that the office safe is open and empty. The officers then proceed to the rear of the building and use the rear staircase to reach the ground floor. They open the rear door and go out onto the street, where they observe four individuals running up the street, crossing at the corner. At that point, the police officers get a clear view of the suspects. They are three males and one female. One of the males appears to be white, one is obviously Hispanic, and the other male is black. The female is white.

The white male is bearded. He is dressed in jeans and white sneakers and a red and blue jacket. He is carrying a white duffel bag on his shoulder. The Hispanic male limps slightly, and he has a large, dark moustache. He is wearing brown slacks, a green shirt, and brown shoes. He is carrying a blue duffel bag on his shoulder. The black male is clean shaven and is wearing black pants, a white shirt, a green cap, and black shoes. He is carrying what appears to be a tool box. The white female is carrying a sawed-off shotgun, has long brown hair, and is wearing white jeans, a blue blouse, and blue sneakers. She has a red kerchief around her neck.

The officers chase the suspects for two blocks without being able to catch them. At that point, the suspects separate. The white and black males quickly get into a black 1973 Chevrolet station wagon with Connecticut license plates with the letters AWK and drive away. The Hispanic male and the white female get away in an old, light-blue Dodge van. The van has a prominent CB antenna on top and large yellow streaks running along the doors on both sides. There is a large dent in the right rear fender, and the van bears New Jersey license plates that the officers are unable to read.

The station wagon turns left and enters the expressway headed toward Connecticut. The van makes a right turn and proceeds in the direction of the tunnel headed for New Jersey.

The officers quickly return to their radio car to report what has happened.

1. The officers were able to read the following letters from the license plates on the station wagon
   (A) WAX
   (B) EWK
   (C) AUK
   (D) AWK

2. The van used by the suspects had a dented
   (A) left front fender
   (B) right front fender
   (C) right rear fender
   (D) left rear fender

3. The officers observed that the van was headed in the direction of
   (A) Long Island
   (B) Pennsylvania
   (C) New Jersey
   (D) Connecticut

4. The best description of the female suspect's hair is
   (A) short and light in color
   (B) long and light in color
   (C) short and dark in color
   (D) long and dark in color

5. The suspect who was wearing a white shirt is the
   (A) white male
   (B) Hispanic male
   (C) black male
   (D) white female

6. The suspect who wore white jeans is the
   (A) white male
   (B) Hispanic male
   (C) black male
   (D) white female

7. The Hispanic male suspect carried a duffel bag of what color?
   (A) yellow
   (B) red
   (C) blue
   (D) brown

8. Of the following, the best description of the shoes worn by the Hispanic suspect is
   (A) white sneakers
   (B) black shoes
   (C) black boots
   (D) brown shoes

9. The suspect who was carrying the white duffel bag was the
   (A) white female
   (B) black male
   (C) Hispanic male
   (D) white male

10. The suspect who was carrying the shotgun was the
    (A) white female
    (B) black male
    (C) Hispanic male
    (D) white male

11. The green cap was worn by the
    (A) white female
    (B) black male
    (C) Hispanic male
    (D) white male

12. The suspect who limped when he or she ran was the
    (A) white female
    (B) black male
    (C) Hispanic male
    (D) white male

13. Of the following, the best description of the station wagon used by the suspects is a
    (A) 1973 black Chevrolet station wagon
    (B) 1971 blue Ford
    (C) 1971 green Dodge
    (D) 1976 red Ford

14. The best description of the suspects who used the station wagon to depart is
    (A) a black male and a white female
    (B) a black male and a white male
    (C) a white female and a Hispanic male
    (D) a black male and a Hispanic male

15. The van's license plate was from which of the following states?
    (A) New York
    (B) Delaware
    (C) New Jersey
    (D) Connecticut

QUESTIONS 16–19 ARE BASED ON THE FOLLOWING PASSAGE.

Court officers have the responsibilities of maintaining order in the courtroom and ensuring that the judicial process is carried out fairly and impartially. Sometimes this means that parties, spectators, attorneys, jurors, and other court personnel are prohibited from accessing desired information or saying or doing what they would like to in a case.

16. If an attorney calls a court officer and asks what the judge's written decision will be on the case and the court officer knows the decision, the court officer should:
    (A) tell the attorney, since he or she will find out anyway
    (B) refer the attorney to the judge
    (C) decline to tell the attorney
    (D) go ask the judge if he can tell the attorney

17. If a witness stands to take the oath to testify in a case, but fails to leave the courtroom when requested to do so by the judge, and the court officer notices this, the court officer's preferred response is to:
    (A) ignore the problem and wait for an attorney to notice
    (B) tell the attorneys of the situation
    (C) tell the judge of the situation
    (D) ask the witness to leave the courtroom based on the judge's instruction

18. When a court officer receives a call from a litigant in his court asking for legal advice, the court officer should:
    (A) give the best advice possible, whether he is sure of the answer or not
    (B) only give advice if he knows the answer
    (C) refer the caller to the judge
    (D) not give any advice

19. When a trial is in progress, what is the best method of asking a member of the gallery to stop talking?
    (A) remove the person from the courtroom
    (B) walk to the aisle and tell the person to hush
    (C) stand, make eye contact with the person, and, with a quick motion, bring your finger to your lips and be seated, showing no anger or emotion
    (D) make eye contact and frown at the spectator

QUESTIONS 20–23 ARE BASED ON THE FOLLOWING PASSAGE.

A court officer shall give reasonable aid to a sick or injured person. He or she shall summon an ambulance, if necessary, by telephoning the Police Department, which shall notify the hospital concerned. He or she shall wait in a place where the arriving ambulance can see him or her, if possible, so as to direct the ambulance doctor or attendant to the patient. If the ambulance does not arrive within a half hour, the court officer should call a second time, telling the department that this is a second call. However, if the injured person is conscious, the court officer should ask whether such person is willing to go to a hospital before calling for an ambulance.

20. According to the preceding paragraph, the court officer who wishes to summon an ambulance should telephone the
   (A) nearest hospital
   (B) Department of Hospitals
   (C) Police Department
   (D) nearest police precinct

21. According to the preceding paragraph, if an ambulance doesn't arrive within half an hour, the court officer should
   (A) ask the person injured if he or she wants to go to the hospital in a cab
   (B) call the Police Department
   (C) call the nearest police precinct
   (D) call the nearest hospital

22. According to the preceding paragraph, a court officer who is called to help a person who has fallen on the courthouse steps and apparently has a broken leg should
   (A) put the leg in traction so that the doctor will have no difficulty setting it
   (B) ask the person, if he or she is conscious, whether he or she wishes to go to a hospital
   (C) attempt to get the story behind the injury to determine if the city is involved
   (D) put in a call for an ambulance at once

23. According to the preceding paragraph, a court officer who is present when a witness becomes ill while waiting to testify should
   (A) wait in front of the room until the ambulance arrives
   (B) send a bystander to the courtroom to page a doctor
   (C) ask the witness if he or she wishes to go to a hospital
   (D) call the court clerk for instructions

QUESTIONS 24–26 ARE BASED ON THE FOLLOWING PASSAGE.

Accident proneness is a subject that deserves much more objective and competent study than it has received to date. In discussing accident proneness, it is important to differentiate between the employee who is a "repeater" and one who is truly accident prone. It is obvious that any person assigned to work without thorough training in safe practice is liable to injury until he or she does learn the "how" of it. Few workers left to their own devices develop adequate safe practices; therefore, they must be trained. Only those who fail to respond to proper training should be regarded as accident prone. The repeater whose accident record can be explained by a correctable physical defect, by correctable plant or machine hazards, or by assignment to work for which he or she is not suited because of physical deficiencies or special abilities cannot be fairly called accident prone.

24. According to the preceding paragraph, people are considered accident prone if
    (A) they have accidents regardless of the fact that they have been properly trained
    (B) they have many accidents
    (C) it is possible for them to have accidents
    (D) they work at a job where accidents are possible

25. According to the preceding paragraph
    (A) workers learn the safe way of doing things if left to their own intelligence
    (B) most workers must be trained to be safe
    (C) a worker who has had more than one accident has not been properly trained
    (D) intelligent workers are always safe

26. According to the preceding paragraph, a person would not be called accident prone if the cause of the accident were
    (A) a lack of interest in the job
    (B) recklessness
    (C) high-speed machinery
    (D) eyeglasses that don't fit properly

27. "A sufficient quantity of material supplied as evidence enables the laboratory expert to determine the true nature of the substance, whereas an extremely limited specimen may be an abnormal sample containing foreign matter not indicative of the true nature of the material." On the basis of this statement alone, it may be concluded that a reason for giving an adequate sample of material for evidence to a laboratory expert is that
    (A) a limited specimen spoils more quickly than a larger sample
    (B) a small sample may not truly represent the evidence
    (C) he or she cannot analyze a small sample correctly
    (D) he or she must have enough material to keep a part of it untouched to show in court

28. "Upon retirement from service a member shall receive a retirement allowance that shall consist of an annuity that shall be the actuarial equivalent of his accumulated deductions at the time of his retirement; a pension in addition to this annuity that shall be equal to one service-fraction of his final compensation, multiplied by the number of years of city service since he last became a member credited to him; and a pension that is the actuarial equivalent of the 'reserve-for-increased-take-home-pay' to which he may then be entitled, if any." According to this selection, a retirement allowance shall consist of
    (A) an annuity plus a pension plus an actuarial equivalent
    (B) an annuity plus a pension reserve-for-increased-take-home-pay, if any
    (C) an annuity plus reserve-for-increased-take-home-pay, if any, plus final compensation
    (D) a pension plus reserve-for-increased-take-home-pay, if any, plus accumulated deductions

QUESTIONS 29–31 ARE BASED ON THE FOLLOWING PASSAGE.

What is required is a program that will protect our citizens and their property from criminal and antisocial acts, will effectively restrain and reform juvenile delinquents, and will prevent the further development of antisocial behavior. Discipline and punishment of offenders must necessarily play an important part in any such program. Serious offenders cannot be mollycoddled merely because they are under 21. Restraint and punishment necessarily follow serious antisocial acts. But punishment, if it is to be effective, must be a planned part of a more comprehensive program of treating delinquency.

29. A goal not included among those listed in the paragraph is to
   (A) stop young people from defacing public property
   (B) keep homes from being broken into
   (C) develop an intra-city boys' baseball league
   (D) change juvenile delinquents into useful citizens

30. According to the preceding paragraph, punishment is
   (A) not satisfactory in any program dealing with juvenile delinquents
   (B) the most effective means by which young vandals and hooligans can be reformed
   (C) not used sufficiently when dealing with serious offenders who are under 21
   (D) of value in reducing juvenile delinquency only if it is part of a complete program

31. With respect to serious offenders who are under 21 years of age, the paragraph suggests that they
   (A) be mollycoddled
   (B) be dealt with as part of a comprehensive program to punish mature criminals
   (C) should be punished
   (D) be prevented, by brute force if necessary, from performing antisocial acts

QUESTIONS 32–34 ARE BASED ON THE FOLLOWING PASSAGE.

A number of crimes, such as robbery, assault, rape, and certain forms of theft and burglary, are high-visibility crimes in that it is apparent to all concerned that they are criminal acts prior to or at the time they are committed. In contrast to these, check forgeries, especially those committed by first offenders, are low visibility. Little in the criminal act or in the interaction between the check passer and the person cashing the check identifies it as a crime. Closely related to this special quality of a forgery is the fact that, while it is formally defined and treated as a felonious or infamous crime, it is informally held by the legally untrained public to be a relatively harmless form of crime.

32. According to the preceding paragraph, crimes of "high visibility"
   (A) are immediately recognized as crimes by the victims
   (B) take place in public view
   (C) always involve violence or the threat of violence
   (D) usually are committed after dark

33. According to the preceding paragraph,
   (A) the public regards check forgery as a minor crime
   (B) the law regards check forgery as a minor crime
   (C) the law distinguishes between check forgery and other forgery
   (D) it is easier to spot inexperienced check forgers than other criminals

34. As used in this paragraph, an "infamous" crime is
- **(A)** more serious than a felony
- **(B)** less serious than a felony
- **(C)** more or less serious than a felony, depending on circumstances
- **(D)** the same as a felony

35. "The housing authority not only faces every problem of the private developer, it must also assume responsibilities of which a private builder is free. The authority must account to the community; it must conform to federal regulations and it must overcome the prejudices of contractors, bankers, and prospective tenants against public operations. These authorities are being watched by antihousing enthusiasts for the first error of judgment or the first evidence of high costs that can be torn to bits before a congressional committee." On the basis of this selection, which statement would be most correct?
- **(A)** Private builders do not have the opposition of contractors, bankers, and prospective tenants.
- **(B)** Congressional committees impede the progress of public housing by petty investigations.
- **(C)** A housing authority must deal with all the difficulties encountered by the private builder.
- **(D)** Housing authorities are no more immune to errors in judgment than private developers.

36. "If you are in doubt as to whether any matter is properly mailable, you should ask the postmaster. Even though the Post Office has not expressly declared any matter to be nonmailable, the sender of such matter may be held fully liable for violation of law if he does actually send nonmailable matter through the mails." Of the following, the most accurate statement made concerning this selection is:
- **(A)** nonmailable matter is not always clearly defined
- **(B)** ignorance of what constitutes nonmailable matter relieves the sender of all responsibility
- **(C)** though doubt may exist about the mailability of any matter, the sender is fully liable for law violation if such matter should be nonmailable
- **(D)** the Post Office Department is not explicit in its position on the violation of the nonmailable matter law

37. "Statistics tell us that heart disease kills more people than any other illness, and the death rate continues to rise. People over 30 have a 50-50 chance of escaping, for heart disease is chiefly an illness of people in late middle age and advanced years. Since more people in this age group are living today than were some years ago, heart disease is able to find more victims." On the basis of this selection, the one of the following statements most nearly correct is that
- **(A)** half of the people over 30 years of age have heart disease today
- **(B)** more people die of heart disease than of all other diseases combined
- **(C)** older people are the chief victims of heart disease
- **(D)** the rising birth rate has increased the possibility that the average person will die of heart disease

38. Assume that you borrowed $2,000 on November 1, 2000, for the use of which you were required to pay simple interest semiannually at 7% a year. By May 1, 2006, you would have paid interest amounting to

(A) $140
(B) $700
(C) $770
(D) $280

QUESTIONS 39–41 ARE BASED ON THE FOLLOWING TABLE.

	2005	2006	Numerical Increase
Clerical staff	1,226	1,347	
Court officers		529	34
Deputy sheriffs	38	40	
Supervisors			
Total	2,180	2,414	

39. The number in the "supervisors" group in 2005 was most nearly

(A) 500
(B) 475
(C) 450
(D) 425

40. The largest percentage increase from 2005 to 2006 was in the group of

(A) clerical staff
(B) court officers
(C) deputy sheriffs
(D) supervisors

41. In 2006, the ratio of the number of clerical staff to the total of the other three categories of employees was most nearly

(A) 1:1
(B) 2:1
(C) 3:1
(D) 4:1

42. A courtroom contains 72 persons, which is two fifths of its capacity. The number of persons that the courtroom can hold is

(A) 28
(B) 180
(C) 129
(D) greater than 200 and less than 300

43. The total cost of thirty pencils at 18¢ a dozen, twelve paper pads at 27½¢ each, and eight boxes of paper clips at 5¼¢ a box is

(A) more than $10
(B) $1.50
(C) $4.17
(D) $1.52

44. A worked 5 days on overhauling an old car. Then B worked 4 days to finish the job. After the sale of the car, the net profit was $243. They wanted to divide the profit on the basis of the time spent by each. A's share of the profit was

(A) $108
(B) $135
(C) $127
(D) $143

45. A clock that loses 4 minutes every 24 hours was set at 6 a.m. on October 1. What time was indicated by the clock when the *correct* time was 12 noon on October 6?

(A) 11:36 a.m.
(B) 11:38 a.m.
(C) 11:39 a.m.
(D) 11:40 a.m.

46. A secretary is entitled to 1⅓ days of sick leave for every thirty-two days of work. How many days of work must the secretary have to her credit in order to be entitled to twelve days of sick leave?

(A) 272
(B) 288
(C) 290
(D) 512

FOR QUESTIONS 47–56, COMPARE THE FOUR NAMES OR NUMBERS IN EACH QUESTION AND

Mark **(A)** if all *FOUR* names or numbers are different.
Mark **(B)** if *TWO* names or numbers are exactly the same.
Mark **(C)** if *THREE* names or numbers are exactly the same.
Mark **(D)** if all *FOUR* names or numbers are exactly the same.

47. W.E. Johnston
W.E. Johnson
W.E. Johnson
W.B. Johnson

48. Vergil L. Muller
Vergil L. Muller
Vergil L. Muller
Vergil L. Muller

49. 5261383
5263183
5263183
5623183

50. Atherton R. Warde
Asheton R. Warde
Atherton P. Warde
Athertin P. Warde

51. 8125690
8126690
8125609
8125609

52. E. Owens McVey
E. Owen McVey
E. Owen McVay
E. Owen McVey

53. Emily Neal Rouse
Emily Neal Rowse
Emily Neal Roose
Emily Neal Rowse

54. Francis Ramsdell
Francis Ransdell
Francis Ramsdell
Francis Ramsdell

55. 2395890
2395890
2395890
2395890

56. 1926341
1962341
1963241
1926341

FOR QUESTIONS 57–66, SELECT THE SENTENCE IN EACH QUESTION THAT IS BEST WITH RESPECT TO GRAMMAR AND USAGE.

57. (A) One of us have to make the reply before tomorrow.
(B) Making the reply before tomorrow will have to be done by one of us.
(C) One of us has to reply before tomorrow.
(D) Anyone has to reply before tomorrow.

58. (A) There is several ways to organize a good report.
(B) Several ways exist in organizing a good report.
(C) To organize a good report, several ways exist.
(D) There are several ways to organize a good report.

59. (A) All employees whose record of service ranged between 51 down to 40 years were retired.
(B) All employees who had served from 40 to 51 years were retired.
(C) All employees serving 40 to 51 years were retired.
(D) Those retired were employees serving 40 to 51 years.

60. (A) Of all the employees, he spends the most time at the office.
(B) He spends more time at the office than that of his employees.
(C) His working hours are longer or at least equal to those of the other employees.
(D) He devotes as much, if not more, time to his work than the rest of the employees.

61. **(A)** She made lots of errors in her typed report, which caused her to be reprimanded.
    (B) The supervisor reprimanded the typist, whom she believed had made careless errors.
    (C) Many errors were found in the report which she typed and could not disregard them.
    (D) The errors in the typed report were so numerous that they could hardly be overlooked.

62. **(A)** He suspects that the service is not so satisfactory as it should be.
    (B) He believes that we should try and find whether the service is satisfactory.
    (C) He believes that the service that we are giving is unsatisfactory.
    (D) He believes that the quality of our services are poor.

63. **(A)** Most all of these statements have been supported by persons who are reliable and can be depended on.
    (B) The persons which have guaranteed these statements are reliable.
    (C) Reliable persons guarantee the facts with regards to the truth of these statements.
    (D) These statements can be depended on, for their truth has been guaranteed by reliable persons.

64. **(A)** The personnel office has charge of employment, dismissals, and employee's welfare.
    (B) The personnel office is responsible for the employment, dismissal, and welfare of employees.
    (C) Employment, together with dismissals and employee's welfare, are handled by the personnel department.
    (D) The personnel office takes care of employment, dismissals, and etc.

65. **(A)** This kind of pen is some better than that kind.
    (B) I prefer having these pens than any other.
    (C) This kind of pen is the most satisfactory for my use.
    (D) In comparison with that kind of pen, this kind is more preferable.

66. **(A)** We often come across people to whom we disagree.
    (B) We often come across people in whom we disagree.
    (C) We often come across people in regard for whom we disagree.
    (D) We often come across people with whom we disagree.

FOR QUESTIONS 67–76, USE THE FOLLOWING TABLE TO COMPARE THE LETTERS AND NUMBERS IN EACH QUESTION. IN SOME OF THE QUESTIONS, AN ERROR EXISTS IN THE CODING. COMPARE THE NUMBERS AND LETTERS IN EACH QUESTION AND

Mark (A) if only one line contains errors.
Mark (B) if two lines contain errors.
Mark (C) if all three lines contain errors.
Mark (D) if none of the lines contains errors.

Code Letter	R	D	F	G	K	Z	E	P	A	T
Number	0	1	2	3	4	5	6	7	8	9

67.   KDEPAPT   4167879
              AGFKZEP   8324567
              RGDKTEZ   0314965

68.   KFPEZT   427659
              FETGEZ   269365
              ZKDEFP   546127

69.   PFDRKTE   7210496
              DETZFKA   1695248
              AKDFEPR   8512670

70.   GDFPKZE   3226456
              KGPTAFG   4379823
              AEGPTRD   6837910

71.   KDPZETG   4175693
              GREKTZE   3065956
              PGARFDG   7380123

72.   ZPGKRGT   5734039
              TFKGPRD   9234710
              KDAPEKZ   4187644

73.   PZKFGET   7452369
              RDPEKGF   0176432
              KDFPTAZ   4172983

74.   PEZKTGE   7654936
              GEPEKDF   3676421
              DFPTAGZ   1399835

75.   KDRTEZ   410965
              GAZFET   385269
              DPETGA   179948

76.   KTEFRAT   4962098
              PGKDEGP   7314637
              ZEPEGKF   5676432

QUESTIONS 77–81 ARE BASED ON THE FOLLOWING DUTIES OF A COURT OFFICER.

Throughout the session of the court, the officer must see that proper order and decorum are maintained in the courtroom. Above everything else, silence must be constantly observed, and every possible distraction must be eliminated so as not to delay the most efficient functioning of the court.

The officer must carry out such duties as may be required by the court and clerk. Examples of such duties are directing witnesses to the witness stand and assisting the court clerk and counsel in the handling of exhibits. At times, the officer must act as a messenger in procuring any books from the court library that are required by the attorneys and ordered by the court clerk.

The enforcement of the rules of the court requires courteous behavior on the part of the court officer, although firmness and strictness are necessary when the occasion requires such an attitude.

77. Testimony has been given, the witnesses have been cross-examined, and the attorneys have given their summations. Now the judge is charging the jury. A court officer has been stationed outside the courtroom door to prevent anyone from entering during the charge. The president of the City Council arrives, accompanied by a woman, and attempts to enter the courtroom. The court officer should

   (A) apologize and explain why they cannot be permitted to enter
   (B) permit the man to enter, since he is the president of the City Council, but exclude the woman
   (C) permit them to enter because surely the judge would make an exception for such important people
   (D) send a note in to the judge to ask whether they may be permitted to enter

78. A witness who is waiting to be called to the stand appears to be very nervous. He wiggles and squirms, stands and stretches, looks over his shoulder at the courtroom door, and waves to spectators and television cameras. The court officer should

   (A) tell the witness to leave the courtroom at once
   (B) handcuff the witness
   (C) ask the witness to please sit still and try to restrain himself
   (D) suggest to the judge that he call this witness next

79. During the course of cross-examination, a defendant frequently refers to a book that she claims has had a great influence on her life and that she claims justifies her behavior in the instance for which she is charged. In the jury box, two jurors begin a lively discussion of whether the defendant is quoting accurately. The best action for the court officer is to

   (A) ask the court clerk for permission to go to the library to get the book
   (B) send a messenger to get the book
   (C) assure the jurors that the book is being accurately quoted and that only the interpretation is in question
   (D) remind the jurors that they are not to converse in the courtroom

80. A group of spectators, friends of the plaintiff, is seated near the rear of the courtroom. As the trial progresses, they raise inoffensive but loud shouts of encouragement, such as "Right on" and "Way to go." Stern looks mute their enthusiasm for only a moment or two, and then they continue with their verbal support. In this case, the court officer should

(A) warn them that they are prejudicing their friend's case

(B) ask the group to leave the courtroom

(C) take each member by the hand and forcibly eject him or her from the courtroom

(D) call a police officer to arrest the noisy spectators

81. The judge has asked the court clerk to hand her Exhibit B, a document that she identifies by its title as well as by its Exhibit B designation. The court clerk requests that the court officer transmit the document to the judge. The court officer goes to the exhibit table and discovers that Exhibit B is an entirely different document and that the document that the judge has requested is really Exhibit F. The court officer should

(A) bring the judge Exhibit B

(B) bring the judge Exhibit F

(C) bring both Exhibits B and F

(D) tell the judge of her error and ask which document she really wants

QUESTIONS 82–85 ARE BASED ON THE FOLLOWING LEGAL DEFINITIONS.

Burglary is committed when a person enters a building to commit a crime therein.

Larceny is committed when a person wrongfully takes, obtains, or withholds the property of another.

Robbery is the forcible stealing of property. If a person, while committing a larceny, uses or threatens the immediate use of force, the crime changes from larceny to robbery.

Sexual abuse is committed when a person subjects another person to sexual contact without the second person's consent or when a person has sexual contact with another person less than 17 years of age. (A person less than 17 years of age cannot legally consent to any sexual conduct.) "Sexual contact" may be defined as touching the sexual or other intimate parts of a person to achieve sexual gratification.

Assault is committed when a person unlawfully causes a physical injury to another person.

82. James Kelly enters the home of Mary Smith with the intention of taking Mary's portable TV set. While Kelly is in the apartment, Mary wakes up and attempts to retrieve her TV set from Kelly. Kelly punches Mary in the face and flees with the TV set. Kelly can be charged with

(A) burglary and larceny

(B) burglary only

(C) robbery and larceny

(D) burglary and robbery

83. John Brown enters a department store with the intention of doing some shopping. Brown has a .38 caliber revolver in his coat pocket and also has a criminal conviction for armed robbery. As he passes the jewelry counter, he notices an expensive watch lying on the showcase. He checks to see whether anyone is watching him and, when he feels that he is not being observed, he slips the watch into his pocket and leaves the store. Brown could be charged with

(A) larceny

(B) burglary and larceny

(C) burglary and robbery

(D) robbery

84. Tom Murphy enters a crowded subway car. He positions himself behind a woman and starts to touch her buttocks with his hand. The woman becomes very annoyed and starts to move away. As she does so, Murphy reaches into her pocketbook and removes $10. He then exits the train at the next station. Murphy could be charged with
   (A) robbery, larceny, and sexual abuse
   (B) burglary, robbery, and sexual abuse
   (C) burglary, larceny, and sexual abuse
   (D) larceny and sexual abuse

85. Ed Saunders entered the apartment of Jane Roberts with the intent to rob and sexually abuse her. However, Roberts was not at home and Saunders left the apartment without taking anything. Saunders could be charged with
   (A) sexual abuse
   (B) robbery
   (C) burglary
   (D) none of the above, as a crime did not take place

QUESTIONS 86 AND 87 ARE BASED ON THE FOLLOWING PASSAGE.

Certain inmate types are generally found in prisons. These types are called gorillas, toughs, hipsters, and merchants. Gorillas deliberately use violence to intimidate fearful inmates into providing favors. Toughs are swift to explode into violence against prisoners because of real or imagined insult. Exploitation of others is not their major goal. Hipsters are bullies who choose victims with caution in order to win acceptance among inmates by demonstrating physical bravery. Their bravery, however, is false. Merchants exploit other inmates through manipulation in sharp trading of goods stolen from prison supplies or in trickery in gambling.

86. Martins frequently beats up Smith and Brooks. Smith and Brooks provide Martins with extra cigarettes and coffee. Martins is a
   (A) tough
   (B) gorilla
   (C) merchant
   (D) hipster

87. White and Miller are in the same cell block and are often assigned to be in the same place at the same time. They are scheduled for the same kitchen duty and the same exercise group. White is cross-eyed. It is often difficult to determine exactly where he is looking, and it often appears that he is directing his gaze in one direction. One day, Miller trips White and beats him about the head with a board. Miller is a
   (A) tough
   (B) gorilla
   (C) merchant
   (D) hipster

ANSWER KEY AND EXPLANATIONS

1. D	19. C	37. C	54. C	71. B
2. C	20. C	38. C	55. D	72. B
3. C	21. B	39. D	56. B	73. B
4. D	22. B	40. D	57. C	74. B
5. C	23. C	41. A	58. D	75. A
6. D	24. A	42. B	59. B	76. C
7. C	25. B	43. C	60. A	77. A
8. D	26. D	44. B	61. D	78. C
9. D	27. B	45. C	62. C	79. D
10. A	28. B	46. B	63. D	80. B
11. B	29. C	47. B	64. B	81. C
12. C	30. D	48. D	65. C	82. D
13. A	31. C	49. B	66. D	83. A
14. B	32. A	50. A	67. D	84. D
15. C	33. A	51. B	68. A	85. C
16. C	34. D	52. B	69. A	86. B
17. D	35. C	53. B	70. B	87. A
18. D	36. C			

1–15. **If you made any errors in answering questions 1–15, reread the description of the event and the questions. Confirm the correctness of the given answer.**

16. **The correct answer is (C).** One attorney should never be given information not given to other side. Also, the judge should not be placed in a situation where both parties to a lawsuit are not given equal access to the judge.

17. **The correct answer is (D).** If the witness will not leave based on the court officer's request, then the judge and attorneys should be notified.

18. **The correct answer is (D).** The court officer should not get involved with giving litigants in his court legal advice even if he thinks he knows the answer.

19. **The correct answer is (C).** This method will get the point across to the gallery member without causing a scene. However, if the talking persists, walk to the aisle and motion for the spectator to step outside the courtroom. At that time, inform the person to be quiet, and if he cannot be quiet, bar him from the courtroom.

20. **The correct answer is (C).** The court officer must telephone the Police Department, which, in turn, will notify a hospital to send an ambulance.

21. **The correct answer is (B).** The court officer must wait patiently for half an hour and then call the Police Department again.

22. **The correct answer is (B).** The last sentence says that the court officer should ask a conscious person if he or she is willing to go to a hospital.

23. **The correct answer is (C).** Assuming that the ill witness is conscious, the witness must be asked whether he or she wishes to go to the hospital before any further action is taken.

24. **The correct answer is (A).** Accident proneness is defined as susceptibility to frequent accidents despite proper training.

25. **The correct answer is (B).** Since few workers develop adequate safe practices on their own, most must be trained to be safe.

26. **The correct answer is (D).** The fitting of eyeglasses is a correctable situation. The person whose accidents are eliminated by the refitting of eyeglasses is not accident prone.

27. **The correct answer is (B).** "... a limited specimen may be an abnormal sample ... not indicative of the true nature of the material."

28. **The correct answer is (B).** The three components of the retirement allowance are separated by semicolons. They are an annuity, a pension, and a pension that is the actuarial equivalent of the reserve-for-increased-take-home pay.

29. **The correct answer is (C).** While participation in sports may help to turn youths from antisocial behavior, the paragraph specifically addresses crime, punishment, and reform.

30. **The correct answer is (D).** The last sentence makes this point very clearly.

31. **The correct answer is (C).** The paragraph states that serious young offenders should be punished and should not be mollycoddled because of their age. It does not suggest treating them as mature criminals.

32. **The correct answer is (A).** Without a doubt, victims of robbery, assault, rape, theft, and burglary immediately recognize that they have been victims of crimes.

33. **The correct answer is (A).** The law considers check forgery to be a felony, but the layman considers forgery to be relatively minor, probably because it is nonviolent.

34. **The correct answer is (D).** This definition is given in the last sentence.

35. **The correct answer is (C).** See the first sentence.

36. **The correct answer is (C).** The sender of nonmailable material is fully liable for violation of the law even though he or she may not have known that the material was not mailable. In other words, ignorance of the law is no excuse. When in doubt, ask.

37. **The correct answer is (C).** "... heart disease is chiefly an illness of people in late middle age and advanced years."

38. **The correct answer is (C).** November 1, 2000 to May 1, 2006 is 5½ years. $2,000 × 7% = $140 × 5.5 = $770.

39. **The correct answer is D.** You will need almost all the figures to calculate answers to the three questions, so begin by completing the table.

	2005	2006	Numerical Increase
Clerical staff	1,226	1,347	121
Court officers	495	529	34
Deputy sheriffs	38	40	2
Supervisors	421	498	77
Totals	2,180	2,414	234

40. **The correct answer is (D).** To find percentage increase, divide the numerical increase by the original number. The approximate percentage increases are clerical staff 10%; court officers 7%; deputy sheriffs 5%; supervisors 18%.

41. **The correct answer is (A).** The total of employees other than clerical staff in 2006 was 1,067. The ratio of others to clerical staff was closest to 1:1.

42. **The correct answer is (B).** If $\frac{2}{5}$ = 72, then $\frac{1}{5}$ = 36 and $\frac{5}{5}$ or a full courtroom = 180.

43. **The correct answer is (C).** 30 pencils = $2\frac{1}{2}$ dozen × $.18 dozen = $ .45

$$12 \text{ pads} \times \$.275 = 3.30$$
$$8 \text{ boxes paper clips} \times \$.0525 = \underline{\quad.42}$$
$$= \$4.17$$

44. **The correct answer is (B).** *A* and *B* worked on the car for nine days.
$243 ÷ 9 = $27 profit per day. *A*'s five days were worth $27 × 5 = $135.

45. **The correct answer is (C).** From 6 a.m. October 1 to noon on October 6 is $5\frac{1}{4}$ days.
$4 \times 5.25 = 21$
21 minutes were lost; noon minus 21 = 11:39 a.m.

46. **The correct answer is (B).** The secretary gets $1\frac{1}{3}$ days of sick leave for 32 days of work.
She therefore gets one day of sick leave for 24 days' work.
$24 \times 12 = 288$ days of work for twelve days' sick leave.

47. **The correct answer is (B).** The second and third names are the same.

48. **The correct answer is (D).** All four names are the same.

49. **The correct answer is (B).** The second and third numbers are the same.

50. **The correct answer is (A).** All four last names are the same, but only the first and third first names are the same, and those two have different middle initials.

51. **The correct answer is (B).** The third and fourth numbers are the same.

52. **The correct answer is (B).** The second and fourth names are exactly the same.

53. **The correct answer is (B).** The second and fourth names are the same.

54. **The correct answer is (C).** The first, third, and fourth names are the same.

55. **The correct answer is (D).** All four numbers are exactly the same.

56. **The correct answer is (B).** The first and fourth numbers are the same.

57. **The correct answer is (C).** Choice (A) incorrectly uses the plural verb form *have* with the singular subject *one*. Choice (B) is awkward and wordy. Choice (D) incorrectly changes the subject from *one of us* to *anyone*.

58. **The correct answer is (D).** Choice (A) incorrectly uses the singular verb form *is* with the plural subject *ways*. In choice (B), *in organizing* should be *to organize*. The inverted construction in choice (C) is not as direct or as clear as the expression in choice (D).

59. **The correct answer is (B).** This sentence is most specific and therefore best.

60. **The correct answer is (A).** Answer choices (B) and (D) contain faulty comparisons; the working hours must be compared with those of any *other* employee. Choice (C) requires the phrase *longer than or equal to*.

61. **The correct answer is (D).** Choices (A), (B), and (C) all contain glaring grammatical errors.

62. **The correct answer is (C).** In choice (A), *suspects* is incorrectly used as a verb. Choice (B) incorrectly uses *try and find* for *try to find out*. Choice (D) has an error in subject-verb agreement *(quality are)*.

63. **The correct answer is (D).** Choice (A) contains the unacceptable expression *most all*. Choice (B) incorrectly uses *which* to refer to persons. Choice (C) includes the unacceptable expression *with regards to*.

64. **The correct answer is (B).** Choice (A) is not parallel. Choice (C) contains an error in agreement between subject and verb *(employment are)*. Choice (D) uses the unacceptable combination *and etc.*

65. **The correct answer is (C).** Choices (A) and (D) use the unacceptable expressions *some better* and *more preferable*. Choice (B) is awkward.

66. **The correct answer is (D).** The correct idiom is *to disagree with*.

67. **The correct answer is (D).** There are no errors in these three lines of code.

68. **The correct answer is (A).** The numbers of D and E are reversed in the third line.

69. **The correct answer is (A).** K is miscoded in the third line.

70. **The correct answer is (B).** D and P are miscoded in the first line. In the third line, there are code reversals for A and E and for R and D.

71. **The correct answer is (B).** K is miscoded in the second line. In the third line, the code numbers for F and D are reversed.

72. **The correct answer is (B).** In the second line, there are code reversals for K and G and for R and D. In the third line, Z is miscoded.

73. **The correct answer is (B).** In the first line, there is code reversal for Z and K. In the third line, there is code reversal for F and P and miscoding of Z.

74. **The correct answer is (B).** In the second line, there is code reversal for D and F. In the third line, F and P are both miscoded.

75. **The correct answer is (A).** In the third line, E and G are miscoded.

76. **The correct answer is (C).** In the first line, there is code reversal for A and T. In the second line, there is code reversal for K and D. In the third line, there is code reversal for G and K.

77. **The correct answer is (A).** If the court officer has been stationed outside the courtroom door to prevent anyone from entering, that is what the court officer must do. The court officer does not have the authority to make exceptions. Sending a note to the judge would be distracting and would impede efficient operation of that court.

78. **The correct answer is (C).** The duty of the court officer is to maintain order and decorum in the courtroom. Certainly the first step the officer should take is to advise the witness that his behavior is distracting and to request that the witness sit quietly. It is not the place of the court officer to make suggestions to the judge. If the witness continues to be distracting, the judge may ask the court officer to remove him, but the court officer may not make such a decision on his or her own.

79. **The correct answer is (D).** The court officer is charged with maintaining silence and order. He or she must admonish the jurors to keep silent. If the judge wants the book in the courtroom, he or she may order it.

80. **The correct answer is (B).** Since attending a trial is a privilege, not a right or a duty, noisy spectators must be asked to leave. Polite asking precedes forcible ejection.

81. **The correct answer is (C).** The court officer must follow directions yet must also be sensible and discreet. Exhibit B is the document requested by label, so it must be delivered. Exhibit F is the document requested by name; it also must be delivered. The court officer should do this in such a manner as not to embarrass the judge nor disrupt proceedings in any way.

82. **The correct answer is (D).** The situation fits both the definition of burglary (to enter a building to commit a crime) and of robbery (stealing by force—in this case, the punch in the face).

83. **The correct answer is (A).** John Brown can be charged with larceny only, as there was no intent to commit a crime when he entered the store and there was no force used. Brown may also be open to a weapons charge, but that is beyond the scope of this question.

84. **The correct answer is (D).** The charges are sexual abuse (touching of the buttocks) and larceny (taking $10 from the pocketbook). No force was used to remove the money, thereby eliminating the charge of robbery.

85. **The correct answer is (C).** To charge a person with burglary, it must only be shown that the building was entered with the intention of committing a crime therein. (In this case, the crimes were robbery and sexual abuse.) Despite the fact that Saunders did not commit the crimes he intended, the intention was there.

86. **The correct answer is (B).** Beating other inmates so as to extract cigarettes and coffee from them is using violence to intimidate and to gain favors, behavior typical of the gorilla.

87. **The correct answer is (A).** White is so cross-eyed that it is difficult to determine just where he is looking, but Miller imagines that White is staring and insulting him and so erupts into violence.

ANSWER SHEET PRACTICE TEST 2

1. Ⓐ Ⓑ Ⓒ Ⓓ	21. Ⓐ Ⓑ Ⓒ Ⓓ	41. Ⓐ Ⓑ Ⓒ Ⓓ	61. Ⓐ Ⓑ Ⓒ Ⓓ	81. Ⓐ Ⓑ Ⓒ Ⓓ
2. Ⓐ Ⓑ Ⓒ Ⓓ	22. Ⓐ Ⓑ Ⓒ Ⓓ	42. Ⓐ Ⓑ Ⓒ Ⓓ	62. Ⓐ Ⓑ Ⓒ Ⓓ	82. Ⓐ Ⓑ Ⓒ Ⓓ
3. Ⓐ Ⓑ Ⓒ Ⓓ	23. Ⓐ Ⓑ Ⓒ Ⓓ	43. Ⓐ Ⓑ Ⓒ Ⓓ	63. Ⓐ Ⓑ Ⓒ Ⓓ	83. Ⓐ Ⓑ Ⓒ Ⓓ
4. Ⓐ Ⓑ Ⓒ Ⓓ	24. Ⓐ Ⓑ Ⓒ Ⓓ	44. Ⓐ Ⓑ Ⓒ Ⓓ	64. Ⓐ Ⓑ Ⓒ Ⓓ	84. Ⓐ Ⓑ Ⓒ Ⓓ
5. Ⓐ Ⓑ Ⓒ Ⓓ	25. Ⓐ Ⓑ Ⓒ Ⓓ	45. Ⓐ Ⓑ Ⓒ Ⓓ	65. Ⓐ Ⓑ Ⓒ Ⓓ	85. Ⓐ Ⓑ Ⓒ Ⓓ
6. Ⓐ Ⓑ Ⓒ Ⓓ	26. Ⓐ Ⓑ Ⓒ Ⓓ	46. Ⓐ Ⓑ Ⓒ Ⓓ	66. Ⓐ Ⓑ Ⓒ Ⓓ	86. Ⓐ Ⓑ Ⓒ Ⓓ
7. Ⓐ Ⓑ Ⓒ Ⓓ	27. Ⓐ Ⓑ Ⓒ Ⓓ	47. Ⓐ Ⓑ Ⓒ Ⓓ	67. Ⓐ Ⓑ Ⓒ Ⓓ	87. Ⓐ Ⓑ Ⓒ Ⓓ
8. Ⓐ Ⓑ Ⓒ Ⓓ	28. Ⓐ Ⓑ Ⓒ Ⓓ	48. Ⓐ Ⓑ Ⓒ Ⓓ	68. Ⓐ Ⓑ Ⓒ Ⓓ	88. Ⓐ Ⓑ Ⓒ Ⓓ
9. Ⓐ Ⓑ Ⓒ Ⓓ	29. Ⓐ Ⓑ Ⓒ Ⓓ	49. Ⓐ Ⓑ Ⓒ Ⓓ	69. Ⓐ Ⓑ Ⓒ Ⓓ	89. Ⓐ Ⓑ Ⓒ Ⓓ
10. Ⓐ Ⓑ Ⓒ Ⓓ	30. Ⓐ Ⓑ Ⓒ Ⓓ	50. Ⓐ Ⓑ Ⓒ Ⓓ	70. Ⓐ Ⓑ Ⓒ Ⓓ	90. Ⓐ Ⓑ Ⓒ Ⓓ
11. Ⓐ Ⓑ Ⓒ Ⓓ	31. Ⓐ Ⓑ Ⓒ Ⓓ	51. Ⓐ Ⓑ Ⓒ Ⓓ	71. Ⓐ Ⓑ Ⓒ Ⓓ	91. Ⓐ Ⓑ Ⓒ Ⓓ
12. Ⓐ Ⓑ Ⓒ Ⓓ	32. Ⓐ Ⓑ Ⓒ Ⓓ	52. Ⓐ Ⓑ Ⓒ Ⓓ	72. Ⓐ Ⓑ Ⓒ Ⓓ	92. Ⓐ Ⓑ Ⓒ Ⓓ
13. Ⓐ Ⓑ Ⓒ Ⓓ	33. Ⓐ Ⓑ Ⓒ Ⓓ	53. Ⓐ Ⓑ Ⓒ Ⓓ	73. Ⓐ Ⓑ Ⓒ Ⓓ	93. Ⓐ Ⓑ Ⓒ Ⓓ
14. Ⓐ Ⓑ Ⓒ Ⓓ	34. Ⓐ Ⓑ Ⓒ Ⓓ	54. Ⓐ Ⓑ Ⓒ Ⓓ	74. Ⓐ Ⓑ Ⓒ Ⓓ	94. Ⓐ Ⓑ Ⓒ Ⓓ
15. Ⓐ Ⓑ Ⓒ Ⓓ	35. Ⓐ Ⓑ Ⓒ Ⓓ	55. Ⓐ Ⓑ Ⓒ Ⓓ	75. Ⓐ Ⓑ Ⓒ Ⓓ	95. Ⓐ Ⓑ Ⓒ Ⓓ
16. Ⓐ Ⓑ Ⓒ Ⓓ	36. Ⓐ Ⓑ Ⓒ Ⓓ	56. Ⓐ Ⓑ Ⓒ Ⓓ	76. Ⓐ Ⓑ Ⓒ Ⓓ	96. Ⓐ Ⓑ Ⓒ Ⓓ
17. Ⓐ Ⓑ Ⓒ Ⓓ	37. Ⓐ Ⓑ Ⓒ Ⓓ	57. Ⓐ Ⓑ Ⓒ Ⓓ	77. Ⓐ Ⓑ Ⓒ Ⓓ	97. Ⓐ Ⓑ Ⓒ Ⓓ
18. Ⓐ Ⓑ Ⓒ Ⓓ	38. Ⓐ Ⓑ Ⓒ Ⓓ	58. Ⓐ Ⓑ Ⓒ Ⓓ	78. Ⓐ Ⓑ Ⓒ Ⓓ	
19. Ⓐ Ⓑ Ⓒ Ⓓ	39. Ⓐ Ⓑ Ⓒ Ⓓ	59. Ⓐ Ⓑ Ⓒ Ⓓ	79. Ⓐ Ⓑ Ⓒ Ⓓ	
20. Ⓐ Ⓑ Ⓒ Ⓓ	40. Ⓐ Ⓑ Ⓒ Ⓓ	60. Ⓐ Ⓑ Ⓒ Ⓓ	80. Ⓐ Ⓑ Ⓒ Ⓓ	

answer sheet

Practice Test 2

97 QUESTIONS • 3 HOURS

Directions: Questions 1–15 are based on the three pictures that follow. You will have 10 minutes to study the three pictures. Then you will have to answer the 15 questions without referring back to the pictures.

QUESTIONS 1–5 ARE BASED ON THE FOLLOWING PICTURE.

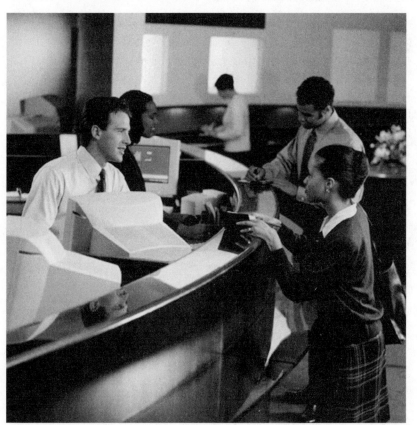

1. The teller is
   (A) wearing a tie
   (B) wearing glasses
   (C) making change
   (D) left-handed

2. The female customer is wearing
   (A) a floral dress
   (B) light-colored pants
   (C) short sleeves
   (D) a plaid skirt

3. The male customer is
   (A) handing money to the teller
   (B) wearing a bow tie
   (C) talking to another man in line
   (D) writing a check

4. How many computer terminals are visible in the picture?
   (A) three
   (B) five
   (C) six
   (D) four

5. The floral arrangement in the picture is
   (A) in front of the teller
   (B) behind the male customer
   (C) next to the computer terminal
   (D) next to the window

QUESTIONS 6–10 ARE BASED ON THE FOLLOWING PICTURE.

6. The ratio of *women* to *men* in the picture is
   (A) 3:4
   (B) 5:4
   (C) 4:3
   (D) 3:5

7. Which of the following items is NOT shown on the table?
   (A) a laptop computer
   (B) a vase
   (C) a water pitcher
   (D) a glass of water

8. The woman directly in front of the laptop computer is
   (A) pointing to the computer screen
   (B) reading the papers in front of her
   (C) typing on the keyboard
   (D) taking notes

9. The man speaking to the woman in the background is
   (A) holding a pencil
   (B) wearing glasses
   (C) drinking a glass of water
   (D) wearing a dark suit

10. All of the following statements are true EXCEPT
    (A) There are seven people at the table.
    (B) The pitcher of water is at the head of the table.
    (C) One person is holding a pencil.
    (D) Three people are standing.

QUESTIONS 11–15 ARE BASED ON THE FOLLOWING PICTURE.

11. The number of people in this picture is
    (A) 6
    (B) 5
    (C) 7
    (D) 4

12. The student with sunglasses
    (A) is sitting cross-legged
    (B) has blond hair
    (C) is male
    (D) is reading a book

13. The item in the far left background is likely a
    (A) hockey stick
    (B) guitar
    (C) tennis racket
    (D) none of these

14. Of the female students in the group,
    (A) two are speaking to each other
    (B) all are taking notes
    (C) two are wearing ponytails
    (D) one is wearing a hat

15. The time of day is likely
    (A) early evening
    (B) mid afternoon
    (C) morning
    (D) cannot tell from this picture

16. "Ideally, a correctional system should include several types of institutions to provide different degrees of custody." On the basis of this statement, one could most reasonably say that
    (A) as the number of institutions in a correctional system increases, the efficiency of the system increases
    (B) the difference in degree of custody for the inmate depends on the types of institutions in a correctional system
    (C) the greater the variety of institutions, the stricter the degree of custody that can be maintained
    (D) the same type of correctional institution is not desirable for the custody of all prisoners

17. "The enforced idleness of a large percentage of adult men and women in our prisons is one of the direct causes of the tensions that burst forth in riot and disorder." On the basis of this statement, a good reason why inmates should perform daily work of some kind is that
    (A) better morale and discipline can be maintained when inmates are kept busy
    (B) daily work is an effective way of punishing inmates for the crimes they have committed
    (C) law-abiding citizens must work; therefore, labor should also be required of inmates
    (D) products of inmates' labor will in part pay the cost of their maintenance

QUESTIONS 18-21 ARE BASED ON THE FOLLOWING STATEMENT.

The court officer's job is not only to maintain order in the courtroom but also to impress upon the public the seriousness of the court proceedings in a pleasant way.

18. During a jury trial, if the court officer urgently needs to speak with the judge what must he do?
    (A) raise his hand until called upon
    (B) write a note and have one of the trial lawyers place it on the bench
    (C) stand up and make eye contact with the judge and ask to approach the bench
    (D) stand and ask the judge to take a recess

19. When a high-profile case is set to be-gin, what is the best method for set-ting the "tone" or rules prior to opening court?
    (A) have extra uniformed deputies assigned to the courtroom
    (B) stand at the entrance to the courtroom, and do not let anyone enter who is not properly dressed
    (C) step to the side of the bench and, in a firm but pleasant voice, ask that no talking, shaking of heads, gestures, clapping, nor constant leaving and returning to the courtroom take place while court is in session
    (D) arrest the first person who misbehaves to set an example for everyone present

20. If the court officer and the judge are lifelong friends, how should the court officer address the judge in the court-room setting?
    (A) by his first name
    (B) Mr./Ms./Mrs.
    (C) boss
    (D) judge

21. Why is the manner in which the court officer opens court important?
    (A) it sets the tone of the proceedings
    (B) it shows that the court officer is important
    (C) it tells the attorneys court is about to begin
    (D) it tells the witnesses to remove themselves from the courtroom

22. A study shows that juvenile delin-quents are equal in intelligence but up to three school grades behind juvenile nondelinquents. On the basis of this information only, it is most reasonable to say that
    (A) a delinquent usually progresses to the educational limit set by intelligence
    (B) educational achievement depends on intelligence only
    (C) educational achievement is closely associated with delinquency
    (D) lack of intelligence is closely associated with delinquency

23. "Prevention of crime is of greater value to the community than the pun-ishment of crime." If this statement is accepted as true, greatest emphasis should be placed on
    (A) execution
    (B) medication
    (C) imprisonment
    (D) rehabilitation

QUESTIONS 24–27 ARE BASED ON THE FOLLOWING PASSAGE.

All automotive accidents, no matter how slight, are to be reported to the Safety Divi-sion by the employee involved on Accident Report Form S-23 in duplicate. When the accident is of such a nature that it requires the filling out of the State Motor Vehicle Report Form MV-104, this form is also pre-pared by the employee in duplicate and sent to the Safety Division for comparison with Form S-23. The Safety Division forwards both copies of Form MV-104 to the Corpora-tion Counsel, which sends one copy to the State Bureau of Motor Vehicles. When the information on Form S-23 indicates that the employee may be at fault, an investigation is made by the Safety Division. If this investi-gation shows that the employee was at fault, the employee's dispatcher is asked to file a complaint on Form D-11. The foreman of me-chanics prepares a damage report on Form D-8 and an estimate of the cost of repairs on Form D-9. The dispatcher's complaint, the damage report, the repair estimate, and the employee's previous accident record are sent to the Safety Division where they are studied together with the accident report. The Safety Division then recommends whether disciplinary action should be taken against the employee.

24. According to the preceding paragraph, the Safety Division should be notified whenever an automotive accident has occurred by means of
    (A) Form S-23
    (B) Forms S-23 and MV-104
    (C) Forms S-23, MV-104, D-8, D-9, and D-11
    (D) Forms S-23, MV-104, D-8, D-9, D-11, and the employee's accident record

25. According to the preceding paragraph, the forwarding of Form MV-104 to the State Bureau of Motor Vehicles is done by the
    (A) Corporation Counsel
    (B) dispatcher
    (C) employee involved in the accident
    (D) Safety Division

26. According to the preceding paragraph, the Safety Division investigates an automotive accident if the
    (A) accident is serious enough to be reported to the State Bureau of Motor Vehicles
    (B) dispatcher files a complaint
    (C) employee appears to have been at fault
    (D) employee's previous accident record is poor

27. Of the forms mentioned in the preceding paragraph, the dispatcher is responsible for preparing the
    (A) accident report form
    (B) damage report
    (C) complaint form
    (D) estimate of cost of repairs

28. A painter being instructed in his duties was told by his foreman, "Experience is the best teacher." The one of the following that most nearly expresses the meaning of this quotation is
    (A) a good teacher will make a hard job look easy
    (B) bad experience does more harm than good
    (C) lack of experience will make an easy job hard
    (D) the best way to learn to do a thing is by doing it

29. "Once the purposes or goals of an organization have been determined, they must be communicated to subordinate levels of supervisory staff." On the basis of this quotation, the most accurate of the following statements is that
    (A) supervisory personnel should participate in the formulation of the goals of an organization
    (B) the structure of an organization should be considered in determining the organization's goals
    (C) the goals that have been established for the different levels of an organization should be reviewed regularly
    (D) information about the goals of an organization should be distributed to supervisory personnel

30. "Close examination of traffic accident statistics reveals that traffic accidents are frequently the result of violations of traffic laws—and usually the violations are the result of illegal and dangerous driving behavior, rather than the result of mechanical defects or poor road conditions." According to this statement, the majority of dangerous traffic violations are caused by
    (A) poor driving
    (B) bad roads
    (C) unsafe cars
    (D) unwise traffic laws

QUESTIONS 31–33 ARE BASED ON THE FOLLOWING PASSAGE.

The supervisor gains the respect of his staff members and increases his influence over them by controlling his temper and avoiding criticizing anyone publicly. When a mistake is made, the good supervisor will talk it over with the employee quietly and privately. The supervisor listens to the employee's story, suggests a better way to do the job, and offers help so the mistake won't happen again. Before closing the discussion, the supervisor should try to find something good to say about other aspects of the employee's work. Some praise and appreciation, along with instruction, are likely to encourage an employee to improve in those areas where he is weakest.

31. A good title that would show the meaning of this entire paragraph would be
    (A) How to Correct Employee Errors
    (B) How to Praise Employees
    (C) Mistakes Are Preventable
    (D) The Weak Employee

32. According to the preceding paragraph, the work of an employee who has made a mistake is more likely to improve if the supervisor
    (A) avoids criticizing him
    (B) gives him a chance to suggest a better way of doing the work
    (C) listens to the employee's excuses to see if he is right
    (D) praises good work at the same time he corrects the mistake

33. According to the preceding paragraph, when a supervisor needs to correct an employee's mistake, it is important that he
    (A) allow some time to go by after the mistake is made
    (B) do so when other employees are not present
    (C) show his influence by his tone of voice
    (D) tell other employees to avoid the same mistake

34. "Determination of total, or even partial, guilt and responsibility as viewed by law cannot be made solely on the basis of a consideration of the external factors of the case, but rather should be made mainly in the light of the individual defendant's history and development." The above statement reflects a philosophy of law that requires that
    (A) the punishment fit the crime
    (B) the individual, rather than the crime, be considered first
    (C) motivations behind a crime are relatively unimportant
    (D) the individual's knowledge of right and wrong be the sole determinant of guilt

35. A city traffic regulation says, "No driver shall enter an intersection unless there is sufficient unobstructed space beyond the intersection to accommodate the vehicle he or she is operating, notwithstanding any traffic-control signal indication to the contrary." This regulation means that
    (A) a driver should not go through an intersection if there are no parking spaces available in the next block
    (B) a driver should not enter an intersection when the traffic light is red
    (C) a driver should not enter an intersection if traffic ahead is so badly backed up that he or she would not be able to go ahead and would block the intersection
    (D) a driver should ignore traffic signals completely whenever there are obstructions in the road ahead

QUESTIONS 36–37 ARE BASED ON THE FOLLOWING PASSAGE.

A large proportion of people behind bars are not convicted criminals, but people who have been arrested and are being held until their trial in court. Experts have often pointed out that this detention system does not operate fairly. For instance, a person who can afford to pay bail usually will not get locked up. The theory of the bail system is that the person will make sure to show up in court when he or she is supposed to; otherwise, bail will be forfeited—the person will lose the money that was put up. Sometimes a person who can show that he or she is a stable citizen with a job and a family will be released on "personal recognizance" (without bail). The result is that the well-to-do, the employed, and the family men can often avoid the detention system. The people who do wind up in detention tend to be the poor, the unemployed, the single, and the young.

36. According to the preceding passage, people who are put behind bars

    (A) are almost always dangerous criminals

    (B) include many innocent people who have been arrested by mistake

    (C) are often people who have been arrested but have not yet come to trial

    (D) are all poor people who tend to be young and single

37. The passage says that the detention system works unfairly against people who are

    (A) rich

    (B) old

    (C) married

    (D) unemployed

38. Occasionally, a court officer will have to work during a trial for a judge from another jurisdiction because of a conflict of interest. This is referred to as interchange. To facilitate the transition, and accommodate the "new" judge as much as possible, a court officer should:

    (A) ask to be transferred to another courtroom

    (B) adapt to the "new" judge's style when possible

    (C) consider it a vacation since the "new" judge will bring his own court officer with him

    (D) tell the "new" judge the "normal" procedures and adjust nothing

39. Suppose that half the peace officers in a department have served for fewer than ten years and one third have served for more than fifteen years. The fraction of peace officers in the department who have served between ten and fifteen years is

    (A) $\dfrac{1}{3}$

    (B) $\dfrac{1}{5}$

    (C) $\dfrac{1}{6}$

    (D) $\dfrac{1}{12}$

40. Suppose that 10% of those who commit serious crimes are convicted and that 15% of those convicted are sentenced for more than three years. The percentage of those committing serious crimes who are sentenced for more than three years is

    (A) 15 %

    (B) 1.5%

    (C) 0.15%

    (D) 0.015%

41. Assume that there are 1,100 employees in a state agency. Of these, 15% are peace officers, 80% of whom are attorneys. Of the attorneys, two fifths have been with the agency more than five years. The number of peace officers who are attorneys and have more than five years' experience with the agency is most nearly

    (A) 45

    (B) 53

    (C) 132

    (D) 165

42. An employee who has 500 cartons of supplies to pack can pack them at the rate of 50 an hour. After this employee has worked for a half hour, he is joined by another employee, who can pack 45 cartons an hour. Assuming that both employees can maintain their respective rates of speed, the total number of hours required to pack all the cartons is

(A) $4\frac{1}{2}$

(B) 5

(C) $5\frac{1}{2}$

(D) $6\frac{1}{2}$

43. Thirty-six officers can complete an assignment in twenty-two days. Assuming that all officers work at the same rate of speed, the number of officers that would be needed to complete this assignment in twelve days is

(A) 42

(B) 54

(C) 66

(D) 72

QUESTIONS 44–47 ARE BASED ON THE FOLLOWING TABLE.

Age Composition in the Labor Force in City A (1995-2005)

	Age Group	1995	2000	2005
Men	14-24	8,430	10,900	14,340
	25-44	22,200	22,350	26,065
	45+	17,550	19,800	21,970
Women	14-24	4,450	6,915	7,680
	25-44	9,080	10,010	11,550
	45+	7,325	9,470	13,180

44. The greatest increase in the number of people in the labor force between 1995 and 2000 occurred among

(A) men between the ages of 14 and 24

(B) men age 45 and over

(C) women between the ages of 14 and 24

(D) women age 45 and over

45. If the total number of women of all ages in the labor force increases from 2005 to 2010 by the same number as it did from 2000 to 2005, the total number of all women of all ages in the labor force in 2010 will be

(A) 27,425

(B) 29,675

(C) 37,525

(D) 38,425

46. The total increase in number of women in the labor force from 1995 to 2000 differs from the total increase in number of men in the same years by being

(A) 770 less than that of men

(B) 670 more than that of men

(C) 770 more than that of men

(D) 1,670 more than that of men

47. In 1995, the proportion of married women in each group was as follows: 1/5 of the women in the 14-24 age group, 1/4 of those in the 25-44 age group, and 2/5 of those 45 and over. How many married women were in the labor force in 1995?

(A) 4,625

(B) 5,990

(C) 6,090

(D) 7,910

FOR QUESTIONS 48–57, CHOOSE THE ONE ANSWER THAT HAS EXACTLY THE SAME IDENTIFICATION NUMBER AND NAME AS THOSE IN THE QUESTION.

48.   176823   KATHERINE BLAU
- **(A)**   176823   CATHERINE BLAU
- **(B)**   176283   KATHERINE BLAU
- **(C)**   176823   KATHERIN BLAU
- **(D)**   176823   KATHERINE BLAU

49.   673403   BORIS T. FRAME
- **(A)**   673403   BORIS P. FRAME
- **(B)**   673403   BORIS T. FRAME
- **(C)**   673403   BORIS T. FRAIM
- **(D)**   673430   BORIS T. FRAME

50.   498832   HYMAN ZIEBART
- **(A)**   498832   HYMAN ZEIBART
- **(B)**   498832   HIRAM ZIEBART
- **(C)**   498832   HYMAN ZIEBARDT
- **(D)**   498832   HYMAN ZIEBART

51.   506745   BARBARA O'DEY
- **(A)**   507645   BARBARA O'DAY
- **(B)**   506745   BARBARA O'DAY
- **(C)**   506475   BARBARA O'DAY
- **(D)**   506745   BARBARA O'DEY

52.   344223   MORTON SKLAR
- **(A)**   344223   MORTON SKLAR
- **(B)**   344332   NORTON SKLAR
- **(C)**   344332   MORTON SKLAAR
- **(D)**   343322   MORTON SKLAR

53.   816040   BETSY B. VOIGHT
- **(A)**   816404   BETSY B. VOIGHT
- **(B)**   814060   BETSY B. VOIGHT
- **(C)**   816040   BETSY B. VOIGHT
- **(D)**   816040   BETSEY B. VOIGHT

54.   913576   HAROLD HOWRITZ
- **(A)**   913576   HAROLD HORWITZ
- **(B)**   913576   HAROLD HOWRITZ
- **(C)**   913756   HAROLD HOWRITZ
- **(D)**   913576   HARALD HOWRITZ

55.   621190   JAYNE T. DOWNS
- **(A)**   621990   JANIE T. DOWNS
- **(B)**   621190   JANIE T. DOWNS
- **(C)**   622190   JANIE T. DOWNS
- **(D)**   621190   JAYNE T. DOWNS

56. 004620 GEORGE MCBOYD
    (A)   006420   GEORGE MCBOYD
    (B)   006420   GEORGE MACBOYD
    (C)   006420   GEORGE MCBOID
    (D)   004620   GEORGE MCBOYD

57. 723495 ALICE APPLETON
    (A)   723495   ALICE APPLETON
    (B)   723594   ALICA APPLETON
    (C)   723459   ALICE APPLETON
    (D)   732495   ALICE APPLETON

FOR QUESTIONS 58–67, SELECT THE SENTENCE THAT IS BEST WITH RESPECT TO GRAMMAR AND USAGE.

58. **(A)** You have got to get rid of some of these people if you expect to have the quality of the work improve.
    (B) The quality of the work would improve if they would leave fewer people do it.
    (C) I believe it would be desirable to have fewer persons doing this work.
    (D) If you had planned on employing fewer people than this to do the work, this situation would not have arose.

59. **(A)** This kind of worker achieves success through patience.
    (B) Success does not often come to men of this type except they who are patient.
    (C) Because they are patient, these sort of workers usually achieve success.
    (D) This worker has more patience than any man in his office.

60. **(A)** Nobody but you and your brother know the reason for my coming.
    (B) The reason for my coming is only known to you and your brother.
    (C) My reason for coming is known by nobody except you and your brother.
    (D) My reason for coming is known only by you and your brother.

61. **(A)** They are alike in this respect.
    (B) They are both alike in this respect.
    (C) He is alike to him in this respect.
    (D) They are alike to this respect.

62. **(A)** It is they.
    (B) It is them.
    (C) It is us.
    (D) It is me.

63. **(A)** Where is he at?
    (B) At where is he?
    (C) Where is he?
    (D) What place is he at now?

64. **(A)** I cannot believe but what he is guilty.
    (B) I cannot believe but where he is guilty.
    (C) I cannot believe but how he is guilty.
    (D) I cannot but believe that he is guilty.

65. **(A)** This data is correct.
    (B) Them data is correct.
    (C) These data are correct.
    (D) Those data is correct.

66. **(A)** The one is different with the other.
    (B) The one is different to the other.
    (C) The one is different from the other.
    (D) The one is different than the other.

67. (A) The draperies were not hanged well.
    (B) The draperies were not hanged good.
    (C) The draperies were not hung well.
    (D) The draperies were not hung good.

FOR QUESTIONS 68–77, YOU ARE GIVEN A LIST OF TAGS IN THE LEFT-HAND COLUMN BASED ON CODE 1. FROM AMONG THE CHOICES IN THE RIGHT-HAND COLUMN, CHOOSE THE LETTERS CALLED FOR BY CODE 2.

CODE 1

F	I	N	D		B	Y		Z	E	A	L
1	2	3	4		5	6		7	8	9	0

CODE 2

W	R	I	T	E	S		A	B	L	Y
1	2	3	4	5	6		7	8	9	0

	CODE 1		CODE 2		
68.	dnb	(A) tie	(B) ris	(C) ati	(D) wit
69.	nba	(A) eil	(B) bir	(C) iel	(D) ieb
70.	blz	(A) tls	(B) bai	(C) elb	(D) eya
71.	lzdy	(A) stay	(B) ybia	(C) yats	(D) lwab
72.	ife	(A) wrb	(B) brw	(C) rbw	(D) rwb
73.	fye	(A) wsb	(B) ral	(C) wbs	(D) iwb
74.	alzd	(A) layt	(B) lyat	(C) layt	(D) bayt
75.	nel	(A) tay	(B) rab	(C) ibl	(D) iby
76.	ilza	(A) rial	(B) liar	(C) lair	(D) ryal
77.	ndb	(A) rit	(B) ite	(C) tes	(D) rte

QUESTIONS 78–82 ARE BASED ON THE FOLLOWING DUTIES OF A COURT OFFICER.

The court officer has important functions in connection with the control of the jury. He or she must confirm that every juror has the proper place in the box and must be constantly on watch to prevent any juror from leaving the jury box while the trial is in progress. Should a juror desire to leave the box while the case is going on, the court officer must first inform the judge of the juror's desire to determine whether the judge will grant or refuse the juror's wish. If the judge approves, the trial is stopped and the court officer is instructed to accompany the juror while he or she is out of the jury box. In order to prevent any stoppage or mistrial, the court officer must not allow the juror to get out of the range of sight or hearing. The officer must always bear in mind that the juror should be returned as quickly as possible, without any unnecessary delay. The juror must not enter into any conversation with anybody or read any matter that he or she may have or that may be given by another person.

The court officer must be particularly careful when placed in charge of a jury that has retired to deliberate. The court officer must conduct the jury to the jury room and see to it that no juror talks with anyone on the way. If a juror does talk with someone, the event may afford grounds for a mistrial.

78. A juror has requested and received permission to go to the men's room. As he approaches the door, he takes out a sports magazine he has brought from home as "bathroom literature." The court officer who has accompanied him should

(A) permit the juror to read his sports magazine
(B) check the magazine for papers that might be hidden between the pages, then let the juror read it
(C) offer the juror something of his own to read, something that the court officer knows will not influence the juror in any way
(D) tell the juror that reading in the men's room is not permitted

79. While leading a jury from the courtroom to the jury room, a court officer notices a person leaning against a corridor wall making active hand motions as a juror stares intently. The first thing for the court officer to do is to

(A) tell the juror to look straight ahead and keep walking
(B) step between the juror and the person making the hand motions so as to interrupt the juror's line of vision
(C) ask the juror what he is looking at
(D) call a police officer to arrest the person with the active hands

80. This question is based on the scenario described in question 79. A court officer ascertains that a message was being transmitted by an outside person to a juror. It would be best for the court officer to

(A) keep this information secret
(B) ask the juror what the message was all about
(C) deliver the jury to the jury room, then discuss the matter with the court clerk
(D) accompany the juror to the judge, and tell the judge exactly what the court officer observed

81. During the course of testimony, a juror begins to cough uncontrollably. The coughing is loud and distressing. The court officer should

(A) summon a doctor at once
(B) lead the juror from the courtroom as quickly and as quietly as possible
(C) bring the juror a glass of water
(D) ask the judge what to do

82. On the third day of a trial, a court officer notices that an alternate is sitting in the front row in the seat of one of the regular jurors while the juror is sitting in the alternate's seat. When questioned, the alternate explains that he is very short and has trouble watching the action from his assigned seat, while the juror doesn't mind the back row. The court officer should

   (A) tell them that they are required to sit in their assigned seats at all times
   (B) permit the switch, since it harms no one
   (C) tell them that the switch of seats involves a change of status and that the alternate is now a juror and the juror an alternate
   (D) threaten to cite them for contempt of court if they do not immediately return to their assigned seats

QUESTIONS 83–86 ARE BASED ON THE FOLLOWING PASSAGE.

The success or failure of a criminal prosecution usually depends on the evidence presented to the court. Evidence may be divided into three major classifications: direct evidence, circumstantial evidence, and real evidence. Evidence must also be admissible, that is, material and relevant. An eyewitness account of a criminal act is direct evidence. Where an eyewitness does not have immediate experience, but reasonably infers what happened, circumstantial evidence is offered. Real evidence comprises objects introduced at a trial to prove or disprove a fact. For example, a gun, fingerprints, or bloodstains are real evidence. Real evidence may be direct or circumstantial. Evidence is immaterial if it is unimportant to the trial. For example, if someone is being tried for larceny of a crate of oranges, it is immaterial that the oranges were yellow in color. Evidence is irrelevant or immaterial if it does not prove the truth of a fact at issue. For example, if a murder has been committed with a bow and arrow, it is irrelevant to show that the defendant was well acquainted with firearms.

83. Jones and Smith go into a room together and close the door. Richards stands outside the door and sees Jones and Smith go in. A shot is heard and Smith rushes out with a smoking gun in his hand. Richards rushes into the room and finds Jones lying on the floor, dead. Richards did not see Smith fire the shot. At Smith's trial for murdering Jones, Richards tells the court what he saw and heard. Richard's story is

   (A) inadmissible evidence
   (B) real evidence
   (C) irrelevant evidence
   (D) circumstantial evidence

84. In Smith's trial for murdering Jones, Smith's attorney could prove that Smith was an excellent student of history in high school. Such evidence would most likely be classified as

   (A) real and material
   (B) direct and relevant
   (C) immaterial and irrelevant
   (D) circumstantial and admissible

85. As Smith's trial for murdering Jones proceeds, the prosecutor proves that Smith owned the gun that killed Jones. Of the following, such evidence is most likely

   (A) direct
   (B) inadmissible
   (C) irrelevant
   (D) material

86. As Smith's trial for murdering Jones continues, the prosecutor introduces a surprise witness, Rogers, who says that, from an apartment across the street, he looked into the window of the room Jones and Smith were in and actually saw Smith point a gun at Jones and shoot him, after which Jones fell to the floor and Smith rushed out of the room. Rogers' story is best described as

   (A) real and circumstantial evidence
   (B) direct and relevant evidence
   (C) circumstantial and admissible evidence
   (D) relevant and real evidence

QUESTIONS 87–97 ARE BASED ON THE FOLLOWING STORY.

Jane and her friend John were walking on Oak Street one rainy day when they noticed three men, one Caucasian, one Hispanic, and one African American, running out of Larry's Sporting Goods Store carrying football, baseball, and basketball equipment. The Caucasian male was approximately 6'2" with brown hair, the Hispanic male was approximately 5'8" with brown hair, and the African-American male was approximately 6'1" with black hair. As they were running, a police car pulled up beside the store and three police officers, two females and one male, began to chase the suspects. The Caucasian male and African-American male were apprehended.

87. The weather conditions on the day of the incident were
    (A) sunny
    (B) cloudy
    (C) rainy
    (D) snowy

88. Jane and John are
    (A) husband and wife
    (B) relatives
    (C) business partners
    (D) friends

89. The total number of suspects and police officers is
    (A) 6
    (B) 5
    (C) 7
    (D) 8

90. The items stolen from the store were
    (A) football, baseball, and soccer equipment
    (B) football, basketball, and baseball equipment
    (C) soccer, football, and baseball equipment
    (D) basketball, golf, and football equipment

91. How many female police officers came to the scene?
    (A) 1
    (B) 2
    (C) 3
    (D) 4

92. Who was the tallest suspect?
    (A) Caucasian male
    (B) Hispanic male
    (C) African-American male
    (D) Caucasian female

93. Which suspect was not apprehended?
    (A) Caucasian male
    (B) Hispanic male
    (C) African-American male
    (D) Caucasian female

94. What time of day did the incident occur?
    (A) morning
    (B) early evening
    (C) late night
    (D) information not provided

95. The name of the sporting goods store was
    (A) Lanny's
    (B) Larry's
    (C) Lonny's
    (D) Louis's

96. The Hispanic male had
    (A) brown hair
    (B) black hair
    (C) blonde hair
    (D) no hair

97. The name of the street on which this incident occurred was
    (A) Vine Street
    (B) Main Street
    (C) Oak Street
    (D) Pine Street

ANSWER KEY AND EXPLANATIONS

1. A	21. A	41. B	60. D	79. B
2. D	22. C	42. C	61. A	80. D
3. D	23. D	43. C	62. A	81. C
4. B	24. A	44. A	63. C	82. A
5. B	25. A	45. D	64. D	83. D
6. C	26. C	46. B	65. C	84. C
7. B	27. C	47. C	66. C	85. D
8. C	28. D	48. D	67. C	86. B
9. D	29. D	49. B	68. A	87. C
10. D	30. A	50. D	69. C	88. D
11. B	31. A	51. D	70. D	89. A
12. B	32. D	52. A	71. C	90. B
13. B	33. B	53. C	72. D	91. B
14. C	34. B	54. B	73. A	92. A
15. B	35. C	55. D	74. B	93. B
16. D	36. C	56. D	75. D	94. D
17. A	37. D	57. A	76. D	95. B
18. C	38. B	58. C	77. B	96. A
19. C	39. C	59. A	78. D	97. C
20. D	40. B			

1–15. **If you made any errors in answering questions 1–15, look back at the pictures and find the relevant details.**

16. **The correct answer is (D).** If the ideal of a correctional system is that different degrees of custody should be provided by different types of institutions, then clearly not all prisoners should be subjected to the same degree of custody. Choice (A) addresses only numbers of institutions; choice (B) reverses the statement; choice (C) does not make sense.

17. **The correct answer is (A).** Daily work reduces the amount of time devoted to enforced idleness, reducing the boredom and tensions that lead to riots and improving morale and discipline.

18. **The correct answer is (C).** The court officer wants to interrupt the court proceedings as little as possible, but not allow other courtroom participants to know what is being discussed.

19. **The correct answer is (C).** The court officer's demeanor and his respect for the system help to maintain the dignity required for a trial atmosphere. Letting the gallery know about appropriate conduct prior to opening court reduces the court officer's admonitions during the trial.

20. **The correct answer is (D).** Even though the two may be friends, in the courtroom setting, respect for the bench and the justice system must be maintained.

21. **The correct answer is (A).** The way in which the court officer opens court tells the participants that this is a serious event and demands respect.

22. **The correct answer is (C).** According to the statement, juvenile delinquents are equal in intelligence but up to three school grades behind juvenile nondelinquents. Therefore, the passage implies that educational achievement is inversely proportionate to juvenile delinquency.

23. **The correct answer is (D).** It is hoped that rehabilitation of prisoners will prevent further crime. Execution also prevents further crime, but its effects cannot be widespread because few criminals are candidates for execution.

24. **The correct answer is (A).** The first sentence states that the first report to the Safety Division, the one filed after every accident, is Form S-23.

25. **The correct answer is (A).** The employee sends two copies of Form MV-104 to the Safety Division, which sends both copies on to the Corporation Counsel. The Corporation Counsel keeps one copy and sends the other to the State Bureau of Motor Vehicles. If you didn't pick up this sequence, look back at the paragraph now.

26. **The correct answer is (C).** If it appears that the employee was at fault, the dispatcher files a complaint on Form D-11, which is sent, along with other papers, to the Safety Division for investigation.

27. **The correct answer is (C).** The dispatcher prepares Form D-11, the complaint form.

28. **The correct answer is (D).** Doing a thing is gaining experience in doing it. The more often one performs a certain act, the more experience one gains and the better one becomes.

29. **The correct answer is (D).** This paragraph is saying that administrators or policymakers determine the purposes and the goals of an organization and should then pass these goals and purposes on to the supervisory personnel. Choice (A) contradicts the statement, in suggesting that supervisory personnel are party to the process of establishing purposes and goals. Choices (B) and (C) have nothing to do with the paragraph.

30. **The correct answer is (A).** Violations of traffic laws and illegal and dangerous driving behavior constitute bad driving.

31. **The correct answer is (A).** The subject of the paragraph is the best approach to take in correcting employee errors and improving work habits.

32. **The correct answer is (D).** See the last two sentences. The paragraph does suggest that the supervisor listen to the employee's story, but only for his own understanding, not to exonerate the employee. The supervisor makes the suggestions for improvement, not the employee. You may feel that asking the employee for suggestions about how he might improve would be a good supervisory policy, but you must answer questions on the basis of what is stated in the paragraph.

33. **The correct answer is (B).** Talking over a mistake quietly and privately is making the correction when other employees are not present. Public embarrassment is not a good supervisory technique.

34. **The correct answer is (B).** The sociological view, as represented in this paragraph, is that the facts are irrelevant in determining guilt and responsibility and that all weight should be given to the history and development of the individual.

35. **The correct answer is (C).** This is the "anti-gridlock" regulation. It has nothing to do with parking spaces. While the anti-gridlock rule requires that the driver not enter the intersection on a green light if he or she has no expectation of clearing the intersection during the duration of the green light, it does not give permission to ignore a red light just because the intersection is clear. A red light must always be obeyed unless a police officer gives contradictory instructions.

36. **The correct answer is (C).** See the first sentence.

37. **The correct answer is (D).** See the last sentence.

38. **The correct answer is (B).** The court officer should ease the transition by making changes when possible to accommodate the "new" judge.

39. **The correct answer is (C).** $\frac{1}{3} \times \frac{1}{2} = \frac{1}{6}$

40. **The correct answer is (B).** Convert to decimals to work out the math. Then return to %. .10 × .15 = .015 = 1.5%

41. **The correct answer is (B).** $1,100 \times .15 = 165$ peace officers
$165 \times .80 = 132$ attorneys
$2/5 \times 132 = 52.8$, which is most nearly 53

42. **The correct answer is (C).** In the first half hour, the employee who can pack 50 cartons per hour packed 25 cartons; 475 cartons remained to be packed. The two employees working together can pack 95 cartons per hour. 475 cartons ÷ 95 per hour = 5 hours. Add to the 5 hours working together the half hour the first employee worked alone, and the total time taken to pack the 500 cartons is $5\frac{1}{2}$ hours.

43. **The correct answer is (C).** Solve this problem by means of a proportion. $36:22 = x:12$. Multiply both sides: $12x = (36 \times 22) = 792$. Divide both sides by 12. $x = 66$ officers needed to complete the assignment in 12 days.

44. **The correct answer is (A).** By subtracting the number of people within each category in the labor force in 1995 from the number in the labor force in 2000, we can determine the size of the increase for each group. The number of men in the 14 to 24 age group increased by 2,470 ($10,900 - 8,430 = 2,470$). The increases in the other groups suggested are smaller (men age 45 and over by 2,250, women between the ages of 14 and 24 by 2,465, and women age 45 and over by 2,145).

45. **The correct answer is (D).** First add the numbers of women in the three age groups in 2005 to learn that there were 32,410 women in the labor force in 2005. Then in the same way, find that the number of women in the labor force in 2000 was 26,395. To find the increase from 2000 to 2005 subtract 26,395 from 32,410. The result is 6,015. If the increase from 2005 to 2010 is to be the same, then add 6,015 to 32,410 to learn that in 2010 there will be 38,425 women of all ages in the labor force.

46. **The correct answer is (B).** The procedure for figuring the answer to this question is similar to that used in answering question 45. The number of women in the labor force increased from 20,855 in 1995 to 26,395 in 2000, a total increase of 5,540. The number of men increased from 48,180 in 1995 to 53,050 in 2000, a total increase of 4,870. The difference between the increases is 670, and the number of women increased more than the number of men.

47. **The correct answer is (C).**

$\frac{1}{5}$ (20%) of $4,450 = 890$

$\frac{1}{4}$ (25%) of $9,080 = 2,270 + \frac{2}{5}$ (40%) of $7,325 = 2,930$

6,090 married women in 1995

48–57. **If you made any errors in questions 48–57, look back at the questions and carefully compare middle initials, the spelling of both first and last names, and the order of the numbers.**

58. **The correct answer is (C).** Choice (A) is wordy. In choice (B), the correct verb should be *have* in place of *leave*. In choice (D), the word *arose* should be *arisen*.

59. **The correct answer is (A).** In choice (B), *they* is incorrect. Choice (C) contains an error of number; to be correct, the phrase must read either *this sort of worker or these sorts of workers*. In choice (D), the comparison is incomplete. It must read *than any other man*.

60. **The correct answer is (D).** In choice (A), the subject is *nobody,* which is singular and requires the singular verb *knows*. Choices (B) and (C) are awkward and poorly written.

61. **The correct answer is (A).** In choice (B), the term *both alike* is a meaningless redundancy. In choice (C), the phrase *alike to him* is awkward. Choice (C) might be correctly stated, "He is like him in this respect." In choice (D), *to this respect* is an incorrect idiom.

answers

62. **The correct answer is (A).** The verb *is* is a linking verb, which takes no object. The noun following a linking verb must be in the nominative case. Only choice (A) meets this requirement.

63. **The correct answer is (C).** Use the fewest possible words to make your message clear. "Where is he?" is perfectly adequate.

64. **The correct answer is (D).** All four sentences are somewhat awkward, but choice (D) is correct and does say what it means. Improvements might read: "I can believe only that he is guilty." "I cannot believe that he is not guilty." "I cannot believe anything, except that he is guilty."

65. **The correct answer is (C).** The word *data* is plural and must take a plural verb. The singular of *data* is *datum*.

66. **The correct answer is (C).** The proper idiom is *different from*.

67. **The correct answer is (C).** The past tense *hanged* is used only with reference to people. Things, including draperies, are *hung*. Choice (C) is correct because the adverb *well* is needed to describe how the draperies were hung. Choice (D) incorrectly uses the adjective *good*.

68. **The correct answer is (A).** dnb - 435 – tie

69. **The correct answer is (C).** nba - 359 – iel

70. **The correct answer is (D).** blz - 507 – eya

71. **The correct answer is (C).** lzdy - 0746 – yats

72. **The correct answer is (D).** ife - 218 – rwb

73. **The correct answer is (A).** fye - 168 – wsb

74. **The correct answer is (B).** alzd - 9074 – lyat

75. **The correct answer is (D).** nel - 380 – iby

76. **The correct answer is (D).** ilza - 2079 – ryal

77. **The correct answer is (B).** ndb - 345 – ite

78. **The correct answer is (D).** The juror is not allowed to read any matter that he or she may have or that may be given by any other person, including a court officer. That is an absolute rule. Furthermore, since the court is awaiting the prompt return of the juror, the distraction of the juror by reading material might constitute an extra, unnecessary delay.

79. **The correct answer is (B).** The alert court officer notices everything going on around the jurors and interprets it as well as he or she can. Unobtrusive intervention is the most diplomatic yet effective way to deal with an ambiguous situation. The person with the active hands may or may not be communicating by sign language, which the juror may or may not understand. If the juror cannot see the hands, no message can be transmitted. Questioning can then follow.

80. **The correct answer is (D).** If there is any possibility that there was communication from an outsider to a juror, the judge must know immediately. Since sign language communication is outside the usual communication against which a court officer must be on guard, the officer need not feel guilty. However, having noticed the event, even if it was of short duration, the court officer is bound to report it at once.

81. **The correct answer is (C).** The court officer must maintain silence in the courtroom, yet must keep all jurors in the jury box unless authorized to remove them. Perhaps a glass of water is all that is needed to calm the coughing. If not, the judge will most certainly take the initiative and suggest a respite.

82. **The correct answer is (A).** The court officer must confirm that every juror has his or her proper place in the box. The court officer does not have the authority to make or to permit changes.

83. **The correct answer is (D).** Richards was not an actual eyewitness to the shooting, so his testimony cannot be considered direct evidence, but what he did hear and see before and after the shooting constitutes circumstantial evidence.

84. **The correct answer is (C).** Smith's academic record has absolutely nothing to do with his guilt or innocence in this murder case.

85. **The correct answer is (D).** Smith's ownership of the murder weapon is very important evidence in this trial.

86. **The correct answer is (B).** The testimony of an eyewitness is direct evidence; if Rogers actually witnessed the murder, his testimony is certainly relevant.

87. **The correct answer is (C).** The first sentence indicates that the day was rainy.

88. **The correct answer is (D).** The first sentence indicates that Jane and John are friends.

89. **The correct answer is (A).** There were 3 suspects and 3 police officers.

90. **The correct answer is (B).** The first sentence indicates that three men were running out of Larry's Sporting Goods Store carrying football, baseball, and basketball equipment.

91. **The correct answer is (B).** The next-to-last sentence states that three police officers, two females and one male, began to chase the suspects.

92. **The correct answer is (A).** The Caucasian male was approximately 6'2"; the Hispanic male was approximately 5'8"; the African-American male was approximately 6'1".

93. **The correct answer is (B).** The last sentence indicates that the Caucasian male and African-American male were apprehended.

94. **The correct answer is (D).** There is no mention of the time of day the incident took place.

95. **The correct answer is (B).** The first sentence states that the three suspects were carrying sports equipment from Larry's Sporting Goods Store.

96. **The correct answer is (A).** The second sentence mentions that the Hispanic male had brown hair.

97. **The correct answer is (C).** The first sentence mentions that the witnesses, Jane and John, were walking along Oak Street when they saw three men running out of Larry's Sporting Goods Store.

ANSWER SHEET PRACTICE TEST 3

1. Ⓐ Ⓑ Ⓒ Ⓓ	21. Ⓐ Ⓑ Ⓒ Ⓓ	41. Ⓐ Ⓑ Ⓒ Ⓓ	61. Ⓐ Ⓑ Ⓒ Ⓓ	81. Ⓐ Ⓑ Ⓒ Ⓓ
2. Ⓐ Ⓑ Ⓒ Ⓓ	22. Ⓐ Ⓑ Ⓒ Ⓓ	42. Ⓐ Ⓑ Ⓒ Ⓓ	62. Ⓐ Ⓑ Ⓒ Ⓓ	82. Ⓐ Ⓑ Ⓒ Ⓓ
3. Ⓐ Ⓑ Ⓒ Ⓓ	23. Ⓐ Ⓑ Ⓒ Ⓓ	43. Ⓐ Ⓑ Ⓒ Ⓓ	63. Ⓐ Ⓑ Ⓒ Ⓓ	83. Ⓐ Ⓑ Ⓒ Ⓓ
4. Ⓐ Ⓑ Ⓒ Ⓓ	24. Ⓐ Ⓑ Ⓒ Ⓓ	44. Ⓐ Ⓑ Ⓒ Ⓓ	64. Ⓐ Ⓑ Ⓒ Ⓓ	84. Ⓐ Ⓑ Ⓒ Ⓓ
5. Ⓐ Ⓑ Ⓒ Ⓓ	25. Ⓐ Ⓑ Ⓒ Ⓓ	45. Ⓐ Ⓑ Ⓒ Ⓓ	65. Ⓐ Ⓑ Ⓒ Ⓓ	85. Ⓐ Ⓑ Ⓒ Ⓓ
6. Ⓐ Ⓑ Ⓒ Ⓓ	26. Ⓐ Ⓑ Ⓒ Ⓓ	46. Ⓐ Ⓑ Ⓒ Ⓓ	66. Ⓐ Ⓑ Ⓒ Ⓓ	86. Ⓐ Ⓑ Ⓒ Ⓓ
7. Ⓐ Ⓑ Ⓒ Ⓓ	27. Ⓐ Ⓑ Ⓒ Ⓓ	47. Ⓐ Ⓑ Ⓒ Ⓓ	67. Ⓐ Ⓑ Ⓒ Ⓓ	87. Ⓐ Ⓑ Ⓒ Ⓓ
8. Ⓐ Ⓑ Ⓒ Ⓓ	28. Ⓐ Ⓑ Ⓒ Ⓓ	48. Ⓐ Ⓑ Ⓒ Ⓓ	68. Ⓐ Ⓑ Ⓒ Ⓓ	88. Ⓐ Ⓑ Ⓒ Ⓓ
9. Ⓐ Ⓑ Ⓒ Ⓓ	29. Ⓐ Ⓑ Ⓒ Ⓓ	49. Ⓐ Ⓑ Ⓒ Ⓓ	69. Ⓐ Ⓑ Ⓒ Ⓓ	89. Ⓐ Ⓑ Ⓒ Ⓓ
10. Ⓐ Ⓑ Ⓒ Ⓓ	30. Ⓐ Ⓑ Ⓒ Ⓓ	50. Ⓐ Ⓑ Ⓒ Ⓓ	70. Ⓐ Ⓑ Ⓒ Ⓓ	90. Ⓐ Ⓑ Ⓒ Ⓓ
11. Ⓐ Ⓑ Ⓒ Ⓓ	31. Ⓐ Ⓑ Ⓒ Ⓓ	51. Ⓐ Ⓑ Ⓒ Ⓓ	71. Ⓐ Ⓑ Ⓒ Ⓓ	91. Ⓐ Ⓑ Ⓒ Ⓓ
12. Ⓐ Ⓑ Ⓒ Ⓓ	32. Ⓐ Ⓑ Ⓒ Ⓓ	52. Ⓐ Ⓑ Ⓒ Ⓓ	72. Ⓐ Ⓑ Ⓒ Ⓓ	92. Ⓐ Ⓑ Ⓒ Ⓓ
13. Ⓐ Ⓑ Ⓒ Ⓓ	33. Ⓐ Ⓑ Ⓒ Ⓓ	53. Ⓐ Ⓑ Ⓒ Ⓓ	73. Ⓐ Ⓑ Ⓒ Ⓓ	93. Ⓐ Ⓑ Ⓒ Ⓓ
14. Ⓐ Ⓑ Ⓒ Ⓓ	34. Ⓐ Ⓑ Ⓒ Ⓓ	54. Ⓐ Ⓑ Ⓒ Ⓓ	74. Ⓐ Ⓑ Ⓒ Ⓓ	94. Ⓐ Ⓑ Ⓒ Ⓓ
15. Ⓐ Ⓑ Ⓒ Ⓓ	35. Ⓐ Ⓑ Ⓒ Ⓓ	55. Ⓐ Ⓑ Ⓒ Ⓓ	75. Ⓐ Ⓑ Ⓒ Ⓓ	95. Ⓐ Ⓑ Ⓒ Ⓓ
16. Ⓐ Ⓑ Ⓒ Ⓓ	36. Ⓐ Ⓑ Ⓒ Ⓓ	56. Ⓐ Ⓑ Ⓒ Ⓓ	76. Ⓐ Ⓑ Ⓒ Ⓓ	96. Ⓐ Ⓑ Ⓒ Ⓓ
17. Ⓐ Ⓑ Ⓒ Ⓓ	37. Ⓐ Ⓑ Ⓒ Ⓓ	57. Ⓐ Ⓑ Ⓒ Ⓓ	77. Ⓐ Ⓑ Ⓒ Ⓓ	97. Ⓐ Ⓑ Ⓒ Ⓓ
18. Ⓐ Ⓑ Ⓒ Ⓓ	38. Ⓐ Ⓑ Ⓒ Ⓓ	58. Ⓐ Ⓑ Ⓒ Ⓓ	78. Ⓐ Ⓑ Ⓒ Ⓓ	98. Ⓐ Ⓑ Ⓒ Ⓓ
19. Ⓐ Ⓑ Ⓒ Ⓓ	39. Ⓐ Ⓑ Ⓒ Ⓓ	59. Ⓐ Ⓑ Ⓒ Ⓓ	79. Ⓐ Ⓑ Ⓒ Ⓓ	99. Ⓐ Ⓑ Ⓒ Ⓓ
20. Ⓐ Ⓑ Ⓒ Ⓓ	40. Ⓐ Ⓑ Ⓒ Ⓓ	60. Ⓐ Ⓑ Ⓒ Ⓓ	80. Ⓐ Ⓑ Ⓒ Ⓓ	100. Ⓐ Ⓑ Ⓒ Ⓓ

answer sheet

Practice Test 3

> **Directions:** Questions 1–15 are based on the following memorandum. You will have 10 minutes to read and note the details. Then you will have to answer the 15 questions without referring back to it.

May 10

TO: All Court Officers
FROM: Clerk of the Court
SUBJECT: Assignment of Duties

Each of you will start a new assignment on May 13. You will be assigned to either Part 1, Part 2, or Part 4. Definite assignments will be made on Monday.

Those of you who are assigned to Part 4, at which the murder trial of George Jackson is now in progress, are cautioned to be especially alert. Information has been received from the office of the Police Commissioner that the accused may attempt to escape from the courtroom, aided by members of the "Blue Circle" gang with which the accused was connected prior to his arrest.

Known members of this gang include: Patsy "Boots" Brescia, a short, swarthy individual who invariably dresses conservatively. Although this member of the gang has no arrest record, he is known to carry firearms at all times and is now wanted by authorities in this state.

Fred Fick, alias Frederick Fidens: This individual is 6 feet 4 inches tall, weighs 230 pounds, and may be identified by a knife scar on the right cheek. He has been convicted of felonious assault, manslaughter, and burglary.

Patrick Ahern: This individual is 6 feet, 2 inches tall and weighs 145 pounds. He is known to be extremely dangerous when under the influence of drugs. Ahern's convictions include those for robbery, breaking and entering, and Sullivan Law violation. He is wanted for kidnapping by the California authorities.

All court officers, including those not assigned to the murder trial, are, of course, expected to be on the lookout for anyone acting peculiarly. If you observe anyone who answers any of the descriptions given above, or anyone else whose actions are such as to arouse your suspicion, send another officer to call the chief court officer. Avoid any indication that you are suspicious. Above all, avoid any action that may even remotely jeopardize the safety of spectators. While every precaution will be taken to prevent the admission to the courtroom of anyone carrying arms, do not gamble on the success of these precautions. These men are dangerous and, if convinced that their own safety is in peril, will have no hesitancy in using their weapons should they be able to smuggle them in.

1. The memorandum you have just read was issued by the
   - (A) Clerk of the Court
   - (B) Presiding Justice
   - (C) Chief Court Attendant
   - (D) Chief of Police

2. The number of members in the "Blue Circle" gang is
   - (A) 1 or 2
   - (B) 3 to 5
   - (C) 6 to 9
   - (D) not definitely stated in the memorandum

3. According to the memorandum, the man accused of murder is named
   - (A) Johnson
   - (B) Jamison
   - (C) Jackson
   - (D) Johnston

4. Information concerning the possibility of the attempted escape of the accused was received from
   - (A) the office of the District Attorney
   - (B) the office of the Police Commissioner
   - (C) a member of the underworld
   - (D) not stated in the memorandum

5. The memorandum indicates that, of the members of the "Blue Circle" gang mentioned,
   - (A) all have been arrested at least once
   - (B) only one has never been arrested
   - (C) two have never been arrested
   - (D) three have never been arrested

6. The murder trial mentioned in the memorandum
   - (A) has already begun
   - (B) will begin some time next week
   - (C) will begin on Monday
   - (D) will begin on May 13

7. According to the memorandum, all officers
   - (A) are to be on the alert for escaped prisoners
   - (B) assigned to the murder trial are to personally search all spectators for concealed weapons immediately upon entering the courtroom
   - (C) will be assigned, at one time or another, to duty at the murder trial
   - (D) will receive definite new assignments on Monday

8. Of the members of the gang mentioned in the memorandum
   - (A) at least one, if apprehended, may be extradited (returned to another state)
   - (B) at least two are said to be wanted by authorities in other states
   - (C) at least three have been guilty of felonies
   - (D) any one is likely to act peculiarly

9. The memorandum does not state that Fred Fick has ever been convicted of
   - (A) burglary
   - (B) manslaughter
   - (C) robbery
   - (D) felonious assault

10. From information given in the memorandum, Patrick Ahern may best be described as
    - (A) short and stocky
    - (B) tall and heavy
    - (C) tall and thin
    - (D) short and thin

11. According to the memorandum, the member of the "Blue Circle" gang who is known to use drugs is

(A) "Boots" Brescia
(B) Patrick Ahern
(C) Fred Fick
(D) George Jackson

12. "Boots" Brescia may most readily be identified by

(A) his swarthy complexion
(B) the scar on his right cheek
(C) his flashy clothes
(D) his footwear

13. According to instructions contained in the memorandum, if a court officer observes anyone acting suspiciously he or she should

(A) sound an alarm
(B) report the situation in person to the Chief Court Officer
(C) keep the suspect under surveillance until he or she can turn the job over to another court officer
(D) send another court officer to summon the Chief Court Officer

14. On the basis of the information contained in the memorandum, it may be positively stated that

(A) most members of the "Blue Circle" gang habitually carry firearms
(B) two or more members of the gang are armed at all times
(C) at least one member of the gang is always armed
(D) the murder was committed with a handgun

15. In dealing with any suspicious characters seen in the courtroom, a court officer's first concern should be with

(A) maintenance of order
(B) protection of spectators
(C) detention of the suspect
(D) confiscation of arms

16. "Referees of the Civil Court are former judges of this court who have served at least ten years and whose term of office terminated at the age of 55 or over, or any judge who has served in a court of record and has retired." According to this statement, a person can be a referee of the Civil Court only if he or she

(A) has been a judge
(B) has retired
(C) has served at least ten years in the court
(D) meets certain age requirements

17. "One theory states that all criminal behavior is taught by a process of communication within small, intimate groups. An individual engages in criminal behavior if the number of criminal patterns that he or she has acquired exceeds the number of non-criminal patterns." This statement indicates that criminal behavior is

(A) learned
(B) instinctive
(C) hereditary
(D) reprehensible

18. "The law enforcement staff of today requires training and mental qualities of a high order. The poorly or partially prepared staff member lowers the standard of work, retards personal earning power, and fails in a career meant to provide a livelihood and social improvement." According to this statement,

(A) an inefficient member of a law enforcement staff will still earn a good livelihood
(B) law enforcement officers move in good social circles
(C) many people fail in law enforcement careers
(D) persons of training and ability are essential to a law enforcement staff

19. "In New York State, no crime can occur unless there is a written law forbidding the act or omission in question, and even though an act may not be exactly in harmony with public policy, such act is not a crime unless it is expressly forbidden by legislative enactment." According to the above statement

(A) a crime is committed with reference to a particular law

(B) acts not in harmony with public policy should be forbidden by law

(C) noncriminal activity will promote public welfare

(D) legislative enactments frequently forbid actions in harmony with public policy

20. "The unrestricted sale of firearms is one of the main causes of our shameful crime record." According to this statement, one of the causes of our crime record is the

(A) development of firepower

(B) ease of securing weapons

(C) increased skill in using guns

(D) scientific perfection of firearms

21. "Every person must be informed of the reason for arrest unless arrested in the actual commission of a crime. Sufficient force to effect the arrest may be used, but the courts frown on brutal methods." According to this statement, a person does not have to be informed of the reason for arrest if

(A) brutal force was not used in effecting it

(B) the courts will later turn the defendant loose

(C) the person arrested knows force will be used if necessary

(D) the reason for it is clearly evident from the circumstances

22. "An important duty of a court officer is to keep order in the court." On the basis of this statement, it is probably true that

(A) it is more important for a court officer to be strong than to be smart

(B) people involved in court trials are noisy if not kept in check

(C) not every duty of a court officer is important

(D) the maintenance of order is important for the proper conduct of court business

23. "The criminal is rarely or never reformed." Acceptance of this statement as true would mean that greatest emphasis should be placed on

(A) imprisonment

(B) parole

(C) probation

(D) malingering

QUESTIONS 24–35 ARE BASED ON THE FOLLOWING FACT PATTERN.

Two Hispanic males in their early 30s were on the corner of Chestnut Street and Vine Street when two Caucasian males and a Caucasian female in a red Mustang approached them. One male was dressed in a black shirt and blue jeans, one male was dressed in a white shirt and blue jeans, and the female was dressed in a blue shirt and blue jeans. The Caucasian males pulled out their guns, opened their car doors, and yelled at the Hispanic men to hand over their money. One Hispanic man ran from the scene and was shot at three times by the Caucasian male in the black shirt. The shots did not hit the man. The other Hispanic male gave the men his wallet, which contained $50, all in $10 bills. The Caucasian men then got back in the car and fled the scene with the female driving.

24. How old were the Hispanic men?

(A) 20s

(B) 30s

(C) 40s

(D) 50s

25. What was the order of events?
- **(A)** The Caucasian males got out of the car, yelled at the other men, and pulled out their guns.
- **(B)** The Caucasian males fired their guns, got out of the car, and yelled at the Hispanic males.
- **(C)** The Caucasian males opened their doors, pulled out their guns, and fired at the Hispanic male.
- **(D)** The Caucasian males pulled out their guns, opened their doors, and yelled at the Hispanic males.

26. How many of the robbers wore black shirts?
- **(A)** 1
- **(B)** 2
- **(C)** 3
- **(D)** none

27. How many of the victims were female?
- **(A)** 1
- **(B)** 2
- **(C)** 3
- **(D)** none

28. Where did the incident occur?
- **(A)** Chestnut Street and Vine Street
- **(B)** Oak Street and Vine Street
- **(C)** Oak Street and Chestnut Street
- **(D)** Vine Street and Carter Street

29. What color was the car driven by the robbers?
- **(A)** black
- **(B)** red
- **(C)** blue
- **(D)** brown

30. The man who shot at the victim was wearing what color shirt?
- **(A)** blue
- **(B)** white
- **(C)** brown
- **(D)** black

31. How many $10 bills did the robbers steal?
- **(A)** 2
- **(B)** 3
- **(C)** 4
- **(D)** 5

32. What color shirt did the female robber wear?
- **(A)** red
- **(B)** blue
- **(C)** white
- **(D)** black

33. How many shots did the robbers fire?
- **(A)** 3
- **(B)** 4
- **(C)** 5
- **(D)** 6

34. The person driving the car after the robbery was wearing what color shirt?
- **(A)** red
- **(B)** blue
- **(C)** black
- **(D)** white

35. How many people were shot in the robbery?
- **(A)** none
- **(B)** 1
- **(C)** 2
- **(D)** 3

36. "It shall be unlawful for any person to manufacture, pack, possess, sell, offer for sale, and/or expose for sale any compound or blended oil of any kind that purports to be an olive oil mixture unless the container be permanently and conspicuously labeled a "compound oil" or "blended oil" with a statement of the different ingredients thereof and the specific percentage of olive oil, the total percentage of other vegetable oils, and the specific percentage of each other ingredient comprising more than one half of 1 percent of the mixture." According to this paragraph, a mixture consisting of olive oil and other oils that is offered for sale
- **(A)** may be labeled as "olive oil" if it contains at least 98 1/2% olive oil
- **(B)** may not contain more than half of 1% of other oils
- **(C)** must be labeled "compound oil" or "blended oil"
- **(D)** must contain only olive oil and other vegetable oils

QUESTIONS 37–40 ARE BASED ON THE FOLLOWING PASSAGE.

"Because of the importance of preserving physical evidence, the officer should not enter a scene of a crime if it can be examined visually from one position and if no other pressing duty requires his presence there. There are some responsibilities, however, that take precedence over preservation of evidence. Some examples are as follows: rescue work, disarming dangerous persons, and quelling a disturbance. The officer should learn how to accomplish these more vital tasks while at the same time preserving as much evidence as possible. If he finds it necessary to enter upon the scene, he should quickly study the place of entry to learn if any evidence will suffer by his contact; then he should determine the routes to use in walking to the spot where his presence is required. Every place where a foot will fall or where a hand or other part of his body will touch should be examined with the eye. Objects should not be touched or moved unless there is a definite and compelling reason. For identification of most items of physical evidence at the initial investigation, it is seldom necessary to touch or move them.

37. The one of the following titles that is the most appropriate for the above paragraph is
  (A) Determining the Order of Tasks at the Scene of a Crime
  (B) The Principal Reasons for Preserving Evidence at the Scene of a Crime
  (C) Precautions to Take at the Scene of a Crime
  (D) Evidence to be Examined at the Scene of a Crime

38. When an officer feels that it is essential for him to enter the immediate area where a crime has been committed, he should
  (A) quickly but carefully glance around to determine whether his entering the area will damage any evidence present
  (B) remove all objects of evidence from his predetermined route in order to avoid stepping on them
  (C) carefully replace any object immediately if it is moved or touched by his hands or any other part of his body
  (D) use only the usual place of entry to the scene in order to avoid disturbing any possible clues left on rear doors and windows

39. The one of the following that is the least urgent duty of an officer who has just reported to the scene of a crime is to
  (A) disarm the hysterical victim who is wildly waving a loaded gun in all directions
  (B) give first aid to a possible suspect who has been injured while attempting to leave the scene of the crime
  (C) prevent observers from attacking and injuring the persons suspected of having committed the crime
  (D) preserve from damage or destruction any evidence necessary for the proper prosecution of the case against the criminals

40. An officer has just reported to the scene of a crime in response to a phone call. The best of the following actions for him to take with respect to objects of physical evidence present at the scene is to

- **(A)** make no attempt to enter the crime scene if his entry will disturb any vital physical evidence
- **(B)** map out the shortest straight path to follow in walking to the spot where the most physical evidence may be found
- **(C)** move such objects of physical evidence as are necessary to enable him to assist the wounded victim of the crime
- **(D)** quickly examine all objects of physical evidence in order to determine which objects may be touched and which may not

QUESTIONS 41–49 ARE BASED ON THE FOLLOWING TABLE.

Court	Arraignments	Fines	Summonses	Warrants
Lower Manhattan	48,175	$ 74,386	6,388	6,926
Upper Manhattan	20,953	45,183	10,745	5,721
Bay Ridge	6,943	14,238	2,674	1,457
Coney Island	8,481	16,805	2,076	1,476
Flatbush	8,935	15,354	3,301	1,090
Williamsburg	8,017	13,170	4,454	1,412
Flushing	3,527	8,297	1,971	708
Long Island City	2,261	4,855	1,719	552
Criminal Court, Manhattan	10,521	200,617	2,312	1,324
Criminal Court, Bronx	4,450	78,625	273	683
Criminal Court, Brooklyn	11,242	164,482	1,782	1,342
Criminal Court, Queens	2,680	31,658	576	365
Total		$667,670	38,271	23,056

41. The total of the arraignments for all the courts listed in the table is most nearly
    (A) 138,000
    (B) 137,000
    (C) 136,000
    (D) 135,000

42. The difference between the total collected in fines in Criminal Court, Brooklyn, and the total collected in fines in Criminal Court, Bronx, is most nearly
    (A) $85,860
    (B) $85,855
    (C) $85,850
    (D) $85,845

43. The number of summonses for Criminal Court, Bronx, when multiplied by 36, is most nearly equal to the number of arraignments for
    (A) Lower Manhattan
    (B) Flatbush
    (C) Criminal Court, Brooklyn
    (D) Criminal Court, Manhattan

44. The average collected in fines per court for the twelve courts listed is most nearly
    (A) $55,640
    (B) $55,635
    (C) $55,630
    (D) $55,625

45. Of the following, the court with the greatest amount in fines in proportion to the number of arraignments is
    (A) Lower Manhattan
    (B) Upper Manhattan
    (C) Criminal Court, Queens
    (D) Coney Island

46. Of the following, the court that has most nearly a 4:1 ratio of arraignments to summonses is
    (A) Flatbush
    (B) Criminal Court, Brooklyn
    (C) Criminal Court, Manhattan
    (D) Flushing

47. Of the courts with more than 8,000 arraignments, the one that had more than three times as many summonses as warrants is
    (A) Williamsburg
    (B) Coney Island
    (C) Upper Manhattan
    (D) Lower Manhattan

48. Of the criminal courts,
    (A) Manhattan had fewer arraignments but more summonses than Brooklyn
    (B) Bronx had more summonses but fewer arraignments than Queens
    (C) Queens had fewer arraignments, fewer summonses, and fewer warrants than any other court
    (D) Brooklyn had more arraignments, more summonses, and more warrants than any other court

49. With fewer than 3,000 summonses and more than 5,000 arraignments, the court that had the smallest number of warrants is
    (A) Flatbush
    (B) Criminal Court, Queens
    (C) Criminal Court, Manhattan
    (D) Criminal Court, Brooklyn

50. At a forced sale, a bankrupt farmer sold his farm for $7,500. If this amount was 33 1/3% less than its real value, the value of the farm would be
    (A) $11,250
    (B) $5,000
    (C) $7,500
    (D) $10,000

FOR QUESTIONS 51 TO 60, COMPARE EACH LINE OF COLUMN I WITH ITS CORRESPONDING LINE IN COLUMN II AND DECIDE HOW MANY LINES IN COLUMN II ARE EXACTLY THE SAME AS THEIR COUNTERPARTS IN COLUMN I. MARK YOUR ANSWERS AS FOLLOWS.

MARK (A) IF ONLY *ONE* LINE IN COLUMN II IS EXACTLY THE SAME AS ITS CORRESPONDING LINE IN COLUMN I.
MARK (B) IF *TWO* LINES IN COLUMN II ARE EXACTLY THE SAME AS THEIR CORRESPONDING LINES IN COLUMN I.
MARK (C) IF *THREE* LINES IN COLUMN II ARE EXACTLY THE SAME AS THEIR CORRESPONDING LINES IN COLUMN I.
MARK (D) IF ALL *FOUR* LINES IN COLUMN II ARE EXACTLY THE SAME AS THEIR CORRESPONDING LINES IN COLUMN I.

	Column I	Column II
51.	3816	3816
	5283	5832
	4686	4868
	1252	1252
52.	acdt	acdt
	xuer	xuer
	ltbf	Ibtf
	oypn	oypn
53.	9063	9063
	itop	itop
	nzne	nzne
	7549	7549
54.	TYBF	TYIF
	5631	5361
	BcOp	BcOP
	ag7B	ag7B
55.	lbct	lbct
	1803	1830
	Xtux	Xtux
	45NM	45NM

	Column I	Column II
56.	AbuR	AbuR
	52VC	52VC
	rehg	rehg
	3416	3416
57.	awg3	awg3
	tyE3	ty3E
	abhn	abnh
	24po	24op
58.	6tru	6tru
	sw4k	sw4K
	lgh8	lgh8
	u2up	u2up
59.	agxp	agXp
	ruy5	ruy5
	aglb	agLb
	8a9c	8z9c
60.	agbt	agbt
	1LiI	1liI
	ty4f	ty4f
	arwd	erwd

FOR QUESTIONS 61–70, SELECT THE SENTENCE IN EACH QUESTION THAT IS BEST WITH RESPECT TO GRAMMAR AND USAGE.

61. **(A)** The receptionist must answer courteously the questions of all them callers.
    (B) The receptionist must answer courteously the questions what are asked by the callers.
    (C) There would have been no trouble if the receptionist had have always answered courteously.
    (D) The receptionist should answer courteously the questions of all callers.

62. **(A)** This letter, together wrath the reports, are to be sent to the principal.
    (B) The reports, together with this letter, is to be sent to the principal.
    (C) The reports and this letter is to be sent to the principal.
    (D) This letter, together with the reports, is to be sent to the principal.

63. **(A)** One of us have to make the reply before tomorrow.
    (B) Making the reply before tomorrow will have to be done by one of us.
    (C) One of us has to reply before tomorrow.
    (D) Anyone has to reply before tomorrow.

64. **(A)** According to the preceding paragraph, the laws have no effect on practice.
    (B) The laws have no effect on practice, according to the preceding paragraph.
    (C) The laws have, according to the preceding paragraph, no effect on practice.
    (D) The preceding paragraph states no effect is made by law on practice.

65. **(A)** Brown's & Company employees have recently received increases in salary.
    (B) Brown & Company recently increased the salaries of all its employees.
    (C) Recently Brown & Company has increased their employees' salaries.
    (D) Brown & Company have recently increased the salaries of all its employees.

66. **(A)** Since the report lacked the needed information, it was of no use to him.
    (B) This report was useless to him because there were no needed information in it.
    (C) Since the report did not contain the needed information, it was not real useful to him.
    (D) Being that the report lacked the needed information, he could not use it.

67. **(A)** If properly addressed, the letter will reach my mother and I.
    (B) The letter had been addressed to myself and my mother.
    (C) I believe the letter was addressed to either my mother or I.
    (D) My mother's name, as well as mine, was on the letter.

68. **(A)** The supervisor reprimanded the typist, whom she believed had made careless errors.
    (B) The typist would have corrected the errors had she of known that the supervisor would see the report.
    (C) The errors in the typed report were so numerous that they could hardly be overlooked.
    (D) Many errors were found in the report which she typed and could not disregard them.

69. **(A)** It is quite possible that we shall reemploy anyone whose training fits them to do the work.
    (B) It is probable that we shall reemploy those who have been trained to do the work.
    (C) Such of our personnel that have been trained to do the work will be again employed.
    (D) We expect to reemploy the ones who have training enough that they can do the work.

70. **(A)** The paper we use for this purpose must be light, glossy, and stand hard usage as well.
    (B) Only a light and a glossy, but durable, paper must be used for this purpose.
    (C) For this purpose, we want a paper that is light, glossy, but that will stand hard wear.
    (D) For this purpose, paper that is light, glossy, and durable is essential.

FOR QUESTIONS 71 TO 80, COMPARE EACH LINE OF LETTERS AND NUMBERS CAREFULLY TO SEE IF EACH LETTER HAS THE CORRECT MATCHING NUMBER BASED ON THE TABLE BELOW. MARK YOUR ANSWER BASED ON HOW MANY LINES IN EACH QUESTION ARE CORRECTLY MATCHED.

MARK (A) IF *NONE* OF THE LINES MATCHES.
MARK (B) IF ONLY *ONE* OF THE LINES MATCHES.
MARK (C) IF *TWO* OF THE LINES MATCH.
MARK (D) IF ALL *THREE* LINES MATCH.

Letter	Y	J	X	C	M	B	V	W	U	L
Number	0	1	2	3	4	5	6	7	8	9

71.   BXUC   5283

         JLMB   1945

         CYWM   3074

72.   MXWB   4285

         CUJL   3819

         MYVX   4073

73.   XWLB   2695

         MUBY   5860

         LXJB   9215

74.   CWLY   3790

         MXJV   4216

         YWMC   0473

75.	LMXB	9452
	BCWY	5370
	JBWU	1587
76.	MWCJ	4731
	VYBU	6085
	LXMB	9254
77.	UCJL	8419
	WXYB	7206
	CWMX	3842
78.	LMWX	9472
	BYCU	5038
	XULJ	2891
79.	JBVW	1576
	YXLM	0295
	WXCJ	7213
80.	JUWL	1897
	CBXW	3527
	JVYB	1065

QUESTIONS 81–85 ARE BASED ON THE FOLLOWING DUTIES OF A COURT OFFICER.

The jury room must be properly ventilated, heated, and lighted, and the jurors must have an ample supply of paper, pens, and any other needed stationery items. The court officer immediately locks the door when leaving the jury room and remains at calling or hearing distance. If any jury member requires services, the officer must respond at a moment's notice. In all cases, two officers are assigned to guard a jury. This ensures constant guard over the jury. Should one court officer be dispatched with a message or sent to the courtroom for an exhibit, the other would remain on guard. If only one guard were assigned, the chances of wrongdoing would be heightened.

There arises, at times, a situation in which a jury member desires to communicate with some family member while the jury is behind closed doors. The court officer cannot allow this except with the permission of the judge or the clerk. If the jury member requires the sending of a message to the judge or court, it must be put in writing with the request that it be delivered by the court officer.

81. In a civil case, the jurors are sometimes instructed to deliver a sealed verdict. In such case, the jurors deliberate until they reach a verdict, put it in writing, and seal it in an envelope. The envelope may be delivered to the court the next morning. After a sealed verdict has been ordered and the judge has gone home for the day, a juror asks permission to telephone his wife to tell her that he will be late. The court officer should

    (A) not permit the juror to use the phone
    (B) permit the juror to use the phone
    (C) call the juror's wife and let the juror talk to her
    (D) call the juror's wife and ask her to come to the courthouse to talk to her husband

82. While one court officer assigned to guard a deliberating jury is on her way to the judge's chambers with a request from the jurors for clarification of a point of law, the foreman of the jury knocks on the door and asks the court officer to procure for the jury Exhibits E and G. The court officer should

    (A) shout loudly after the first officer to ask her to return and pick up the additional requests
    (B) complain to the foreman that the jury makes too many requests
    (C) run after the first officer and hand her notes making requests for the exhibits
    (D) wait for the first officer to return and then go for the exhibits

83. A court officer has conscientiously supplied the jury room with paper, pencils, pens, and a generous assortment of office supplies. After several days of deliberation, a member of the jury tells the officer that the jury needs more rubber bands and paper clips. The officer should

    (A) ask the jury what happened to all the supplies
    (B) tell the judge that this jury is costing the taxpayers too much money
    (C) get more rubber bands and paper clips for the jury
    (D) tell the jury that it must get along with what it has

84. A juror tells a court officer that he is claustrophobic and is afraid to remain in a closed and locked jury room. Under these circumstances, the court officer should

    (A) leave the door partly open
    (B) close the door but not lock it
    (C) close and lock the door
    (D) have the juror sit outside the locked door with the court officers

85. A court officer with a 5:30 p.m. appointment has been assigned to a jury room to guard the jury until 4 p.m., at which time she is to be relieved if the jury has not yet come to an agreement. At 4 p.m., the jury is still deliberating, and the relief has not appeared. The court officer should
    (A) ask the foreman of the jury to assume responsibility until the relief arrives
    (B) find out what the jurors may need, get it, and then lock the jurors in for the night
    (C) inform her supervisor but remain on duty until she is relieved
    (D) wait until 5 p.m. and then leave the jury in the care of the of the second court officer, even if the relieving officer has not arrived

QUESTIONS 86–95 ARE BASED ON THE FOLLOWING LEGAL DEFINITIONS.

Larceny is committed when a person wrongfully takes, obtains, or withholds the property of another.

Grand larceny is committed when a person wrongfully takes, obtains, or withholds the property of another and the value of the property is over $250 or the property taken is a credit card.

Theft of services is committed when a person uses a stolen credit card to purchase goods or services or when a person avoids payment for restaurant, hotel, motel, transportation, gas, electric, or telecommunications (telephone) services.

Menacing is committed when a person, by physical menace, places another person in fear of immediate serious injury. "Physical menace" means that a person must have the means available to carry out the threat, i.e., if the person threatens to shoot someone, he must have a gun present; if he threatens to beat someone with a bat, he must have the bat present, etc.

Arson is committed when a person intentionally causes damage to a building or motor vehicle by either setting fire to said building or motor vehicle or by causing an explosion that damages said building or motor vehicle.

86. While riding on a subway train, Thomas Evans reaches into the pocketbook of Janet Brown and removes two credit cards. Evans could be charged with
    (A) larceny
    (B) grand larceny
    (C) theft of services
    (D) no crime, as he did not use the cards

87. John Murphy overslept and because of this he may be late reporting to his job. He has been tardy for work several times in the recent past and has been warned that future lateness may result in his being fired from his job. As John enters the subway station, he hears his train approaching. He does not have a token for the turnstile, and the line to purchase tokens is very long. He knows that if he waits in line he will definitely miss the train and thereby be late for work and perhaps lose his job. John jumps over the turnstile without paying and enters the train. John could be charged with
    (A) larceny and theft of services
    (B) grand larceny and theft of services
    (C) theft of services
    (D) no crime because waiting in the token line could have caused him to lose his job

88. Mary Simmons was doing some shopping in a department store. She observed another customer place a credit card on the counter as she examined some merchandise. Mary took the credit card off the counter and put it in her pocketbook. She then proceeded to another section of the store, where she purchased some articles with the credit card she had just taken. Mary could be charged with
    (A) larceny only
    (B) grand larceny only
    (C) larceny and theft of services
    (D) grand larceny and theft of services

89. John Smith enters an appliance store and takes a portable stereo–cassette player valued at $100 without paying for it. As he starts to exit the store, the manager of the store yells to Smith to stop. Smith turns and puts his hand in his pocket and states, "I'll shoot you if you come near me." Smith does not actually have a gun in his possession. He flees with the cassette player. Smith could be charged with

(A) menacing only
(B) larceny only
(C) grand larceny only
(D) menacing and larceny

90. Mary Johnson enters a jewelry store and takes a watch worth $250 without paying for it. As she is leaving the store, the manager approaches her and Mary starts to run for the front door. While trying to make her escape, Mary accidentally knocks over a portable electric heater, which starts a fire. Mary escapes with the watch, and the store suffers minor damage from the fire. Mary could be charged with

(A) grand larceny only
(B) larceny only
(C) larceny and arson
(D) arson only

91. Bill Walsh was assaulted by the owner of an apartment building. He wants revenge for the injuries he suffered and has decided to burn the apartment house down. Bill does not want to hurt any innocent people, so he calls the superintendent of the building to warn him to get the tenants out. Walsh had to use a slug to make the phone call, as he had no change, only paper money, in his possession. He enters the building and starts a fire, which damages the building extensively before it is extinguished. Walsh could be charged with

(A) arson only
(B) larceny and theft of services
(C) arson and larceny
(D) arson and theft of services

92. Bill enters the basement of John's house and takes a saw worth $250. As he is about to escape, John attempts to stop him. Bill then picks up a baseball bat and says, "If you come one step closer, I'll break your head." John retreats. Just before he flees, Bill tosses a lighted match into a group of paint cans that are stacked in a corner of the basement. A fire starts and causes minor damage to the basement before it is extinguished. Bill could be charged with

(A) grand larceny and arson
(B) larceny and arson
(C) larceny, menacing, and arson
(D) grand larceny, menacing, and arson

93. While visiting Lisa at her apartment, Frank takes a credit card from her pocketbook without Lisa's knowledge. Frank then goes to a restaurant and charges his meal with the credit card he has just taken. He takes a cab to his home and, when he realizes that he does not have enough money to pay the cab fare, he opens the door and flees without paying. Frank could be charged with

(A) larceny and theft of services
(B) grand larceny and theft of services
(C) larceny only
(D) grand larceny only

94. Bill Martin is a passenger in a taxi cab. He lights a cigarette and then proceeds to fall asleep. The lighted cigarette drops between the seat cushions. When Bill awakens, he does not realize that the cigarette has fallen from his mouth. He pays his fare and leaves the cab, taking with him a woman's pocketbook that he found on the seat. A fire starts in the back of the cab and causes minor damage to the rear of the taxi before it is extinguished. Bill could be charged with

(A) larceny
(B) grand larceny
(C) larceny and arson
(D) grand larceny and arson

95. Mike steals a telephone credit card from Joe. He then makes a long-distance phone call to his girlfriend and charges it to the credit card he has just taken. Mike could be charged with

(A) larceny
(B) grand larceny
(C) theft of services
(D) grand larceny and theft of services

QUESTIONS 96–98 ARE BASED ON THE FOLLOWING PASSAGE.

"A person who gives or offers a bribe to any executive officer, or to a person elected or appointed to become an executive officer, of this state with intent to influence him in respect to any act, decision, vote, opinion, or other proceedings as such officer, is subject to punishment by imprisonment in a state prison not exceeding ten years or by a fine not exceeding $5,000 or by both."

96. George Sloan has just been elected to his first term as the county executive. Among the issues facing the county is disposal of solid waste. Phil Crane is a private contractor involved in collection and transportation of garbage from restaurants and businesses. Crane has definite ideas as to methods of solving the solid waste question. Crane offers Sloan a bribe and attempts to convince Sloan of the value of his opinion. Sloan listens politely but refuses to accept the bribe. Crane's attempt comes to the attention of the county prosecutor.

(A) Sloan and Crane could both be subject to fines.
(B) Crane faces imprisonment in the county jail.
(C) Crane could spend five years in a state prison.
(D) Crane could be imprisoned for ten years or be fined $5,000 but not both.

97. Don Williams is an Assistant Attorney General. The Attorney General's office has been investigating an alleged civil rights violation. Joe Marshall, a friend of the suspect, approaches Williams and asks him to use his influence to curtail the investigation and to overlook certain evidence against the accused violator. He backs his request with a cash offer, which Williams accepts. The investigation is later dropped for lack of evidence.

(A) Williams is subject to imprisonment or fine.
(B) Marshall is subject to imprisonment and/or fine.
(C) Williams is subject to imprisonment; Marshall to fine.
(D) Williams is subject to fine; Marshall to imprisonment.

98. Joe White is very eager for the planning commission to give him permission to build a twelve-unit subdivision in an area tentatively designated open space. White speaks at every public meeting, takes out ads in local newspapers, and generally makes himself heard. He also writes and calls the chief of the commission, Jack Fisk, threatening, cajoling, and promising a generous donation to Fisk's favorite charity if Fisk will expedite his application.

(A) White could be fined and/or imprisoned.
(B) White could be fined but not imprisoned.
(C) White could be imprisoned but not fined.
(D) White cannot be imprisoned or fined.

QUESTIONS 99 AND 100 ARE BASED ON THE FOLLOWING PASSAGE.

"A person concerned in the commission of a crime, whether he directly commits the act constituting the offense or aids and abets in its commission, and whether present or absent, and a person who directly or indirectly counsels, commands, induces, or procures another to commit a crime is a 'principal.' A person who, after the commission of a felony, harbors, conceals, or aids the offender, with intent that he may avoid or escape from arrest, trial, conviction, or punishment, having knowledge or reasonable ground to believe that such offender is liable to arrest, has been arrested, is indicted or convicted, or had committed a felony, is an 'accessory' to the felony."

99. Glen Wilson, Tim Tripp, Bob Burns, and Don Ford made elaborate plans to rob the Buy-Rite Liquor Store on Saturday night just before closing. On the designated night, Bob Burns had a bad case of flu and stayed home in bed. Glen Wilson drove Tripp and Ford in his car, then waited with the engine running while Tripp and Ford went in with guns drawn, emptied the cash register, and emerged with the money and two bottles of vodka. Tripp and Ford jumped into Wilson's car. Wilson drove them to the Holiday Inn, where they registered and spent the night.

   (A) Tripp and Ford are principals; Wilson is an accessory.

   (B) Tripp, Ford, and Wilson are principals; Burns is an accessory.

   (C) Tripp, Ford, Wilson, and Burns are principals.

   (D) Tripp, Ford, Wilson, and Burns are principals; the night clerk at the Holiday Inn is an accessory.

100. Ron Johnson is a crack dealer. He has been a regular supplier to Harry Walker, a user introduced to crack by Johnson some months ago. Walker finds his habit increasingly expensive, so Johnson suggests that Walker begin dealing himself in order to make money. Walker takes the suggestion and begins by selling small vials in a corner of the school yard at PS 380. One day, a child accuses Walker of delivering drugs and threatens to tell the principal of Walker's activity. Walker becomes frightened and drives out of the city to the farm of his friend Molly Miller. He tells Molly Miller that he may be in trouble and asks to stay at her home for awhile. Molly refuses to let Harry into her house but tells him he may stay in the barn for as long as he likes.

   (A) Harry Walker is a principal; Ron Johnson and Molly Miller are accessories.

   (B) Harry Walker and Ron Johnson are principals; Molly Miller is an accessory.

   (C) Harry Walker, Ron Johnson, and Molly Miller are all principals.

   (D) Harry Walker and Ron Johnson are principals; Molly Miller and the child are accessories.

ANSWER KEY AND EXPLANATIONS

1. A	21. D	41. C	61. D	81. A
2. D	22. D	42. B	62. D	82. D
3. C	23. A	43. D	63. C	83. C
4. B	24. B	44. A	64. A	84. C
5. B	25. D	45. C	65. B	85. C
6. A	26. A	46. C	66. A	86. B
7. D	27. D	47. A	67. D	87. C
8. A	28. A	48. A	68. C	88. D
9. C	29. B	49. C	69. B	89. B
10. C	30. D	50. A	70. D	90. B
11. B	31. D	51. B	71. D	91. D
12. A	32. B	52. C	72. B	92. C
13. D	33. A	53. D	73. B	93. B
14. C	34. B	54. A	74. C	94. A
15. B	35. A	55. C	75. B	95. D
16. A	36. C	56. D	76. B	96. C
17. A	37. C	57. A	77. A	97. B
18. D	38. A	58. C	78. D	98. D
19. A	39. D	59. A	79. A	99. C
20. B	40. C	60. B	80. B	100. B

1. **The correct answer is (A).** The memorandum was issued by the Clerk of the Court.

2. **The correct answer is (D).** Four members of the gang are named, but the total number of members of the gang is not stated.

3. **The correct answer is (C).** The accused on trial for murder is George Jackson.

4. **The correct answer is (B).** Information concerning the possible escape came from the office of the Police Commissioner (second paragraph).

5. **The correct answer is (B).** Patsy "Boots" Brescia has no arrest record. Fick and Ahearn have previous convictions, so they obviously have been previously arrested. Jackson is under arrest right now.

6. **The correct answer is (A).** A murder trial now in progress has already begun.

7. **The correct answer is (D).** The first paragraph states that all officers will begin new assignments on May 13 and that all will receive definite assignments on Monday.

8. **The correct answer is (A).** Patrick Ahern is wanted for kidnapping in California and, if apprehended, may be extradited to California. No mention is made of any other gang member's being wanted by another state.

9. **The correct answer is (C).** Fred Fick's list of convictions does not include robbery.

10. **The correct answer is (C).** A person who stands 6 feet 2 inches yet weighs only 145 pounds is tall and thin.

11. **The correct answer is (B).** If Patrick Ahern is extremely dangerous when under the influence of drugs, he must be a user.

12. **The correct answer is (A).** Brescia is a conservative dresser with a swarthy complexion. Fick is the one with a knife scar. We were not told how Brescia got his nickname.

13. **The correct answer is (D).** So stated in the last paragraph.

14. **The correct answer is (C).** Brescia is known to carry firearms at all times. Chances are pretty good that others of the gang carry arms as well, but the memorandum does not say so.

15. **The correct answer is (B).** The court officers must avoid any action that may jeopardize the safety of spectators.

16. **The correct answer is (A).** Referees of the civil court are drawn from the ranks of former judges of this court or from the ranks of judges who have retired from any court of record.

17. **The correct answer is (A).** If criminal behavior is taught, then it is learned.

18. **The correct answer is (D).** The law enforcement staff of today requires training and mental qualities of a high order.

19. **The correct answer is (A).** Regardless of how antisocial an act may be, it is not a crime unless it is a violation of a written law.

20. **The correct answer is (B).** Our crime rate is so high because it is so easy for criminals to obtain guns.

21. **The correct answer is (D).** A person who is arrested while in the process of committing a crime knows full well why he or she is being arrested and need not be told.

22. **The correct answer is (D).** If it is important that the court officer keep order in the court, obviously order is important to the functioning of the court.

23. **The correct answer is (A).** If one's attitude is "once a criminal always a criminal," then probation and parole should not be options and imprisonment must be emphasized. Malingering is pretending to be sick to avoid work.

24. **The correct answer is (B).** The first sentence indicates that two Hispanic males were in their early 30s.

25. **The correct answer is (D).** Choice (D) describes the correct order of events.

26. **The correct answer is (A).** The second sentence states that one male was dressed in a black shirt.

27. **The correct answer is (D).** The paragraph does not mention any female victims.

28. **The correct answer is (A).** The first sentence provides information about where the incident took place.

29. **The correct answer is (B).** The first sentence states "two Caucasian males and a Caucasian female in a red mustang...".

30. **The correct answer is (D).** The fourth sentence states that one Hispanic male was shot at three times by the Caucasian male in the black shirt.

31. **The correct answer is (D).** The wallet handed over to the robbers contained $50, all in $10 bills.

32. **The correct answer is (B).** The second sentence states that the female was dressed in a blue shirt.

33. **The correct answer is (A).** The fourth sentence states that one Hispanic male was shot at three times.

34. **The correct answer is (B).** The female, who was wearing a blue shirt, drove the getaway car.

35. **The correct answer is (A).** No one was shot.

36. **The correct answer is (C).** As long as the oil is properly labeled, any blend may be packed and sold.

37. **The correct answer is (C).** The paragraph discusses the precautions that must be taken at the scene of the crime so as to disturb as little evidence as possible.

38. **The correct answer is (A).** Danger to persons is more compelling than preservation of evidence, but the officer should size up the situation so as to do as little damage as possible.

39. **The correct answer is (D).** Preservation of evidence is important, but it pales in the face of danger to any person, victim, or perpetrator.

40. **The correct answer is (C).** The same point is repeated. Save lives.

41. **The correct answer is (C).** Add up arraignments in all twelve courts. The total is 136,185, which is closest to 136,000.

42. **The correct answer is (B).** $164,482 − $78,625 = $85,857, which is most nearly $85,855.

43. **The correct answer is (D).** 273 × 36 = 9,828, which is closest to the 10,521 arraignments in Manhattan.

44. **The correct answer is (A).** $667,670 ÷ 12 = $55,639.17, which is most nearly $55,640.

45. **The correct answer is (C).** In Criminal Court, Queens, the amount of fines is nearly 12 times the number of arraignments. In the other three courts, fines outpace arraignments by only about 2 to 1.

46. **The correct answer is (C).** By inspection, it is clear that the 10,521 to 2,312 in Criminal Court, Manhattan, is much closer to 4 to 1 than is the 8,935 to 3,301 of Flatbush; the 11,242 to 1,782 of Criminal Court, Brooklyn; or the 3,527 to 1,971 of Flushing.

47. **The correct answer is (A).** 1,412 × 3 = 4,236, which is very close to 4,454.

48. **The correct answer is (A).** Manhattan had 10,521 arraignments, while Brooklyn had 11,242; on the other hand, Manhattan had 2,312 summonses, while Brooklyn had only 1,782.

49. **The correct answer is (C).** Study the table. The court that meets the criteria of the question is Criminal Court, Manhattan.

50. **The correct answer is (A).** $7,500 is $33\frac{1}{3}\%$ less than its real value, so it is $66\frac{2}{3}\%$ or $\frac{2}{3}$ of its real value. If $\frac{2}{3}$ = $7,500, then $\frac{1}{3}$ = $3,750, and $\frac{3}{3}$ or the full value is $3,750 × 3 = $11,250.

51. **The correct answer is (B).** Lines 1 and 4 are exactly the same.

52. **The correct answer is (C).** Lines 1, 2, and 4 are exactly the same.

53. **The correct answer is (D).** All four lines are exactly the same.

54. **The correct answer is (A).** Only the fourth line is exactly the same.

55. **The correct answer is (C).** Lines 1, 3, and 4 are exactly the same.

56. **The correct answer is (D).** All four lines are exactly the same.

57. **The correct answer is (A).** Only the first line is exactly the same.

58. **The correct answer is (C).** Lines 1, 3, and 4 are exactly the same.

59. **The correct answer is (A).** Only the second line is exactly the same.

60. **The correct answer is (B).** Lines 1 and 3 are exactly the same.

61. **The correct answer is (D).** Choices (A), (B), and (C) are written badly and contain extraneous and incorrect words.

62. **The correct answer is (D).** The first three choices contain errors in agreement between subject and verb.

63. **The correct answer is (C).** Choices (B) and (D) are awkward and poorly written. Choice (A) contains an agreement error that is corrected in choice (C).

64. **The correct answer is (A).** The other choices are awkwardly written.

65. **The correct answer is (B).** In referring to the employees of a company in this manner, you need not use a possessive. Choice (A) is incorrect. *Brown & Company* is the singular subject of choices (C) and (D).

66. **The correct answer is (A).** In choice (B), the subject of the second clause is *information,* which is singular. In choice (C), the adverb should be *really. Being that,* in (D), is not an acceptable form.

67. **The correct answer is (D).** In choice (A), *my mother and me* are the objects of the verb *reach,* while in (C), *my mother or me* are the objects of the preposition *to.* In choice (B), the object of the preposition *to* should be *me* not the reflexive *myself,* since I did not address the letter.

68. **The correct answer is (C).** In choice (A), *who* is the subject of *had made.* In choice (B), the word *of* before *known* should be omitted. In choice (D), the second clause is missing a subject.

69. **The correct answer is (B).** In choice (A), *them* should be *him* because it refers to *anyone,* which is singular. Choices (C) and (D) are very awkward.

70. **The correct answer is (D).** The first three sentences lack parallel construction. All the words that modify *paper* must appear in the same form.

71. **The correct answer is (D).** All three lines are correctly coded.

72. **The correct answer is (B).** In the first line, W is miscoded; in the third line, V and X are both miscoded.

73. **The correct answer is (B).** In the first line, W is miscoded; in the second line, M and B are miscoded.

74. **The correct answer is (C).** In the third line, the code numbers for W and M are reversed.

75. **The correct answer is (B).** In the first line, the code numbers for X and B are reversed; in the third line, the code numbers for W and U are reversed.

76. **The correct answer is (B).** In the second line, the code numbers for B and U are reversed; in the third line, the code numbers for M and B are reversed.

77. **The correct answer is (A).** In the first line, C is miscoded; in the second line, B is miscoded; in the third line, W is miscoded.

78. **The correct answer is (D).** All three lines are correctly coded.

79. **The correct answer is (A).** In the first line, the code numbers for V and W are reversed; in the second line, M is miscoded; in the third line, the code numbers for C and J are reversed.

80. **The correct answer is (B).** In the first line, the code numbers for W and L are reversed; in the third line, the code numbers for V and Y are reversed.

81. **The correct answer is (A).** The sealed verdict has been ordered, and the jury is now deliberating. This is a period of time during which no juror may communicate with anyone outside, unless with the permission of the judge. Since the judge has left the courthouse, permission cannot be requested nor granted, so the juror cannot use the telephone. (Since the message is a simple "I'll be home late," a court officer might make the call and give this information to the wife. Court officers, who are not privy to deliberations, are not under the same tight restrictions concerning communication.)

82. **The correct answer is (D).** The jury must never be left unguarded, so both court officers must not run errands at the same time. Courthouse decorum suggests that shouting down the corridor is not appropriate. The jury must wait until one request is filled before a court officer can leave to fill the next one.

83. **The correct answer is (C).** The court officer must provide the jury with whatever supplies its members feel that they need.

84. **The correct answer is (C).** Rules demand that the court officer closes and locks the door of the jury room and remains outside the door within easy calling distance of the jurors.

85. **The correct answer is (C).** Two officers are assigned to guard the jury at all times. This job cannot be delegated to any other person. If, for some reason, a relieving officer does not arrive on time, both officers must remain with the jury, even if doing so interferes with personal responsibility.

86. **The correct answer is (B).** Evans took two credit cards, thereby committing grand larceny.

87. **The correct answer is (C).** John Murphy avoided payment for transportation. He thus committed theft of services.

88. **The correct answer is (D).** By taking the credit card, Mary committed grand larceny. In using the credit card, Mary committed theft of services as well.

89. **The correct answer is (B).** Refer to the definition of larceny. There is no charge of menacing because Smith did not have the means to carry out the threat.

90. **The correct answer is (B).** Larceny is the only charge that could be brought against Mary. Grand larceny and arson are discounted as possible answers because the former involves values over $250 and the latter requires the fire to be set intentionally.

91. **The correct answer is (D).** Bill could be charged with arson and theft of services because the fire was started intentionally and because he used a slug to make a phone call.

92. **The correct answer is (C).** The charges that could be brought against Bill are larceny, because the saw was not worth more than $250; arson, because the fire was started intentionally; and menacing, because he had the means available to carry out his threat.

93. **The correct answer is (B).** In taking Lisa's credit card, Frank committed grand larceny. Frank committed theft of services two times, once when he used the credit card to pay for his dinner and again when he did not pay for the cab ride.

94. **The correct answer is (A).** Bill Martin's taking the pocketbook constituted larceny. He cannot be charged with arson because the fire was not started intentionally.

95. **The correct answer is (D).** Mike's stealing the credit card constitutes grand larceny; his using it is theft of services.

96. **The correct answer is (C).** Sloan has been elected to become an executive officer of the county. Bribing or attempting to bribe him is a crime. Crane has attempted to bribe this elected officer. If convicted, Crane could serve five years in a state prison. He could even serve up to ten years and be fined as well. Sloan, in refusing the bribe, has done no wrong.

97. **The correct answer is (B).** Joe Marshall has bribed a public officer. He is subject to imprisonment and/or fine. Don Williams is clearly guilty of accepting a bribe and probably of delivering the action for which the bribe was made. The paragraph, however, deals only with penalties for the person who offers the bribe. Williams's punishment cannot enter into the answer.

98. **The correct answer is (D).** White is trying very hard and may be obnoxious, but he really is not offering a bribe to a public official. There is no basis for punishment in the context of the quoted paragraph.

99. **The correct answer is (C).** All four men conspired to commit an armed robbery and, as such, contributed to its success. The fact that Bob Burns was unable to physically participate does not make him any less party to the crime. Likewise, Wilson, who did not actually enter the liquor store, was a participant and principal in the action. The night clerk at the Holiday Inn had no reason to suspect that three men seeking accommodations for the night were fugitives from justice. He is not an accessory.

100. **The correct answer is (B).** Ron Johnson is a crack dealer. Selling crack is a crime. Further, Johnson has counseled and induced Walker to commit the same crime. Both are principals. Hiding Harry in the barn is aiding him to avoid detection, even though he is not in her house. Molly is an accessory.

ANSWER SHEET PRACTICE TEST 4

Part One

1. Ⓐ Ⓑ Ⓒ Ⓓ	7. Ⓐ Ⓑ Ⓒ Ⓓ	13. Ⓐ Ⓑ Ⓒ Ⓓ	19. Ⓐ Ⓑ Ⓒ Ⓓ	25. Ⓐ Ⓑ Ⓒ Ⓓ
2. Ⓐ Ⓑ Ⓒ Ⓓ	8. Ⓐ Ⓑ Ⓒ Ⓓ	14. Ⓐ Ⓑ Ⓒ Ⓓ	20. Ⓐ Ⓑ Ⓒ Ⓓ	26. Ⓐ Ⓑ Ⓒ Ⓓ
3. Ⓐ Ⓑ Ⓒ Ⓓ	9. Ⓐ Ⓑ Ⓒ Ⓓ	15. Ⓐ Ⓑ Ⓒ Ⓓ	21. Ⓐ Ⓑ Ⓒ Ⓓ	27. Ⓐ Ⓑ Ⓒ Ⓓ
4. Ⓐ Ⓑ Ⓒ Ⓓ	10. Ⓐ Ⓑ Ⓒ Ⓓ	16. Ⓐ Ⓑ Ⓒ Ⓓ	22. Ⓐ Ⓑ Ⓒ Ⓓ	28. Ⓐ Ⓑ Ⓒ Ⓓ
5. Ⓐ Ⓑ Ⓒ Ⓓ	11. Ⓐ Ⓑ Ⓒ Ⓓ	17. Ⓐ Ⓑ Ⓒ Ⓓ	23. Ⓐ Ⓑ Ⓒ Ⓓ	29. Ⓐ Ⓑ Ⓒ Ⓓ
6. Ⓐ Ⓑ Ⓒ Ⓓ	12. Ⓐ Ⓑ Ⓒ Ⓓ	18. Ⓐ Ⓑ Ⓒ Ⓓ	24. Ⓐ Ⓑ Ⓒ Ⓓ	30. Ⓐ Ⓑ Ⓒ Ⓓ

Part Two

1. Ⓐ Ⓑ Ⓒ Ⓓ	15. Ⓐ Ⓑ Ⓒ Ⓓ	29. Ⓐ Ⓑ Ⓒ Ⓓ	43. Ⓐ Ⓑ Ⓒ Ⓓ	57. Ⓐ Ⓑ Ⓒ Ⓓ
2. Ⓐ Ⓑ Ⓒ Ⓓ	16. Ⓐ Ⓑ Ⓒ Ⓓ	30. Ⓐ Ⓑ Ⓒ Ⓓ	44. Ⓐ Ⓑ Ⓒ Ⓓ	58. Ⓐ Ⓑ Ⓒ Ⓓ
3. Ⓐ Ⓑ Ⓒ Ⓓ	17. Ⓐ Ⓑ Ⓒ Ⓓ	31. Ⓐ Ⓑ Ⓒ Ⓓ	45. Ⓐ Ⓑ Ⓒ Ⓓ	59. Ⓐ Ⓑ Ⓒ Ⓓ
4. Ⓐ Ⓑ Ⓒ Ⓓ	18. Ⓐ Ⓑ Ⓒ Ⓓ	32. Ⓐ Ⓑ Ⓒ Ⓓ	46. Ⓐ Ⓑ Ⓒ Ⓓ	60. Ⓐ Ⓑ Ⓒ Ⓓ
5. Ⓐ Ⓑ Ⓒ Ⓓ	19. Ⓐ Ⓑ Ⓒ Ⓓ	33. Ⓐ Ⓑ Ⓒ Ⓓ	47. Ⓐ Ⓑ Ⓒ Ⓓ	61. Ⓐ Ⓑ Ⓒ Ⓓ
6. Ⓐ Ⓑ Ⓒ Ⓓ	20. Ⓐ Ⓑ Ⓒ Ⓓ	34. Ⓐ Ⓑ Ⓒ Ⓓ	48. Ⓐ Ⓑ Ⓒ Ⓓ	62. Ⓐ Ⓑ Ⓒ Ⓓ
7. Ⓐ Ⓑ Ⓒ Ⓓ	21. Ⓐ Ⓑ Ⓒ Ⓓ	35. Ⓐ Ⓑ Ⓒ Ⓓ	49. Ⓐ Ⓑ Ⓒ Ⓓ	63. Ⓐ Ⓑ Ⓒ Ⓓ
8. Ⓐ Ⓑ Ⓒ Ⓓ	22. Ⓐ Ⓑ Ⓒ Ⓓ	36. Ⓐ Ⓑ Ⓒ Ⓓ	50. Ⓐ Ⓑ Ⓒ Ⓓ	64. Ⓐ Ⓑ Ⓒ Ⓓ
9. Ⓐ Ⓑ Ⓒ Ⓓ	23. Ⓐ Ⓑ Ⓒ Ⓓ	37. Ⓐ Ⓑ Ⓒ Ⓓ	51. Ⓐ Ⓑ Ⓒ Ⓓ	65. Ⓐ Ⓑ Ⓒ Ⓓ
10. Ⓐ Ⓑ Ⓒ Ⓓ	24. Ⓐ Ⓑ Ⓒ Ⓓ	38. Ⓐ Ⓑ Ⓒ Ⓓ	52. Ⓐ Ⓑ Ⓒ Ⓓ	66. Ⓐ Ⓑ Ⓒ Ⓓ
11. Ⓐ Ⓑ Ⓒ Ⓓ	25. Ⓐ Ⓑ Ⓒ Ⓓ	39. Ⓐ Ⓑ Ⓒ Ⓓ	53. Ⓐ Ⓑ Ⓒ Ⓓ	67. Ⓐ Ⓑ Ⓒ Ⓓ
12. Ⓐ Ⓑ Ⓒ Ⓓ	26. Ⓐ Ⓑ Ⓒ Ⓓ	40. Ⓐ Ⓑ Ⓒ Ⓓ	54. Ⓐ Ⓑ Ⓒ Ⓓ	68. Ⓐ Ⓑ Ⓒ Ⓓ
13. Ⓐ Ⓑ Ⓒ Ⓓ	27. Ⓐ Ⓑ Ⓒ Ⓓ	41. Ⓐ Ⓑ Ⓒ Ⓓ	55. Ⓐ Ⓑ Ⓒ Ⓓ	69. Ⓐ Ⓑ Ⓒ Ⓓ
14. Ⓐ Ⓑ Ⓒ Ⓓ	28. Ⓐ Ⓑ Ⓒ Ⓓ	42. Ⓐ Ⓑ Ⓒ Ⓓ	56. Ⓐ Ⓑ Ⓒ Ⓓ	

answer sheet

Practice Test 4

PART ONE

30 QUESTIONS • 45 MINUTES

Directions: For questions 1–20, each question consists of three sets of information appearing in three columns. In some of the questions, the same information appears on the same line in all three sets. In other questions, the information appears on a different line in each set. The position of the information is irrelevant. You are to compare the information in the three sets, searching for any differences in the information presented. Any difference at all makes the sets different. Mark your answer sheet as follows.

Mark (A) if *ALL THREE* sets are exactly alike.
Mark (B) if only the *FIRST* and *THIRD* sets are exactly alike.
Mark (C) if only the *FIRST* and *SECOND* sets are exactly alike.
Mark (D) if *NONE* of the sets is exactly like another.

1. Petrillo, A T Co Inc.
    1-201-748-4999
    Troy: Red and Tan
    PG683.D781045
    Peiser, Isadore

2. Uniform Commercial Code
    ISBN 0-13-18476-2-8
    Moscovitz, Simeon
    Guaranty Title Co.
    155 East 3300 South

3. Manhattan Referral Svce
    XT9846.L4010
    H. Kauffman & Sons
    011-34-52-882291
    Maison Sapho School

4. Harvey Geary Assocs Inc
    9-1-817-625-3394
    Deluxe Courier & Air
    BX44182.J908764
    McGregor, Angus W.

5. Spadaro and Heller, PC
    Rent-A-Mailbox Inc.
    ISBN 0-668-05604-5
    NY Civil Practice Law
    33164,8972.7

6. Misericordia Hospital
    619-60-4683
    PTB3.9760.G109
    Schildwachter Fuel Oil
    Summer-Wiggins, Ltd.

7. Montessori-Piaget
    ISBN 0-8120-3886-X
    Bouregy, Thomas PC
    TT980.765,412
    Ohaus Itin Scales

8. First Megasafe Indus.
    D703Y380-SAI-413
    Black's Law Dictionary
    22 Street Electronics
    708.732DWI/4168

9. Title L 205.00-205.65
    Cirabella, Carmen Mi
    Alco Grauvre Inc.
    Miller & bollard
    ISBN 0-931794-14-5

10. Corbin on Contracts
    9-O11-021-28-17-33
    ISBN 0-913094-37-4
    Scheichet and Elger
    Bunting and Lyon, Inc.

11. Immigration Law & Proc.
    Jofram Ambulette Serv.
    Biegeleisen, J. Co.
    11th '89 $17.95
    FH3281.K27919

Petrillo, A T Co Inc.
1-201-748-4999
Troy:Red and Tan
PG683.D781045
Peiser, Isadore

Uniform Commercial Code
ISBN 0-13-18476-2-8
Moscowitz, Simeon
Guaranty Title Co.
155 East 3300 South

Manhattan Referral Svce
XT9846.L4010
H. Kauffman & Sons
011-34-52-882291
Maison Sapho School

Harvey Geary Assocs Inc
9-1-817-625-3394
Deluxe Courier & Air
BX44182.J908764
McGregor, Angus W.

Spadaro and Heller, PC
Rent-A-Mailbox Inc.
ISBN 668-05604-5
NY Civil Practice Law
33164,8972.7

Misericordia Hospital
619-60-4683
PT83.9760.G109
Schildwachter Fuel Oil
Summer-Wiggins, Ltd.

Bouregy, Thomas PC
ISBN 0-8120-3886-X
Ohaus Itin Scales
TT980.765,412
Montessori-Piaget

22 Street Electronics
708.732DWI/4168
D703Y380-SAI-413
First Megasafe Indus.
Black's Law Dictionary

Miller & bollard
ISBN 0-931794-14-5
Cirabella, Carmen Mi
Alco Grauvre Inc.
Title L 205.00-205.56

Bunting and Lyon, Inc.
Scheichet and Elgar
Corbin on Contracts
ISBN 0-913094-37-4
9-O11-021-28-17-33

11th '89 $19.95
Immigration Law & Proc.
FH3281.K27919
Biegeleisen, J. Co.
Jofram Ambulette Serv.

Petrillo, A T Co Inc.
1-201-748-4999
Troy: Red and Tan
PG683.D781045
Peiser, Isadore

Uniform Commercial Code
ISBN 0-13-184762-8
Moscovitz, Simeon
Guaranty Title Co.
155 East 3300 South

Manhattan Referral Svce
XT9846.L4010
H. Kauffman & Sons
011-34-882291
Maison Sapho School

Harvey Geary Assocs Inc
9-1-817-625-3394
Deluxe Courier & Air
BX44182.J908764
MacGregor, Angus W

Spadaro and Heller, PC
Rent-a-Mailbox Inc.
ISBN 0-668-05604 5
NY Civil Practice Law
33164,8972.7

Misericordia Hospital
619-60-4683
PTB3.9760.G109
Schildwachter Fuel Oil
Sumner-Wiggins, Ltd.

TT980.765,412
Ohaus Itin Scales
Bouregy, Thomas PC
Montessori-Piaget
ISBN 0-8120-3886-x

708.732DWI/4168
Black's Law Dictionary
22 Street Electronics
D703Y380-SAI-413
First Megasafe Indus.

Cirabella, Carmen Mi
Title L 205.00-205.65
ISBN 0-931794-14-5
Miller & bollard
Alco Grauvre Inc.

ISBN 0-913094-37-4
Bunting and Lyon, Inc.
9-O11-021-28-17-33
Corbin on Contracts
Scheichet and Elger

FH3281.K27919
Jofran Ambulette Serv.
Immigration Law & Proc.
11th '89 $17.95
Biegeleisen, J. Co.

12. Spink & Gaborc Inc.
Leavenworth Prison
PE1628.W5633
McKinney's Consol. Laws
2550-923-258-7530

2550-923-258-7530
McKinney's Consol. Laws
Leavenworth Prison
PE1628.W5633
Spink & Gaborc Inc.

Leavenworth Prison
Spink & Gaborc Inc.
McKinney's Consol. Laws
2550-923-258-7530
PE1628.W5633

13. Forzano and Sons, Ltd.
Constitutional Issues
FAX # 302-741-0809
Hwang v. Mathews
ISBN 0-525-03643-1

FAX # 302-741-0809
ISBN 0-525-03543-1
Constitutional Issues
Forzano and Sons, Ltd.
Hwang v. Mathews

Constitutional Issues
Forzano and Sons, Ltd.
ISBN 0-03643-1
Hwang v. Mathews
FAX # 302-741-0809

14. Hohenfels Abstract Svce
Angelika Film Corp.
1487-3.09/865
9-1-723-282-4551x67
Francais, Jacques

9-1-723-282-4451x67
Francais, Jacques
Hohenfels Abstract Svce
Angelika Film Corp.
1487-3.09/865

Angelika Film Corp.
Hohenfels Abstract Svce
Francais, Jacques
9-1-723-282-4551x67
1487-3.09/865

15. Siegel Chalif & Winn
PC1.582-68314EX77531
Hahnemann, Jos. & Bro.
TT46814.3209/5911-7

Siegel Chalif & Winn
PC1.582-63814EX77531
Hahnemann, Jos. & Bro.
TT46814.3209/5911-7

Siegel Chalif & Winn
PC1.582-68314EX77531
Hahnemann, Jos. & Bro.
TT46814.3209/5911-7

16. Criminal Justice Admin.
Amitai, Jonah ben
TZ-39184-672/091.4
Sills Beck Cummins Radin

Criminal Justice Admin.
Amitai, Jonah Ben
TZ-39184-672/091.4
Sills Beck Cummins Radin

Criminal Justice Admin.
Amitai, Johan ben
TZ-39184-672/091.4
Sills Beck Cummins Radin

17. Espejo, Manning & Esposito
Geoghan Tutrone & Grossman
RD45Y,90UPN-0056.2
Kurumazushi Sushi Shoppe

RD45Y,90UPN-0056.2
Kurumazushi Sushi Shoppe
Geoghan Tutrone & Grossman
Espejo, Manning & Esposito

Kurumazushi Sushi Shoppe
RD45Y,90UPN-0056.2
Espejo, Manning & Esposito
Geoghan Tutrone & Grossman

18. White & Snow Beck & Koss
Song Yook Hong Law Offices
118.9FR-9230/10585.6
Lorson Electrical Contractors

Song Yook Hong Law Offices
118.9FR-9230/10585.6
White & Snow Beck & Koss
Lorson Electrical Contractors

118.9FR-9230/10585.6
Lorson Electrical Contractors
Song Yook Hong Law Offices
White Snow Beck & Koss

19. Feet First Reflexology Center
Spagna, Saul & Rose
8976JV765.33/3975WE
475-3412.FPB838/2684

475-3412.FBP838/2684
8976JV765.33/3975WE
Feet First Reflexology Center
Spagna, Saul & Rose

Feet First Reflexology Center
475-3412.FPB838/2684
Spagna, Saul & Rose
8976JV765.33/3975WE

20. Gouverneur Hospital Facility
PT68432.UZ83921-91
ONY Production Centre
Tsigonia Industries Corp.

PT68432.UZ83921-91
Tsigonia Industries Corp.
Gouverneur Hospital Facility
ONY Production Center

ONY Production Centre
Gouverneur Hospital Facility
PT68432.UZ83921-91
Tsigonia Industrial Corp.

FOR QUESTIONS 21–30, ANSWER ON THE BASIS OF THE INFORMATION CONTAINED IN THE FOLLOWING TABLES AND THEIR ACCOMPANYING CODE KEYS. YOU MAY FIND IT HELPFUL TO COMPLETE TABLES 4 AND 5 (THE SUMMARY TABLES) BEFORE YOU ATTEMPT TO ANSWER THE QUESTIONS. USE OF A CALCULATOR IS PERMITTED.

Table 1

Sentences—Wessex County—May 11–15

Offense	Age and Sex of Offender									
	Under 15		15–17		18–21		22–30		Over 30	
	M	F	M	F	M	F	M	F	M	F
Vandalism	c;d;d	c	a;d	c;j	a;e	d	b&e			
Burglary			a&c		b;e&f	b&e	g;h;j	e;f	h;h;j	b&e;f
Larceny	c	c;j	d;d	b&c	b;f;j	a&d	d&f	e&g	b&d;c	e&f;j
Assault	a;b		j;j	a	b;f	a;j	b;e	d;f	g;j	f;h
Robbery			a;b		b;g	b;e	e&f	h;j	g;g;g	d&f;j
Drunk driving			e;j	d;d	b&e	e;j;j	e;f	e&f	b;d;j	e;e
Prostitution		a;j	b	b;d		b;f	e	g;j	d;e	e;g
Manslaughter			j	j	b	a;j	d&f	f	b;g	e;j
Narcotics (sale)	a;a;b		b;e	c;d	e&g;g	e&f	e&h;g	h;j	g;h;j	e;j
Narcotics (possession)	c;c	c	a&c	a;c	b;b;b	b;c	b;j	d;j	b;f;j	b&d;f

Table 2

Sentences—Essex County—May 11–15

Offense	Age and Sex of Offender									
	Under 15		15–17		18–21		22–30		Over 30	
	M	F	M	F	M	F	M	F	M	F
Vandalism	d;j	c	a;e	c	e;e;e	b&d	b;e	d		
Burglary	j		b		b;e;j	d;j	e&g;f	d&f	e&g;h	b&e;d
Larceny	d;c	c	a;c	d;j	a;j	a;b;e	d;g	d&g	e;f;j	a
Assault	b;j	a	b;e;j	b	b&d	a	d&g;f	b	b;e;f	b;j
Robbery	b&e		b;d	a	b;e;j	d&f	e;f;g	e&g	e;h;h	b;f;h
Drunk driving	b		e	j	b;e	a;j	e;f;j	e&f;j	e;e;f	d;g
Prostitution		b;d	a	b&c;j	b;d	a;c;c		d;e	e	b;e;j
Manslaughter			a		b;b;e	b;j	a&e;j	a	b;d	e;j;j
Narcotics (sale)	b;a&d		b;b	a	e;g;h	e&h	h;j	h;h;j	e&h;j	e&h;j
Narcotics (possession)	j	c;j	a;a&d	c;d	b&d	d;d	d;f	e&f	b;j	b&e;j

Code key: a = probation 1 to 2 years   f = imprisonment 1–6 months
            b = probation more than 2 years   g = imprisonment 6 months to 1 year
            c = fine under $100   h = imprisonment over 1 year
            d = fine $100–350   j = acquitted
            e = fine over $350

Table 3
Sentences—Sussex County—May 11–15

Offense	Under 15 M	Under 15 F	15–17 M	15–17 F	18–21 M	18–21 F	22–30 M	22–30 F	Over 30 M	Over 30 F
Vandalism	d;e;e	d	b&e	c;d	a;b;e	b;d	b;e	j		
Burglary	a		b;j		b;f	e&f	e&g	g;j	e&h;h	f
Larceny	a	a&c	d;e	a;c	b;d	c;d	f;f	j;j	e&f;j	e&g;h
Assault	b	a	b;d	d;j	e&f	b;b	b;d;j	d;j	f;f	d;f
Robbery	b		b;e;j	a	e&f	b&d	a;e;h	h;j	e;e&g	e;f;g
Drunk driving		b	b&e	a&c	e;j	d;j	e;e	b;e	f;j	e&f
Prostitution	j	a;b		b;b;j	a	d;e	d	f;j		e&f;j
Manslaughter			a;a		b;e	b;j	e;j	j	e;e;e	e;j
Narcotics (sale)	b	b	b;e	e;j	d&f	f	g;j	e&g	a&h;j	g;h;j
Narcotics (possession)	a&c	a	a&d	a;j	e	d	a&d	b&d	e;e	e;j;j

Code key: a = probation 1 to 2 years   f = imprisonment 1–6 months
            b = probation more than 2 years   g = imprisonment 6 months to 1 year
            c = fine under $100   h = imprisonment over 1 year
            d = fine $100–350   j = acquitted
            e = fine over $350

Table 4
Summary of Disposition of Cases—Three Counties

Disposition	Age and Sex of Offender																	
	Under 15			15–17			18–21			22–30			Over 30			Total		
	M	F	T	M	F	T	M	F	T	M	F	T	M	F	T	M	F	T
Acquitted	卌				卌 IIII						卌卌 IIII							
Probation only								卌卌卌					67					
Fine only		卌卌卌卌								卌卌卌								138
Prison only						0	卌 II						卌卌卌卌	卌卌卌				
Probation & fine				卌 I								IIII						29
Prison & fine																		
Total		21							108									

Table 5

Summary of Dispositions by Offense—Three Counties

Offense		Sentence					
	Acquitted	**Probation Only**	**Fine Only**	**Prison Only**	**Probation & Fine**	**Prison & Fine**	**Total**
Vandalism			卌 卌 / 卌 卌 / 卌 ||				
Burglary							
Larceny		卌 ||||		卌		||||		53
Assault								
Robbery			卌 ||||			卌		
Drunk driving	卌 卌						
Prostitution							
Manslaughter		|卌 卌 ||					39
Narcotics (sale)				卌 卌 ||||			
Narcotics (possession)					卌 ||||		
Total			138	29			

21. The total number of women age 21 and younger who were acquitted is
    - (A) 21
    - (B) 22
    - (C) 23
    - (D) 24

22. The total number of people between the ages of 18 and 21 who will spend more than one year in prison is
    - (A) 0
    - (B) 1
    - (C) 2
    - (D) 3

23. The number of people sentenced to probation only upon conviction for prostitution is
    - (A) 13
    - (B) 14
    - (C) 15
    - (D) 16

24. How many more people were convicted and sentenced for assault than were acquitted?
    - (A) 10
    - (B) 32
    - (C) 42
    - (D) 52

25. The number of men tried for manslaughter is
    - (A) 19
    - (B) 22
    - (C) 24
    - (D) 27

26. How many more women than men in the 18-21 age group were sentenced to pay fines only?
    - (A) 2
    - (B) 3
    - (C) 15
    - (D) 17

27. The number of women over age 30 who will spend any time in prison is
    - (A) 15
    - (B) 16
    - (C) 20
    - (D) 21

28. How many men between the ages of 15 and 30 were convicted of drunk driving?
    - (A) 13
    - (B) 14
    - (C) 16
    - (D) 20

29. The total number of people who paid fines under $100 for narcotics convictions is
    - (A) 8
    - (B) 9
    - (C) 10
    - (D) 11

30. How many more people will serve prison time for burglary than will spend time on probation?
    - (A) 7
    - (B) 9
    - (C) 12
    - (D) 18

PART TWO

69 QUESTIONS • 2 HOURS

> **Directions:** Read and study the story below for 5 minutes. Concentrate on the details and try to remember as many as possible. Answer questions 1–10 on the basis of the story as you remember it. After answering the memory questions, proceed directly to question 11 without waiting for a signal.

On Tuesday, March 13, Supreme Court of Princess County was gearing up for trial in the latest of a series of bias-related crimes. Two Korean merchants, UnJin Ehee and Ed Paik, had been badly beaten in their store on the evening of July 12, and Ehee remained in a coma eight months after the attack.

Three black teenagers, Harry Wilson, George Jones, and Glenda Pratt, had been indicted, and jury selection for their trial was scheduled to begin at 10 a.m. All court personnel were alert to the possibility of demonstrations, disruptions, and even violence.

Court Officers Maria Martinez, Monty Pipko, and Ben Bradson stood just inside the door of the courthouse, manning the front desk and the metal detector. Senior Court Officer Warren Chen stood on the front steps of the courthouse with Court Officers Pat Kelly, John Pinero, Kuniko Parker, and Fred White.

At 9:20 a.m., a large, noisy group, led by Hal Sharkey, rounded the corner and began to converge on the courthouse. Members of the group carried signs demanding justice for all blacks. They shouted that blacks are always singled out, picked on, and accused.

As the group attempted to mount the courthouse steps, Senior Court Officer Chen barred their way and asked them to please congregate in the grassy area directly across the street from the courthouse. Hal Sharkey complained that blacks were never even permitted to express their opinions, but a cordon of court officers and city police slowly moved the group back to the designated area. In the course of this action, one protester hit Court Officer Parker over the head with a sign, opening a nasty gash on Parker's scalp. Officer Parker was assisted by paramedics, who were called to the scene by Officer Pinero.

1. The trial about to take place concerns an incident that occurred on
   (A) July 10
   (B) March 13
   (C) August 8
   (D) July 12

2. The victim who remains in a coma is
   (A) Warren Chen
   (B) UnJin Ehee
   (C) Ed Paik
   (D) Kuniko Parker

3. The trial is being held in
   (A) Criminal Court, Princess County
   (B) Supreme Court, Kent County
   (C) Supreme Court, Princess County
   (D) Superior Court, Prince County

4. The name of one accused teenager is
   (A) Harry Wilson
   (B) Ben Bradson
   (C) Hal Sharkey
   (D) Fred White

5. The location of the metal detector is
   (A) at the top of the courthouse steps
   (B) inside the front door of the courthouse
   (C) outside the door of the courtroom
   (D) in the grassy area across the street from the courthouse

6. The demonstrators approached the courthouse from
   (A) across the street
   (B) around the corner
   (C) the park
   (D) down the block

7. The protest by the demonstrators concerned
   (A) police brutality
   (B) equal justice
   (C) poor medical services
   (D) the right to protest

8. The demonstrators were controlled by
   (A) court officers
   (B) court officers and paramedics
   (C) court officers and city police
   (D) court officers, city police, and paramedics

9. The injury to the officer occurred
   (A) before 9:20 a.m.
   (B) around 9:30 a.m.
   (C) after 10:30 a.m.
   (D) in the evening

10. The paramedics who assisted the injured officer were summoned by
    (A) Officer Pinero
    (B) Officer Parker
    (C) Officer Pipko
    (D) Officer Pratt

QUESTIONS 11–17 ARE BASED ON THE MATERIAL PROVIDED. USE ONLY THE INFORMATION GIVEN AND YOUR OWN COMMON SENSE. DO NOT ALLOW ANY ADDITIONAL OR CONTRARY KNOWLEDGE TO INFLUENCE YOUR ANSWERS.

11. "Many children who are exposed to contacts and experiences of a delinquent nature become educated and trained in crime in the course of participating in the daily life of the neighborhood." From this statement, we may reasonably conclude that
    (A) delinquency passes from parent to child
    (B) neighborhood influences are usually bad
    (C) schools are training grounds for delinquents
    (D) none of the above conclusions is reasonable

12. "Old age insurance, a benefit for which city employees are eligible, is one feature of the Social Security Act that is wholly administered by the federal government." On the basis of this statement, it may most reasonably be inferred that
    (A) all city employees are now drawing old age insurance
    (B) no city employees have elected to become eligible for old age insurance
    (C) the city has no part in administering Social Security old age insurance
    (D) only the federal government administers the Social Security Act

13. A court officer is a peace officer. A peace officer's revolver is a defensive, not an offensive, weapon. From this statement, you know that a court officer should draw a revolver
    (A) to fire at an unarmed burglar
    (B) to force a suspect to confess
    (C) to frighten a juvenile delinquent
    (D) in self-defense

14. "The depositions must set forth the facts tending to establish that an illegal act was committed and that the defendant is guilty." According to this statement, the one of the following that need not be included in a deposition is evidence that establishes the

(A) fact that an illegal act was committed

(B) fact that the defendant committed the illegal act

(C) guilt of the defendant

(D) method of commission of the illegal act

15. "Each court officer should understand how his or her own work helps to accomplish the purpose of the entire agency." This statement means most nearly that the court officer should understand the

(A) efficiency of a small agency

(B) importance of his or her own job

(C) necessity of initiative

(D) value of a large organization

16. "All concerned are most likely to recognize the court officer's authority and cooperate if the officer conveys in his or her manner a complete confidence that they will do so." According to this statement, an effective court officer should display

(A) arrogance

(B) agitation

(C) assurance

(D) excitement

17. "It is a frequent misconception that court officers can be recruited from those registers established for the recruitment of city police or firefighters. While it is true that many common qualifications are found in all of these, specific standards for court officer work are indicated, varying with the size, geographical location, and policies of the office." According to this statement, it may be inferred that

(A) a successful court officer must have some qualifications not required of a police officer or a firefighter

(B) qualifications that make a successful police officer will also make a successful firefighter

(C) the same qualifications are required of a court officer, regardless of the office to which he or she is assigned

(D) the successful court officer is required to be both more intelligent and stronger than a firefighter

QUESTIONS 18 AND 19 ARE BASED ON THE FOLLOWING PASSAGE.

Proper firearms training is one phase of law enforcement that cannot be ignored. No part of the training of a police officer is more important or more valuable. The officer's life and often the lives of his fellow officers depend directly upon his skill with the weapon he is carrying. Proficiency with the revolver is not attained exclusively by the volume of ammunition used and the number of hours spent on the firing line. Supervised practice and the use of training aids and techniques help make the shooter. It is essential to have a good firing range where new officers are trained and older personnel practice in scheduled firearms sessions. The fundamental points to be stressed are grip, stance, breathing, sight alignment, and trigger squeeze. Coordination of thought, vision, and motion must be achieved before the officer gains confidence in his shooting ability. Attaining this ability will make the student a better officer and enhance his value to the force.

18. A police officer will gain confidence in his shooting ability only after he has
    (A) spent the required number of hours on the firing line
    (B) been given sufficient, supervised practice
    (C) learned the five fundamental points
    (D) learned to coordinate revolver movement with his sight and thought

19. Proper training in the use of firearms is one aspect of law enforcement that must be given serious consideration chiefly because it is the
    (A) most useful and essential single factor in the training of a police officer
    (B) one phase of police officer training that stresses mental and physical coordination
    (C) costliest aspect of police officer training, involving considerable expense for the ammunition used in target practice
    (D) most difficult part of police officer training, involving the expenditure of many hours on the firing line

20. "Complaints from the public are no longer regarded by government officials as mere nuisances. Instead, complaints are often welcomed because they frequently bring into the open conditions and faults in operation and service that should be corrected." This selection means most nearly that
    (A) government officials now realize that complaints from the public are necessary
    (B) faulty operations and services are not brought into the open except by complaints from the public
    (C) government officials now realize that complaints from the public are in reality a sign of a well-run organization
    (D) complaints from the public can be useful in indicating need for improvement in operation and service

QUESTIONS 21–25 ARE BASED ON THE FOLLOWING DUTIES OF A COURT OFFICER.

Another important duty of the court officers is to see that no witnesses are left standing while others who have no business in the courtroom have seats. They must also direct witnesses to seats when they present themselves in court to testify. If the case being tried is a criminal case, the court officers must collect all the subpoenas from those who have been summoned and turn them over to the District Attorney.

In order to bring about a smoother conduct of the day's business, it is best that the court officers reserve a portion of the courtroom for the witnesses, thus making it easier to call them to the witness stand. This eliminates much confusion and saves the court much time. When a witness its called to testify, the court officers must direct him or her to the witness stand. The officer at the witness stand should direct the witness to face the court while being sworn. The officer should remain close by to render further assistance.

21. A witness takes his seat in the court-room and hands his subpoena to the court officer who has shown him to his seat. The court officer should
    (A) tell the witness to hold onto the subpoena until he is called to the stand
    (B) accept the subpoena and give it to the attorney for the defense
    (C) accept the subpoena and give it to the District Attorney
    (D) accept the subpoena and put it into his pocket

22. A witness has been called, and the court officer has directed the witness to the stand for swearing in. The court officer should now
    (A) administer the oath to the witness
    (B) leave the courtroom and stand guard outside the jury room
    (C) remain in the courtroom in sight of the judge
    (D) stand guard outside the courtroom door to keep people from entering and thereby disrupting the proceedings

23. With no clear knowledge of how many witnesses are scheduled to testify, a court officer has reserved three rows for witnesses in a sensational trial. Spectators have arrived early, and the courtroom is nearly full when a delegation from the defendant's church, led by their pastor, arrives. The court officer tells the group that there are not enough remaining seats for all their members. The pastor asks that they be seated in the vacant three rows. The court officer should
    (A) refuse, explaining that those seats are reserved for witnesses
    (B) seat the church delegation in the three rows but not seat any further spectators so as to have seats in the courtroom for witnesses
    (C) seat the church group telling them that they may be asked to leave as witnesses arrive
    (D) seat part of the delegation and hold one row for witnesses

24. As people enter the courtroom before the hour of trial, the court officer should
    (A) ask them to remain standing until all witnesses are seated
    (B) ask them why they are in the courtroom and seat them according to their business
    (C) ask them how long they plan to stay and seat those who will leave early near the back of the courtroom
    (D) direct them to seats near the front of the courtroom, reserving the back for latecomers

25. During the course of testimony by a witness, an attorney raises a point of information. The judge requests that the court officer who has been stationed near the witness go to her chambers and bring a specific book that might clarify the point. The court officer should
    (A) refuse because his duty is to remain near the witness
    (B) go for the book
    (C) send a messenger for the book
    (D) ask the judge for a clarification of the duties of a court officer

QUESTIONS 26 AND 27 ARE BASED ON THE FOLLOWING PASSAGE.

Criminal acts are classified according to several standards. One is whether the crime is major or minor. A major offense, such as murder, would be labeled a felony, whereas a minor offense, such as reckless driving, would be considered a misdemeanor. Another standard of classification is the specific kind of crime committed. Examples are burglary and robbery, which are terms often used incorrectly by individuals who are not aware of the actual difference as defined by law. A person who breaks into a building to commit a theft or other major crime is guilty of burglary, while robbery is the felonious taking of an individual's property from his person or in his immediate presence by the use of violence or threat. Other common criminal acts with distinct legal definitions are those of larceny and assault. The unlawful taking away of another's property without his consent and with the intent of depriving him belongs to the first classification, while a violent attack on someone or an unlawful threat or attempt to do physical harm belongs to the second category.

26. A young woman was threatened at knifepoint by a criminal who demanded that she give him her pocketbook and gold watch. The woman screamed and the criminal, frightened, ran off without taking anything. According to the information in the above paragraph, the crime committed was
    (A) assault
    (B) robbery
    (C) larceny
    (D) burglary

27. A man who has been asleep on a bus awakes to find that $350 in cash has been taken from him. According to the above passage, he was subjected to
    (A) robbery
    (B) burglary
    (C) larceny
    (D) assault

QUESTIONS 28–30 ARE BASED ON THE FOLLOWING PASSAGE.

"A person, who, with intent to effect or facilitate the escape of a prisoner, whether the escape is effected or attempted or not, enters a prison, or conveys to a prisoner any information, or sends into a prison any disguise, instrument, weapon, or other thing, is guilty of felony, if the prisoner is held upon a charge, arrest, commitment, or conviction for a felony; and of a misdemeanor, if the prisoner is held upon a charge, arrest, commitment, or conviction of a misdemeanor."

28. Johnny O. is serving time after conviction for the felony crime of armed robbery. Johnny's friend Frank devises an escape scheme and writes a letter to Johnny detailing the plans. Frank, without telling of the contents of the letter, asks Mary P to deliver the letter for Johnny when she visits her husband, Bob, in on a misdemeanor conviction. The letter is intercepted by a correction officer.
    (A) Frank and Mary are both guilty of felonies.
    (B) Frank is guilty of a felony; Mary is guilty of misdemeanor.
    (C) Frank is guilty of a felony; Mary is not guilty.
    (D) Frank is guilty of a misdemeanor; Mary is not guilty.

29. On a visit to her boyfriend, Bill, who is awaiting trial in the county jail on a felony charge of grand larceny, Joan orally transmits to Bill instructions for fashioning a cutting tool from objects available to him in the jail. This tool had been an invention of Joan's brother, Tom. Bill follows these instructions, creates the tool, and escapes.
    (A) Joan and Tom are both guilty of felonies.
    (B) Joan is guilty of a felony; Tom is guilty of misdemeanor.
    (C) Joan is guilty of a felony; Tom is not guilty.
    (D) Neither Joan nor Tom is guilty.

30. While charming little Debbie, age 4, distracts a guard, Barbara manages to smuggle a gun to Jim, who is completing a sentence on a misdemeanor conviction. In the course of his escape, Jim shoots and severely injures a correction officer.
    (A) Barbara is guilty of a felony; Debbie is guilty of misdemeanor.
    (B) Barbara is guilty of a felony; Debbie is not guilty.
    (C) Barbara and Debbie are both guilty of misdemeanors.
    (D) Barbara is guilty of misdemeanor; Debbie is not guilty.

31. When a person is frustrated in his desires, whether those desires are for economic advancement, for power, influence, love, or simply for getting his work done, one of the most common reactions is to become aggressive. His aggressive thoughts or actions may be directed at the thing or person that frustrated him or at some imagined source of his frustration; or his aggression may be released indiscriminately against some minority group he feels to be different from himself. The frustrated individual seeks a scapegoat as a target for the hostility he cannot safely express toward the real source of his frustration. A group whose members have troubles due to their own shortcomings will not quarrel among themselves; hence the external enemy becomes the target for this hostility. Any visible minority can be made a scapegoat. The chief function of a scapegoat is to
    (A) solve the problems of minorities
    (B) serve as an object of frustration
    (C) counter hostility
    (D) remedy inequalities of economic opportunity

QUESTIONS 32–41 ARE BASED ON THE FOLLOWING FACT PATTERN.

Peggy and Betsy were attending a football game in mid-October. They were sitting on row 26, seats 13 and 14. On row 25, Betsy noticed a man in a red shirt with blue jeans, John, yelling at a man in a white shirt and blue jeans, Sam, about a play in the game. After a few minutes, Peggy saw John hit Sam in the face. Sam then retaliated by hitting John back. Within seconds, John pulled out a knife and stabbed Sam in the shoulder and chest. Sam immediately fell down three rows. At this point, John fled the area, heading for the parking lot. Two policemen stopped John in the parking lot and arrested him. Sam was taken to St. Mary's Hospital, where he died two days later.

32. Where did this incident occur?
    (A) soccer match
    (B) baseball game
    (C) basketball game
    (D) football game

33. In what month did this incident occur?
    (A) September
    (B) October
    (C) November
    (D) January

34. After Sam was stabbed, what row was he on?
    (A) 25
    (B) 24
    (C) 23
    (D) 22

35. What was John wearing on the day of this incident?
    (A) red shirt, blue jeans
    (B) white shirt, blue jeans
    (C) blue shirt, blue jeans
    (D) none of the above

36. What topic were Sam and John arguing about during the game?
    (A) money
    (B) a play
    (C) a girl
    (D) the seating arrangement

37. Sam was stabbed in the
    (A) back and shoulder
    (B) side and shoulder
    (C) chest and side
    (D) chest and shoulder

38. How many policemen arrived at the parking lot to arrest John?
    (A) 1
    (B) 2
    (C) 3
    (D) 4

39. Sam died at what hospital?
    (A) St. Mary's
    (B) St. Timothy's
    (C) St. Peter's
    (D) St. Nicholas'

40. The two friends watching the game who witnessed the event were
    (A) Peggy and Susie
    (B) Peggy and Betsy
    (C) Susie and Betsy
    (D) Peggy and Elizabeth

41. What was the weather on the day of the game?
    (A) rainy
    (B) cloudy
    (C) sunny
    (D) the story did not tell

QUESTIONS 42 AND 43 ARE BASED ON THE FOLLOWING PASSAGE.

"A male between the ages of 16 and 30, convicted of a felony, who has not theretofore been convicted of a crime punishable by imprisonment in a state prison, may, in the discretion of the trial court be sentenced to imprisonment in the state reformatory. Where a male person between the ages of 16 and 21 is convicted of a felony, or where the term of imprisonment of a male convict for a felony is fixed by the trial court at one year or less, the court may direct the convict to be imprisoned in a county penitentiary, instead of a state prison, or in the county jail located in the county where sentence is imposed."

42. Mark, age 20, recently released from state prison after serving time for a felony committed when he was 16, has just been convicted of another felony.
- **(A)** Mark must serve his new term in a state prison.
- **(B)** Mark may not serve his term at the state reformatory.
- **(C)** Mark must serve his term at the county penitentiary.
- **(D)** Mark may serve his term in any one of the following: state penitentiary, county penitentiary, state reformatory, or county jail.

43. George, age 21, has just been convicted of his first crime ever and has been sentenced to a term of 4 to 7 years.
- **(A)** George must serve his term in a state prison.
- **(B)** George may be sentenced to either state prison or the state reformatory.
- **(C)** George may serve his time in a state prison or in the county penitentiary but not in the state reformatory.
- **(D)** George may serve his sentence at a state prison or at the county jail of the county in which he is sentenced.

44. A fracture is a broken bone. In a simple fracture, the skin is not broken. In a compound fracture, a broken end of the bone pierces the skin. Whenever a fracture is feared, the first thing to do is to prevent motion of the broken part. A defendant awaiting trial has just tripped on a stairway and twisted her ankle. She says it hurts badly, but the court officer cannot tell what is wrong merely by looking at it. The court officer should
- **(A)** tell the defendant to stand up and see whether she can walk
- **(B)** move the ankle gently to feel for any broken ends of bones
- **(C)** tell the defendant to rest a few minutes and promise to return later to see whether her condition has improved
- **(D)** tell the defendant not to move her foot and put in a call for medical assistance.

QUESTIONS 45–49 ARE BASED ON THE FOLLOWING COURT PROCEDURES.

When the jurors agree upon a verdict, one of the court officers should make it known to the court and then proceed to announce the court's command, "Return the jury to the courtroom." After delivery of this command, the officers should conduct the jurors back to the jury box and remain near them. The clerk then receives and records the verdict.

A slightly different procedure is followed if the jurors are deliberating on a civil case and are instructed to deliver a sealed verdict. It then becomes necessary for the court officers to procure an envelope and blank form from the clerk. The jurors are instructed to sign the form when they have reached a decision, and the foreman is instructed to seal the envelope and keep it until the following morning or until the opening of the court at the next session. NO one is to read the contents of the envelope, not even the court officers.

45. The jury has been deliberating for a number of hours and has finally agreed upon a verdict. The court officer should

(A) lead the jury back into the courtroom
(B) ask the jury to put their decision in writing
(C) go to the courtroom and announce to the judge that the jury has reached a decision
(D) tell the verdict to the court clerk

46. The jurors deliberating on a civil case have been instructed to deliver a sealed verdict. The jurors have reached their decision. The court officer should

(A) read the decision, then seal the envelope
(B) read the decision, then ask the foreman to seal the envelope
(C) tell the foreman to seal and keep the envelope
(D) tell the foreman to seal the envelope and mail it to the court clerk

47. The jury that has been deliberating a criminal case has reached its decision and has returned to the jury box. The court officer who has accompanied the jury should now

(A) stay in the courtroom with the jury
(B) guard the door to the courtroom so that no one else may enter
(C) tell the defendant about the verdict
(D) go home

48. The jury, having reached its conclusion, has returned to the courtroom and announced its verdict. The clerk of the court must now

(A) hand an envelope and blank form to the court officer for the use of the jury
(B) receive the envelope from the foreman of the jury
(C) poll the jury
(D) record the verdict

49. It is very late at night, and the jurors in a criminal case have finally agreed upon a verdict. The court officer should

(A) tell the jurors to put the verdict in writing and go home
(B) inform the court that the jurors have reached a verdict
(C) tell the jurors to go home to sleep and to return first thing in the morning without telling anyone of their decision
(D) send the jurors home and tell the judge what their verdict is

50. Most employees of foreign governments serving in Embassies, Consulates, or United Nations delegations, above the clerical level, have the privilege of "diplomatic immunity." In dealing with persons with diplomatic immunity, court officers face the same restrictions as do police officers. Persons with diplomatic immunity may not be issued summonses and may not be arrested or otherwise detained.

Court Officer Collins is on duty in the courtroom during the trial of a legally resident national of a foreign country. The defendant has been accused of armed robbery. As a witness is being questioned, a well-dressed gentleman seated in the spectators' section jumps up on his chair and begins shouting obscenities and threats concerning the United States, its people, its government, and this court. His final threat concerns the safety of the prosecuting attorney. As he finishes his diatribe, the man runs from the courtroom. Court Officer Collins follows the man and stops him in the corridor. Collins asks for identification, and the man produces a State Department Diplomat's Identity Card. Satisfied with the card's authenticity,

Collins watches the man exit the courthouse. This action by Collins is

(A) proper; the man did nothing wrong
(B) improper; Collins should have made the man wait until his consulate was summoned
(C) proper; there was nothing more Collins could do
(D) improper; Collins should have turned the man over to a police officer

51. A court officer being called to a disciplinary hearing on any charges is entitled to request that the personnel office produce all documents that the court officer feels could bolster his or her defense.

Court Officer Blakelee's new supervisor has placed charges that Blakelee has reported late on two occasions within the supervisor's three-week tenure. Blakelee's attorney requests Blakelee's attendance records for all seven years of her employment in the court system and copies of all performance reviews. Court Officer Arthur of the court personnel office readily produces the attendance records for all seven years but releases only two years' performance reviews. This action by Officer Arthur is

(A) appropriate; performance reviews are irrelevant to a charge of lateness
(B) inappropriate; Blakelee is entitled to any documents that she feels will be helpful
(C) appropriate; if Blakelee persists in being late, she should be disciplined
(D) inappropriate; two years' worth of attendance records would be adequate

52. The rules governing a court officer's mandate are very clear: maintain order through the use of minimum necessary force.

Court Officer Janssen has been assigned to a jury room during the jury's deliberations in a felony trial. The jury has been sequestered for three days and seems nowhere near reaching a verdict. Tempers are heating up. As he stands outside the jury room, Janssen hears furniture crashing, shouts, and a scuffle. He enters the jury room and finds two jurors involved in a violent struggle on the floor. Other jurors are watching and cheering, and one or two look ready to join the fray. Officer Janssen calls loudly for assistance. The next thing he should do is

(A) shoot into the air
(B) tell the jurors to stop fighting
(C) hit the fighting jurors with his billy club
(D) clear the other jurors to the other side of the room

QUESTIONS 53 AND 54 ARE BASED ON THE FOLLOWING PASSAGE.

"It is not always understood that the term 'physical evidence' embraces any and all objects, living or inanimate. A knife, gun, signature, or burglar tool is immediately recognized as physical evidence. Less often is it considered that dust, microscopic fragments of all types, even an odor, may equally be physical evidence and often the most important of all. It is well established that the most useful types of physical evidence are generally microscopic in dimensions, that is, not noticeable by the eye and therefore most likely to be overlooked by the criminal and by the investigator. For this reason, microscopic evidence persists for months or years after all other evidence has been removed and found inconclusive. Naturally, there are limitations to the time of collecting microscopic evidence as it may be lost or decayed. The exercises of judgment as to the possibility or profit of delayed action in collecting the evidence is a field in which the expert investigator should judge."

53. The one of the following that would not be considered to be physical evidence is

(A) a typewritten note
(B) an odor of raw onions
(C) criminal intent
(D) a minute speck of dust

54. The most accurate of the following statements, according to the above paragraph, is that

- **(A)** a delay in collecting evidence must definitely diminish its value to the investigator
- **(B)** microscopic evidence is generally the most useful type of physical evidence
- **(C)** microscopic evidence exists for longer periods of time than other physical evidence
- **(D)** physical evidence is likely to be overlooked by the criminal and by the investigator

55. "Credibility of a witness is usually governed by his character and is evidenced by his reputation for truthfulness. Personal or financial reasons or a criminal record may cause a witness to give false information to avoid being implicated. Age, sex, physical and mental abnormalities, loyalty, revenge, social and economic status, indulgence in alcohol, and the influence of other persons are some of the many factors that may affect the accuracy, willingness, or ability with which witnesses observe, interpret, and describe occurrences." According to the paragraph, factors that influence the witness of an occurrence may affect

- **(A)** what he sees but not what he describes
- **(B)** what he is willing to see but not what he is able to see
- **(C)** only what he describes and interprets later but not what he actually sees at the time of the event
- **(D)** not only what he says about it but what he was able and wanted to see of it

FOR QUESTIONS 56–69, CHOOSE THE WORD FROM EACH SET THAT BEST FITS THE NUMBERED BLANK.

The criminal _56_ system is generally regarded as having the _57_ objective of reducing crime. However, one must _58_ consider its larger objective of minimizing the total social costs associated with crime and crime control. Both of these components are complex and difficult to measure completely. The social _59_ associated with crime come from the long- and short-term physical damage, psychological harm, and property losses to _60_ as a result of crimes committed. _61_ also creates serious indirect effects. It can induce a feeling of insecurity that is only partially reflected in business losses and economic disruption due to anxiety _62_ venturing into high crime-rate areas.

56. **(A)** behavior
   (B) justice
   (C) action
   (D) patrol

57. **(A)** sole
   (B) occasional
   (C) basic
   (D) peripheral

58. **(A)** never
   (B) consequently
   (C) also
   (D) fortunately

59. **(A)** security
   (B) activities
   (C) resources
   (D) costs

60. **(A)** criminals
   (B) victims
   (C) justice
   (D) prisoners

61. **(A)** Security
   (B) Justice
   (C) Control
   (D) Crime

62. **(A)** about
   (B) into
   (C) for
   (D) and

If the interviewer does not _63_ the witness, it is better to proceed _64_ permitting the witness to know that _65_ statements are being _66_. A _67_ who believes that his deception is successful is encouraged to complete his prepared story by supplementing it with other false details. Only _68_ a witness has completed his story should the interviewer, if the occasion arises, tell him that his story is _69_.

63. **(A)** understand
    (B) like
    (C) know
    (D) believe

64. **(A)** unless
    (B) cautiously
    (C) without
    (D) quickly

65. **(A)** your
    (B) one's
    (C) his
    (D) their

66. **(A)** recorded
    (B) doubted
    (C) changed
    (D) dramatic

67. **(A)** victim
    (B) lawyer
    (C) witness
    (D) liar

68. **(A)** after
    (B) if
    (C) while
    (D) before

69. **(A)** funny
    (B) untrue
    (C) interesting
    (D) well-written

ANSWER KEY AND EXPLANATIONS

Part One

1. B	7. C	13. D	19. B	25. B
2. D	8. A	14. B	20. D	26. A
3. C	9. B	15. B	21. A	27. D
4. C	10. B	16. D	22. C	28. A
5. D	11. D	17. A	23. B	29. C
6. D	12. A	18. C	24. B	30. B

1. **The correct answer is (B).** In the second set, the spacing of Troy:Red and Tan differs from the spacing in the first and third sets.

2. **The correct answer is (D).** The first and third sets differ in the placement of dashes in the ISBN number. The first and second sets differ in the spelling of the person's last name.

3. **The correct answer is (C).** In the third set, fourth line, the digits "52" are omitted.

4. **The correct answer is (C).** In the third set, *MacGregor* differs from the *McGregor* of the first and second sets.

5. **The correct answer is (D).** In the second set, the ISBN number is missing a zero. In the third set, the letter "a" is lowercase.

6. **The correct answer is (D).** The first and third sets differ in the spelling of the last company's name. The first and second sets differ in that PTB3 is not the same as PT83.

7. **The correct answer is (C).** In the third set, the ISBN number ends with a lowercase "x."

8. **The correct answer is (A).** All three sets are exactly alike.

9. **The correct answer is (B).** In the second set, the final two digits of the Title number are reversed.

10. **The correct answer is (B).** In the second set, the spelling of the name *Elgar* differs from the *Elger* of the first set.

11. **The correct answer is (D).** In the third set, the name of the ambulette service differs from that in the first. In the second set, the book price exceeds that in the first set by $2.

12. **The correct answer is (A).** All three sets are exactly alike.

13. **The correct answer is (D).** All three ISBN numbers are different.

14. **The correct answer is (B).** In the second set, the digits "4451" differ from the "4551" of the first set.

15. **The correct answer is (B).** The second set contains a digit reversal: 638 in place of 683.

16. **The correct answer is (D).** In the second set, *Ben* begins with a capital letter. In the third set, *Johan* is substituted for *Jonah*.

17. **The correct answer is (A).** All three sets are exactly alike.

18. **The correct answer is (C).** In the third set, an ampersand has been omitted.

19. **The correct answer is (B).** In the second set, we find the letters "FBP" instead of "FPB" as in the first and third sets.

20. **The correct answer is (D).** In the second set, *Center* differs from *Centre* of the first set. In the third set, *Industrial* differs from *Industries* of the first set.

21. **The correct answer is (A).** If you filled in Table 4, just add together 3 + 9 + 9 from the three columns, "under 15," "15-17," and "18-21." If you chose not to spend time filling in tables 4 and 5, quickly run down the "F" column in the three age categories on Tables 1, 2, and 3, and keep a tally of all the j's.

22. **The correct answer is (C).** The summary tables will not help you here, but the task is not difficult. The code letter *h* refers to imprisonment of more than one year, and the question does not specify whether or not a fine is to be paid in addition. Look straight down both the "M" and "F" columns in the 18-21 range on all three county tables and count the *h*'s.

23. **The correct answer is (B).** If you filled in Table 5, just convert your tally lines to a number. If you skipped over Table 5, remember that both *a* and *b* refer to probation sentences and that the question specifies "probation *only*." Then look across the "probation" line on all three county charts and tally up all appearances of *a* or *b* not in combination with another letter.

24. **The correct answer is (B).** Table 5 is very helpful here. All alleged offenders who were not acquitted were convicted. Ten people were acquitted. The total number of assault cases is 52. 52 − 10 = 42, so 42 were convicted. 42 − 10 = 32, so 32 more were convicted than were acquitted. If you did not fill in Table 5, your best bet is to fill in the "assault" category in conjunction with answering this question.

25. **The correct answer is (B).** You must turn to the three county charts and count. As you count, remember that the question specifies *men,* that the code *j* does not refer to conviction, and that a dual sentence (probation plus fine or prison plus fine) is meted out to one person.

26. **The correct answer is (A).** If you filled in Table 4, follow the "fine only" line across to the 18-21 "M" and "F" columns. Turn your tallies into numbers. 17F - 15M = a difference of 2. Again, if you did not fill out Table 4 in advance, you might deal with just this category now. Remember to count only the single letters *c, d,* and *e.*

27. **The correct answer is (D).** Table 4 gives you a quick answer. Fifteen women over 30 are sentenced to prison only and six to prison and fine. 15 + 6 = 21. You will get the same answer, of course, by doing the counting when you get to the question.

28. **The correct answer is (A).** You have to use the county tables to answer this question. Limit your counting to the three central age categories and to the M columns only. Then, remember that *j* is not a conviction and that a sentence with & is given to one person.

COMPLETED TABLES

Table 4
Summary of Disposition of Cases—Three Counties

Disposition	Age and Sex of Offender																	
	Under 15			15–17			18–21			22–30			Over 30			Totals		
	M	F	T	M	F	T	M	F	T	M	F	T	M	F	T	M	F	T
Acquitted	5	3	8	7	9	16	5	9	14	8	14	22	11	15	26	36	50	86
Probation only	13	9	22	20	10	30	22	15	37	6	3	9	6	4	10	67	41	108
Fine only	12	8	20	16	17	33	15	17	32	15	8	23	17	13	30	75	63	138
Prison only	0	0	0	0	0	0	7	2	9	16	11	27	20	15	35	43	28	71
Probation & fine	3	1	4	6	3	9	3	4	7	3	1	4	1	4	5	16	13	29
Prison & fine	0	0	0	0	0	0	5	4	9	7	8	15	6	6	12	18	18	36
Total	33	21	54	49	39	88	57	51	108	55	45	100	61	57	118	255	213	468

Table 5
Summary of Dispositions by Offense—Three Counties

Offense	Sentence						
	Acquitted	Probation only	Fine only	Prison only	Probation & fine	Prison & fine	Totals
Vandalism	3	8	27	0	3	0	41
Burglary	7	6	4	12	4	7	40
Larceny	9	9	19	6	4	6	53
Assault	10	20	9	10	1	2	52
Robbery	5	12	9	15	2	6	49
Drunk driving	11	6	19	5	3	3	47
Prostitution	8	14	16	4	1	1	44
Manslaughter	12	12	11	2	1	1	39
Narcotics (sale)	11	10	8	14	1	9	53
Narcotics (possession)	10	11	16	3	9	1	50
Total	86	108	138	71	29	36	468

29. **The correct answer is (C).** This is an easy count. Just remember that both categories *narcotics (sale)* and *narcotics (possession)* must be included and that a fine is a fine even when paid in conjunction with a prison or probationary sentence.

30. **The correct answer is (B).** Table 5 is helpful here. Add together the 6 burglars who will serve only probation and the 4 burglars who will pay fines with their probation and subtract those 10 from the 19 burglars who will serve time in prison (12 in prison only + 7 paying fines and serving time as well).

A suggestion: Tables 4 and 5 here, and their counterparts on an actual exam, include a great many categories that are totally irrelevant to answering test questions. And filling out these tables in their entirety is very time-consuming. Some questions must be answered without the summary tables; others can easily be answered bypassing the summaries. Where a summary table might prove useful, as where categories must be combined or comparisons made, use the summary tables as work sheets, tallying as you count along, and fill out only those segments that you need. Remember, only the answer sheet is scored; the summary tables are for your own use even though they will be collected along with the question booklets.

Part Two

1. D	15. B	29. A	43. B	57. C
2. B	16. C	30. D	44. D	58. C
3. C	17. A	31. B	45. C	59. D
4. A	18. B	32. D	46. C	60. B
5. B	19. A	33. B	47. A	61. D
6. B	20. D	34. D	48. D	62. A
7. B	21. C	35. A	49. B	63. D
8. C	22. C	36. B	50. C	64. C
9. B	23. A	37. D	51. B	65. C
10. A	24. B	38. B	52. D	66. B
11. D	25. B	39. A	53. C	67. C
12. C	26. A	40. B	54. B	68. A
13. D	27. C	41. D	55. D	69. B
14. D	28. C	42. B	56. B	

1–10. **If you made any errors on questions 1–10, reread the Memory Passage to confirm the correct answer.**

11. **The correct answer is (D).** The paragraph states that if the neighborhood is composed of people and circumstances that might serve as a breeding ground for crime, then children might gain a criminal education in that neighborhood. Neither choices (A) nor (B) nor (C) may reasonably be concluded from the paragraph.

12. **The correct answer is (C).** Since old age insurance is *wholly* administered by the federal government, the city has no part in it. However, old age insurance is *one feature* of the Social Security Act that is wholly administered by the federal government, so presumably other governments administer other features. In light of this information, choice (D) cannot be correct.

13. **The correct answer is (D).** A defensive weapon is used in self-defense.

14. **The correct answer is (D).** Method of commission of the illegal act is not included among the requirements for the depositions.

15. **The correct answer is (B).** Understanding how one's own work contributes to the effort of the entire agency is appreciating the importance of that job.

16. **The correct answer is (C).** Conveying self-confidence is displaying assurance.

17. **The correct answer is (A).** The paragraph says that a court officer needs specific qualifications that are different from those required of police officers or of firefighters and which may differ from court to court. The paragraph does not spell out the nature of these qualifications. It further does not equate the qualifications of police officers with those of firefighters, saying only that they have many qualifications in common.

18. **The correct answer is (B).** "Supervised practice and the use of training aids and techniques help make the shooter."

19. **The correct answer is (A).** See the second sentence.

20. **The correct answer is (D).** Complaints from the public may be helpful in pointing out areas for improvement, but they are not required.

21. **The correct answer is (C).** One of the duties of court officers is to collect subpoenas and turn them over to the District Attorney.

22. **The correct answer is (C).** While a witness is being sworn in and while that witness is testifying, a court officer should remain close by the witness and in easy distance of the judge so as to render any assistance requested.

23. **The correct answer is (A).** Especially in a crowded courtroom, it is important that the witnesses be seated in one area for easy access. Attending a trial as a spectator is a privilege based on available space; it is not a right, even for a religious delegation.

24. **The correct answer is (B).** Witnesses in a civil case and witnesses for the defense do not come with subpoenas in hand. In order to seat witnesses in the area reserved for them, the court officer must know which people they are.

25. **The correct answer is (B).** Going for a book requested by the judge is precisely the type of assistance for which the court officer is standing nearby.

26. **The correct answer is (A).** An unlawful threat or attempt to do physical harm, even if unsuccessful, constitutes assault.

27. **The correct answer is (C).** Larceny is the taking away of another's property. It differs from robbery because violence is not involved.

28. **The correct answer is (C).** Frank was attempting to help a convicted felon to escape, so Frank is guilty of a felony. Mary was an innocent courier; she did not intend to help Johnny to escape, so, within the scope of the quoted paragraph, she is not guilty.

29. **The correct answer is (A).** The prisoner being assisted to escape is being held on a felony charge, therefore those who assist in his escape are guilty of felonies. While all the assistance is given orally, it is obviously useful. Both Joan and Tom are parties to Bill's escape.

30. **The correct answer is (D).** Debbie is a very young child, far too young to be charged with criminal intent; she is innocent. Since Jim was serving a sentence on a misdemeanor conviction, Barbara is guilty only of a misdemeanor. Jim, on the other hand, is now in serious trouble. The next person who tries to help Jim escape will be guilty of a felony.

31. **The correct answer is (B).** The unsolicited function of a scapegoat is to serve as the object of the frustrations of an impotent person or group. The true value of a scapegoat is, of course, nil. While the scapegoat suffers, the problems remain unsolved.

32. **The correct answer is (D).** The first sentence states that Peggy and Betsy were attending a football game.

33. **The correct answer is (B).** The first sentence states that Peggy and Betsy were attending a football game in mid-October.

34. **The correct answer is (D).** He was originally on row 25 and then he fell 3 rows.

35. **The correct answer is (A).** The third sentence discusses John's wardrobe.

36. **The correct answer is (B).** The third sentence states that Sam and John were arguing about a play in the game.

37. **The correct answer is (D).** The sixth sentence states that Sam was stabbed in the shoulder and chest.

38. **The correct answer is (B).** The next-to-last sentence states that two policemen stopped John in the parking lot and arrested him.

39. **The correct answer is (A).** The last sentence states that Sam died at St. Mary's Hospital.

40. **The correct answer is (B).** The first sentence mentions the name of the two witnesses.

41. **The correct answer is (D).** There is no mention of the weather in the passage.

42. **The correct answer is (B).** Mark, as a second offender, cannot serve his term in the state reformatory. Even though Mark's sentence is for a term well in excess of 1 year, he may serve his time at the county penitentiary or at the county jail because he is between the ages of 16 and 21. Mark may, of course, be sent to a state prison.

43. **The correct answer is (B).** As a first offender between the ages of 16 and 30, George may be sent to the state reformatory. State prison is also an option. George's term is too long for a man his age to serve at the county penitentiary or the county jail.

44. **The correct answer is (D).** If there is any possibility of a fracture, the injured part should not be moved.

45. **The correct answer is (C).** The correct procedure: the jurors tell a court officer that they have reached a decision; the court officer reports to the court that the jury has reached a decision; the judge orders the court officer to return the jury to the courtroom; the court officer leads the jury back.

46. **The correct answer is (C).** The foreman of the jury seals the envelope containing the verdict signed by the jurors. The foreman then personally keeps custody of the envelope until turning it in to the court at the next session. The court officer may know that a verdict has been reached, but not what that verdict is.

47. **The correct answer is (A).** The court officer who accompanies the jury from the jury room back to the courtroom to deliver its verdict remains with that jury in the courtroom.

48. **The correct answer is (D).** If the verdict is announced in open court, it is not a sealed verdict. No forms or envelopes are involved. The clerk receives and records the verdict as announced. The jury is polled only upon request of the judge.

49. **The correct answer is (B).** Only the judge has the authority to send the jurors home. Once the jurors have reached their verdict, the court officer must go to the court and announce that the verdict has been reached.

50. **The correct answer is (C).** The law with respect to diplomatic immunity is clear. The court officer had no choice. The man could not be detained, but follow-up contact with his consulate would not be out of order.

51. **The correct answer is (B).** If the officer or the officer's attorney feels that the documents would be helpful to the defense, the documents should be provided.

52. **The correct answer is (D).** The jurors are unarmed, and assistance has been summoned. Preventing the fight from spreading to other jurors seems adequate for the immediate moment. Shooting always presents a danger and adding to the violence seems unnecessary. However, just asking them to stop fighting is unlikely to be an effective way to restore order. When reinforcements arrive, the fighters can easily be separated.

53. **The correct answer is (C).** Criminal intent is purely mental.

54. **The correct answer is (B).** Microscopic evidence is likely to be the most useful not because of its size per se but because it is likely to have been overlooked and so not to have been disturbed. Choice (C) is not necessarily true. Some microscopic evidence readily dissipates or degenerates; however, that which remains intact and undisturbed may be very useful.

55. **The correct answer is (D).** The answer is in the last line. The factors that influence the witness affect what he observes (what he is able to see), how he interprets (what he wants to see), and how he describes (what he says about it).

56. **The correct answer is (B).** Reducing crime is an objective of the criminal *justice* system.

57. **The correct answer is (C).** Obviously, crime reduction must occur more than occasionally or peripherally. Your choice that reducing crime is its basic objective is based on reading ahead to the next sentence. The word "however" indicates that this is not the sole objective.

58. **The correct answer is (C).** *Also* is the only sensible completion here.

59. **The correct answer is (D).** The losses described are social *costs*.
60. **The correct answer is (B).** Obviously, the people who suffer the losses are the *victims*.
61. **The correct answer is (D).** Read on to the next sentence. *Crime* induces a feeling of insecurity.
62. **The correct answer is (A).** This is an idiomatic phrase, "anxiety *about*."
63. **The correct answer is (D).** You may have to read well into the paragraph to learn that the paragraph is about deception and false details. Then you will know that the paragraph deals with the interviewer who does not *believe* the witness.
64. **The correct answer is (C).** The case is better if filled out with false details; therefore, it is better to proceed *without* letting on that the interviewer is suspicious.
65. **The correct answer is (C).** We are speaking of a single witness. *His* is the only possible word for this blank.
66. **The correct answer is (B).** We don't want him to know that he is being *doubted*.
67. **The correct answer is (C).** The *witness* is telling the story.
68. **The correct answer is (A).** The whole point of the paragraph is to let the witness complete the story and only *after* the testimony to express doubt.
69. **The correct answer is (B).** Deception and false details describe a story that is *untrue*.

ANSWER SHEET PRACTICE TEST 5: PROMOTION EXAM

1. Ⓐ Ⓑ Ⓒ Ⓓ	26. Ⓐ Ⓑ Ⓒ Ⓓ	51. Ⓐ Ⓑ Ⓒ Ⓓ	76. Ⓐ Ⓑ Ⓒ Ⓓ	101. Ⓐ Ⓑ Ⓒ Ⓓ
2. Ⓐ Ⓑ Ⓒ Ⓓ	27. Ⓐ Ⓑ Ⓒ Ⓓ	52. Ⓐ Ⓑ Ⓒ Ⓓ	77. Ⓐ Ⓑ Ⓒ Ⓓ	102. Ⓐ Ⓑ Ⓒ Ⓓ
3. Ⓐ Ⓑ Ⓒ Ⓓ	28. Ⓐ Ⓑ Ⓒ Ⓓ	53. Ⓐ Ⓑ Ⓒ Ⓓ	78. Ⓐ Ⓑ Ⓒ Ⓓ	103. Ⓐ Ⓑ Ⓒ Ⓓ
4. Ⓐ Ⓑ Ⓒ Ⓓ	29. Ⓐ Ⓑ Ⓒ Ⓓ	54. Ⓐ Ⓑ Ⓒ Ⓓ	79. Ⓐ Ⓑ Ⓒ Ⓓ	104. Ⓐ Ⓑ Ⓒ Ⓓ
5. Ⓐ Ⓑ Ⓒ Ⓓ	30. Ⓐ Ⓑ Ⓒ Ⓓ	55. Ⓐ Ⓑ Ⓒ Ⓓ	80. Ⓐ Ⓑ Ⓒ Ⓓ	105. Ⓐ Ⓑ Ⓒ Ⓓ
6. Ⓐ Ⓑ Ⓒ Ⓓ	31. Ⓐ Ⓑ Ⓒ Ⓓ	56. Ⓐ Ⓑ Ⓒ Ⓓ	81. Ⓐ Ⓑ Ⓒ Ⓓ	106. Ⓐ Ⓑ Ⓒ Ⓓ
7. Ⓐ Ⓑ Ⓒ Ⓓ	32. Ⓐ Ⓑ Ⓒ Ⓓ	57. Ⓐ Ⓑ Ⓒ Ⓓ	82. Ⓐ Ⓑ Ⓒ Ⓓ	107. Ⓐ Ⓑ Ⓒ Ⓓ
8. Ⓐ Ⓑ Ⓒ Ⓓ	33. Ⓐ Ⓑ Ⓒ Ⓓ	58. Ⓐ Ⓑ Ⓒ Ⓓ	83. Ⓐ Ⓑ Ⓒ Ⓓ	108. Ⓐ Ⓑ Ⓒ Ⓓ
9. Ⓐ Ⓑ Ⓒ Ⓓ	34. Ⓐ Ⓑ Ⓒ Ⓓ	59. Ⓐ Ⓑ Ⓒ Ⓓ	84. Ⓐ Ⓑ Ⓒ Ⓓ	109. Ⓐ Ⓑ Ⓒ Ⓓ
10. Ⓐ Ⓑ Ⓒ Ⓓ	35. Ⓐ Ⓑ Ⓒ Ⓓ	60. Ⓐ Ⓑ Ⓒ Ⓓ	85. Ⓐ Ⓑ Ⓒ Ⓓ	110. Ⓐ Ⓑ Ⓒ Ⓓ
11. Ⓐ Ⓑ Ⓒ Ⓓ	36. Ⓐ Ⓑ Ⓒ Ⓓ	61. Ⓐ Ⓑ Ⓒ Ⓓ	86. Ⓐ Ⓑ Ⓒ Ⓓ	111. Ⓐ Ⓑ Ⓒ Ⓓ
12. Ⓐ Ⓑ Ⓒ Ⓓ	37. Ⓐ Ⓑ Ⓒ Ⓓ	62. Ⓐ Ⓑ Ⓒ Ⓓ	87. Ⓐ Ⓑ Ⓒ Ⓓ	112. Ⓐ Ⓑ Ⓒ Ⓓ
13. Ⓐ Ⓑ Ⓒ Ⓓ	38. Ⓐ Ⓑ Ⓒ Ⓓ	63. Ⓐ Ⓑ Ⓒ Ⓓ	88. Ⓐ Ⓑ Ⓒ Ⓓ	113. Ⓐ Ⓑ Ⓒ Ⓓ
14. Ⓐ Ⓑ Ⓒ Ⓓ	39. Ⓐ Ⓑ Ⓒ Ⓓ	64. Ⓐ Ⓑ Ⓒ Ⓓ	89. Ⓐ Ⓑ Ⓒ Ⓓ	114. Ⓐ Ⓑ Ⓒ Ⓓ
15. Ⓐ Ⓑ Ⓒ Ⓓ	40. Ⓐ Ⓑ Ⓒ Ⓓ	65. Ⓐ Ⓑ Ⓒ Ⓓ	90. Ⓐ Ⓑ Ⓒ Ⓓ	115. Ⓐ Ⓑ Ⓒ Ⓓ
16. Ⓐ Ⓑ Ⓒ Ⓓ	41. Ⓐ Ⓑ Ⓒ Ⓓ	66. Ⓐ Ⓑ Ⓒ Ⓓ	91. Ⓐ Ⓑ Ⓒ Ⓓ	116. Ⓐ Ⓑ Ⓒ Ⓓ
17. Ⓐ Ⓑ Ⓒ Ⓓ	42. Ⓐ Ⓑ Ⓒ Ⓓ	67. Ⓐ Ⓑ Ⓒ Ⓓ	92. Ⓐ Ⓑ Ⓒ Ⓓ	117. Ⓐ Ⓑ Ⓒ Ⓓ
18. Ⓐ Ⓑ Ⓒ Ⓓ	43. Ⓐ Ⓑ Ⓒ Ⓓ	68. Ⓐ Ⓑ Ⓒ Ⓓ	93. Ⓐ Ⓑ Ⓒ Ⓓ	118. Ⓐ Ⓑ Ⓒ Ⓓ
19. Ⓐ Ⓑ Ⓒ Ⓓ	44. Ⓐ Ⓑ Ⓒ Ⓓ	69. Ⓐ Ⓑ Ⓒ Ⓓ	94. Ⓐ Ⓑ Ⓒ Ⓓ	119. Ⓐ Ⓑ Ⓒ Ⓓ
20. Ⓐ Ⓑ Ⓒ Ⓓ	45. Ⓐ Ⓑ Ⓒ Ⓓ	70. Ⓐ Ⓑ Ⓒ Ⓓ	95. Ⓐ Ⓑ Ⓒ Ⓓ	120. Ⓐ Ⓑ Ⓒ Ⓓ
21. Ⓐ Ⓑ Ⓒ Ⓓ	46. Ⓐ Ⓑ Ⓒ Ⓓ	71. Ⓐ Ⓑ Ⓒ Ⓓ	96. Ⓐ Ⓑ Ⓒ Ⓓ	121. Ⓐ Ⓑ Ⓒ Ⓓ
22. Ⓐ Ⓑ Ⓒ Ⓓ	47. Ⓐ Ⓑ Ⓒ Ⓓ	72. Ⓐ Ⓑ Ⓒ Ⓓ	97. Ⓐ Ⓑ Ⓒ Ⓓ	122. Ⓐ Ⓑ Ⓒ Ⓓ
23. Ⓐ Ⓑ Ⓒ Ⓓ	48. Ⓐ Ⓑ Ⓒ Ⓓ	73. Ⓐ Ⓑ Ⓒ Ⓓ	98. Ⓐ Ⓑ Ⓒ Ⓓ	123. Ⓐ Ⓑ Ⓒ Ⓓ
24. Ⓐ Ⓑ Ⓒ Ⓓ	49. Ⓐ Ⓑ Ⓒ Ⓓ	74. Ⓐ Ⓑ Ⓒ Ⓓ	99. Ⓐ Ⓑ Ⓒ Ⓓ	124. Ⓐ Ⓑ Ⓒ Ⓓ
25. Ⓐ Ⓑ Ⓒ Ⓓ	50. Ⓐ Ⓑ Ⓒ Ⓓ	75. Ⓐ Ⓑ Ⓒ Ⓓ	100. Ⓐ Ⓑ Ⓒ Ⓓ	125. Ⓐ Ⓑ Ⓒ Ⓓ

answer sheet

Practice Test 5: Promotion Exam

Directions: Each question has four possible answers. Choose the letter that best answers the question and mark your answer on the answer sheet.

1. The plaintiff in a lawsuit is
   - **(A)** the person bringing the lawsuit
   - **(B)** the person who is being sued
   - **(C)** a witness in a case
   - **(D)** an alternate juror in a case

2. A pleading titled *Smith v Jones et al* indicates
   - **(A)** two plaintiffs
   - **(B)** two defendants
   - **(C)** more than two defendants
   - **(D)** unknown defendants

3. Which area of law deals with the validity of a will?
   - **(A)** Admiralty law
   - **(B)** Tort law
   - **(C)** Real property law
   - **(D)** Estate and trust law

4. A proper or legal attestation is called a (an)
   - **(A)** verification
   - **(B)** authentication
   - **(C)** oath
   - **(D)** jurat

5. A felony is a crime with a possible sentence of
   - **(A)** 6 months or more
   - **(B)** 1 year or more
   - **(C)** 30 days or more
   - **(D)** 10 years or more

6. When a judge asks the court attendant for a copy of "McKinney's," he or she wants
   - **(A)** federal laws
   - **(B)** Consolidated Laws of N.Y. State
   - **(C)** local ordinances
   - **(D)** rules of evidence

7. A person is entitled to represent himself (provided there are no extenuating circumstances such as mental health concerns)
   - **(A)** only in civil cases
   - **(B)** only in criminal cases
   - **(C)** only in federal cases
   - **(D)** in all cases

8. Statutes that fix the time within which particular actions must be instituted or otherwise be barred are known as
   (A) Statutes of Frauds
   (B) Exclusionary Acts
   (C) Statutes of Limitations
   (D) Unconsolidated Laws

9. If a person is in contempt of court, he did not
   (A) file an answer to a complaint
   (B) bring all of his witnesses to the court
   (C) follow the court's order(s)
   (D) file an appeal in time

10. The basic distinction between an affidavit and a deposition is that
   (A) one is sworn
   (B) the latter is sworn written testimony
   (C) the former is sworn written testimony
   (D) the latter is unsigned

11. The standard of proof in a criminal case is
   (A) beyond a reasonable doubt
   (B) preponderance of the evidence
   (C) beyond all doubt
   (D) clear and convincing evidence

12. The subject matter or property with which the action is concerned is known as the
   (A) fee simple
   (B) freehold
   (C) res
   (D) abstract of title

13. Venue describes
   (A) where a case can be brought
   (B) what kind of case a court hears
   (C) what kind of law applies to a case
   (D) the number of witnesses the court case can have

14. When counsel in a trial takes "exception" to a court ruling, it means that
   (A) an adjournment is required before additional evidence is introduced
   (B) he or she formally objects to the court ruling
   (C) he or she withdraws his or her original objection
   (D) he or she wishes to give reasons for original objections

15. An *ex parte* order is one that is given
   (A) when requested by an attorney
   (B) in all civil cases
   (C) in all criminal cases
   (D) with only one side of a case present

16. Mary stabs Susan to death. Which of the following statements is true?
   (A) Mary can be charged criminally and be sued civilly by Susan's family.
   (B) Mary can only be charged criminally due to double jeopardy principles.
   (C) Mary can only be sued civilly by Susan's family.
   (D) Mary will be committed to a state hospital.

17. Which area of law deals with the ownership of a piece of land?
   (A) Tort law
   (B) Administrative law
   (C) Real property law
   (D) Family law

18. Prosecution of all felonies in County Courts must be by
   (A) petition
   (B) information
   (C) summons
   (D) indictment

19. The First Amendment deals with
   (A) freedom of speech
   (B) the right to a jury trial
   (C) the right to bear arms
   (D) the right to confront witnesses against you

20. "Polling the jury" means
    (A) challenging the jury because of bias
    (B) requiring each juror to declare his or her individual verdict before it is legally recorded
    (C) selecting the jury
    (D) waive of trial by jury

21. Common law or case law
    (A) is enacted by the legislature
    (B) cannot be overturned
    (C) is judge-made law
    (D) is law created by administrative agencies

22. Subject to certain conditions, the one of the following persons who may be permitted to testify in a criminal case without being sworn, is a (an)
    (A) adult over 70 years of age
    (B) justice of a court of record
    (C) court attendant who witnessed a criminal contempt in court
    (D) child under 12 years of age

23. The distinction between a criminal contempt and a civil contempt is
    (A) one occurs in a court of record
    (B) one is punishable by jail
    (C) one is remedial in nature
    (D) one occurs in a criminal court

24. A witness who has conscientious scruples against taking an oath
    (A) shall not be permitted to testify
    (B) may solemnly affirm to tell the truth instead of taking an oath
    (C) may testify if the testimony is corroborated by further evidence
    (D) may testify only in special proceedings

25. Which of the following is true?
    (A) All persons arrested can be released on bail.
    (B) All persons arrested and charged with misdemeanors must be released on bail.
    (C) No one charged with a felony can be released on bail.
    (D) None of the above.

26. A statute is best defined as
    (A) a legislative enactment
    (B) a legal prosecution
    (C) adjective law
    (D) a codification of principles and procedure

27. The United States Supreme Court is comprised of how many members?
    (A) 7
    (B) 9
    (C) 11
    (D) 13

28. When the judge enters the courtroom
    (A) everyone is directed to rise
    (B) only the litigants are directed to rise
    (C) all except court employees are directed to rise
    (D) all court employees are directed to rise

29. A statute of limitations places a restriction on the
    (A) maximum penalty that may be imposed
    (B) time within which an action should be commenced
    (C) number of causes of action that may be pleaded at one time
    (D) amount and quality of evidence that may be introduced

30. According to the Criminal Procedure Law, the one of the following who is not a peace officer is a
    (A) court officer
    (B) criminal investigator attached to District Attorney's office in Westchester County
    (C) state parole officer
    (D) civilian employee of a state prison

practice test

31. The defendant in a criminal case
   (A) must testify if called upon by the prosecution
   (B) has the right to be present in the courtroom during the trial (providing he is not disrupting the case)
   (C) can only call a limited number of witnesses when presenting his case
   (D) must be convicted of the criminal act by a preponderance of the evidence

32. A case that has been adjourned is
   (A) stricken from the calendar
   (B) postponed for a time
   (C) dismissed without prejudice
   (D) tried without a jury

33. An objection to a juror for which no reason is given is called
   (A) an exception
   (B) peremptory challenge
   (C) challenge for cause
   (D) challenge to the favor

34. A trial jury consisting of 12 persons is called a
   (A) struck jury
   (B) special jury
   (C) grand jury
   (D) petit jury

35. A fictitious name used by a person is called a (an)
   (A) alibi
   (B) alias
   (C) facsimile
   (D) alienist

36. A "recidivist" is
   (A) mentally incompetent
   (B) incapable of committing crime
   (C) a psychopath
   (D) a habitual offender

37. If a party to a lawsuit is *pro se,* he is
   (A) a witness in the case
   (B) an expert in the case
   (C) being represented by an attorney at no cost
   (D) representing himself in the case

38. Which statement is *not* true?
   (A) Some cases can be initially brought in federal or state court.
   (B) All cases can be initially brought in federal or state court.
   (C) Some cases can be initially brought only in federal court.
   (D) Some cases can be initially brought only in state court.

39. Which area of law deals with domestic orders of protection?
   (A) Family law
   (B) Contract law
   (C) Estate and trust law
   (D) Administrative law

40. In the trial of a felony action, the court charges the jury
   (A) before People's summation
   (B) before the defendant's summation
   (C) after the summation by both parties
   (D) before the summation of either party

41. In legal parlance, an "alienist" is one who
   (A) has entered this country illegally
   (B) constantly changes his or her name
   (C) specializes in mental disorders
   (D) studies the causes of crime

42. The "polling of a jury" is exercised
   (A) before the jury is impaneled
   (B) after the jurors are sworn
   (C) after the verdict
   (D) after the judge's charge

43. In the trial of a felony action, the jurors must be warned by the court, after each adjournment, that they shall not
   (A) be separated
   (B) converse among themselves
   (C) form any opinion as to the case until the cause is submitted to them
   (D) communicate with other persons

44. In a criminal action, "impeaching a witness" means
   (A) compelling a witness to testify
   (B) rejecting a witness as incompetent
   (C) attacking the credibility of a witness
   (D) holding a witness for perjury

45. Jane punches John in the face. Civilly, this case would come under what type of law?
   (A) Tort law
   (B) Family law
   (C) Defamation law
   (D) Contract law

46. Decisions of the United States Supreme Court
   (A) must be unanimous
   (B) can be by a majority
   (C) must be by a ⅔ majority
   (D) must be by a ¾ majority

47. The number of jury challenges for cause
   (A) depends on the type of case being heard
   (B) is unlimited
   (C) depends on the number of plaintiffs in the case
   (D) depends on the number of defendants in the case

48. A plaintiff is to a complaint as a defendant is to a (an)
   (A) rebuttal
   (B) reply
   (C) answer
   (D) demurrage

49. A person whose negligence has caused damage to another is called a
   (A) tortfeasor
   (B) decedent
   (C) testator
   (D) demurrer

50. A restraining order issued by a court is called a (an)
   (A) subpoena
   (B) injunction
   (C) mandamus
   (D) rescission

51. Appeals from convictions for murder in the first degree go in the first instance to the
   (A) Appellate Term of the Supreme Court
   (B) County Court
   (C) Court of Appeals
   (D) Appellate Division of the Supreme Court

52. Statutory law is
   (A) created by legislatures
   (B) only applicable in civil cases
   (C) only applicable in criminal cases
   (D) judge-made law

53. Which statement is true about leading questions?
   (A) The prosecution in a criminal case never permits them.
   (B) They do not suggest an answer.
   (C) They are usually permitted on cross-examination.
   (D) They usually require a narrative to answer.

54. If an attempt is made to free the defendant at a murder trial by the use of automatic firearms, the court officer's primary obligation is to
   (A) handcuff the defendant to prevent escape
   (B) protect the spectators and court officials from possible harm
   (C) commit to memory a good description of those assisting in the attempted escape of the defendant
   (D) advise the spectators and court officials not to panic

55. The best attitude for a court officer to assume toward the public is to
 - **(A)** be kind and pleasant, ready to assist, and never argumentative
 - **(B)** be very friendly and cultivate all the acquaintances possible as they may prove useful in the future
 - **(C)** hold himself or herself apart and assume a superior manner as the public should be taught to look up to and respect a representative of the law
 - **(D)** be understanding and sympathetic

56. The legal term used to describe all the means by which the truth regarding any alleged matter of fact is established or disproved in court is
 - **(A)** testimony
 - **(B)** exhibit
 - **(C)** evidence
 - **(D)** proof

57. Which statement is *not* true?
 - **(A)** Open-ended questions are usually asked on direct examination.
 - **(B)** Open-ended questions do not suggest an answer.
 - **(C)** Open-ended questions are rarely used on cross-examination.
 - **(D)** The judge is the only person who can ask a witness an open-ended question.

58. A person who, when examined under oath, deliberately gives false information commits the crime of
 - **(A)** barratry
 - **(B)** forgery
 - **(C)** perjury
 - **(D)** slander

59. If a witness under a severe cross-examination becomes indignant and engages the attorney in a heated argument, a court officer should
 - **(A)** await any action the judge may take
 - **(B)** order the witness to be more respectful
 - **(C)** try to attract the attention of the witness
 - **(D)** call for assistance

60. If a spectator in a court room faints and falls to the floor, he or she should be
 - **(A)** placed in a chair in a sitting position
 - **(B)** laid on a flat surface with the head lower than the body
 - **(C)** picked up and removed to a hospital
 - **(D)** placed on the stomach with the head turned to the side

61. Several of the spectators in a courtroom get into a fight and one of them is seriously injured. As a court officer, the *first* thing you should do is to
 - **(A)** get the facts and make a report
 - **(B)** call an ambulance or a physician
 - **(C)** hold the people who engaged in the fight and arrest them for creating a public nuisance
 - **(D)** clear the courtroom

62. Defendants have the right to attorney representation at no cost
 - **(A)** in civil and criminal cases
 - **(B)** in criminal cases only
 - **(C)** in all federal cases
 - **(D)** only in cases where the crime charged is a capital offense

63. Which is the correct order of appeals in the federal system?
    (A) United States Supreme Court, then to the Court of Appeals, then to the United States District Courts
    (B) The United States District Court, then to the Court of Appeals, then to the United States Supreme Court
    (C) The Court of Appeals, then to the United States District Court, then to the United States Supreme Court
    (D) None of the above

64. Which area of law deals with the warranty on a car?
    (A) Contract law
    (B) Tort law
    (C) Administrative law
    (D) Real property law

65. An endorsement signed by the foreman of the grand jury that an indictment has been found on the concurrence of at least twelve grand jurors is known as a (an)
    (A) presentment
    (B) true bill
    (C) commission
    (D) ascertainment

66. An allegation made to a magistrate that a person is guilty of some designated crime is known as a (an)
    (A) charge
    (B) inquest
    (C) incrimination
    (D) information

67. What legal instrument is used by court officers to facilitate testimony of prisoners outside their jurisdiction?
    (A) a faxed subpoena
    (B) a signed order by the presiding judge served on the prisoner
    (C) a subpoena duces tecum
    (D) a writ of habeas corpus

68. A term used in law to describe licentious art or literature is
    (A) pornography
    (B) amercement
    (C) masochism
    (D) didacticism

69. An agreement to conceal a crime or to abstain from prosecuting a crime for some consideration is known in the Penal Law as
    (A) compounding a crime
    (B) compromising a crime
    (C) obstruction of justice
    (D) misprision of crime

70. The one of the following words that means a wrongdoer is
    (A) litigant
    (B) complainant
    (C) tortfeasor
    (D) prosecutor

71. When a presiding judge invokes the "rule" during a trial, what duties does the court officer perform?
    (A) All news media are barred from the courtroom.
    (B) All audible testimony and comments are recorded by the court officer for the judge's trial record.
    (C) Witnesses are removed from the courtroom until the court officer calls them for testimony.
    (D) Witnesses must remain in the courtroom until all witnesses have testified.

72. Prior to trial, who is responsible for setting up visual aids and large exhibits in the courtroom?
    (A) the court officer
    (B) court appointed technicians
    (C) the court reporter
    (D) the attorney who introduces the evidence

73. A Felony is to an Indictment as a Misdemeanor is to a (an)
    (A) Presentment
    (B) Complaint
    (C) Information
    (D) Summons

74. Defendant is to Counterclaim as Plaintiff is to
    (A) Answer
    (B) Denial
    (C) Repay
    (D) Complaint

75. A judgment entered in consequence of the nonappearance of a party in a civil action is called
    (A) interlocutory
    (B) declaratory
    (C) nonsuit
    (D) default

76. The papers containing the names of the jurors who are being impaneled are called
    (A) exhibits
    (B) canons
    (C) ballots
    (D) drafts

77. Sentences imposed by a court on a defendant convicted of several crimes but with the provision that the sentences shall be served at the same time are
    (A) consecutive
    (B) cumulative
    (C) concurrent
    (D) intermittent

78. The science of fingerprint identification is called
    (A) ballistics
    (B) semantics
    (C) dactylography
    (D) anthropometry

79. A designation given to a crime punishable by imprisonment in a state prison is
    (A) malicious
    (B) lascivious
    (C) turpitude
    (D) infamous

80. When a court officer is assigned to a courtroom prior to trial, to whom must he/she report?
    (A) the court's liaison officer
    (B) the presiding judge
    (C) the courtroom bailiff
    (D) the deputy court clerk

81. What is a subpoena?
    (A) a writ requiring appearance in court to give testimony
    (B) a letter notifying potential witnesses to appear in court for testimony
    (C) a mailed request to appear for trial
    (D) an official pass to enter the courtroom

82. What is a subpoena duces tecum?
    (A) a mailed request ordering individuals to report for trial testimony or face imprisonment
    (B) a writ requiring testimony and all records pertaining to a case
    (C) a form allowing a proxy to testify
    (D) formal permission by the trial judge to give unsolicited testimony

83. A guardian ad litem is a guardian for
    (A) the suit
    (B) all purposes
    (C) the purpose of conserving real property
    (D) the purpose of representing a corporation

84. The fundamental basis for allowing people to be free on bail is the
    (A) prevention of overcrowding in prisons
    (B) centralization of administrative responsibility in criminal cases
    (C) detection of violations of the law
    (D) prevention of punishment before trial

85. That system of law that does not rest for its authority on acts passed by the legislature is called
    (A) statutory law
    (B) civil law
    (C) common law
    (D) codified law

86. You are an officer assigned to guard the door in a criminal court where an important robbery case is on trial. A man whom you know not to be a police officer approaches and requests admission. In speaking with him you observe that he has a revolver in his overcoat pocket. You should

   (A) refuse to admit him
   (B) summon another court officer and search him
   (C) ask him to identify himself
   (D) refuse him admittance and call the matter to the attention of a detective who is nearby

87. You are an officer in charge of a prison pen in which there are a large number of men awaiting trial for felony. One of them falls to the floor and cries out that he has been poisoned. You should

   (A) open the door of the pen and, with the assistance of another officer, remove him
   (B) summon other officers to guard the pen while you take him to the doctor's office
   (C) make him as comfortable as possible pending the arrival of a physician
   (D) summon a number of other court officers before opening the pen door

88. As a court officer in charge of a jury that is deliberating, you are approached by one of the attorneys in the case who asks you to inform him as to how the jury is voting. You should

   (A) tell him it is none of his business
   (B) tell him that the rules prohibit your giving him any information
   (C) call another officer and have the attorney arraigned before the court
   (D) procure his name and report him to the judge immediately

89. You are in charge of a jury that is deliberating on a case and one of the jurors becomes seriously ill; you should

   (A) permit the jurors to continue their discussion of the case
   (B) stop all discussion and notify the clerk of the court
   (C) send for an ambulance
   (D) render first aid and, when the juror recovers, return him or her to the jury room

90. An attorney in a case on trial in a court in which you are an officer requests that you refer to him any person who is in need of legal services. You should

   (A) tell him that it is against the rules
   (B) procure his name and address, give it to the judge, and tell the judge what the attorney has said
   (C) immediately arraign him before the court and explain what he has said to you
   (D) agree to do so only if you think he is a good attorney

91. You are assigned, as an officer, to the door of a criminal court while three desperate criminals are being sentenced for robbery. Your instructions are to admit no one to the courtroom. The detective who made the arrest and who is late for the proceeding requests that he be admitted, as the judge may want to speak to him. You should

   (A) admit him
   (B) obey the orders given to the letter
   (C) ask another officer to find out if the judge wants to see the detective
   (D) tell the detective to wait until the sentencing is over

92. You are one of three officers assigned to guard a jury in a hotel where they are confined during the trial of a case. A hotel employee tells you that a physician is on the telephone and wants to speak to one of the jurors as his wife has had a serious accident. You should

    (A) convey the message to the juror immediately
    (B) permit the juror to talk to the physician
    (C) speak to the juror and tell him that he will have to get in touch with the judge
    (D) advise the employee to tell the doctor that you will convey the message as soon as you can get the judge's permission to do so

93. In legal parlance, an "execution" is

    (A) a decree appointing an executor of a decedent's estate
    (B) a summons
    (C) a court process directing the satisfaction of a judgment
    (D) the service of a warrant

94. Direct evidence is required in prosecutions of criminal homicides to prove the

    (A) identity of the victim
    (B) death of the victim
    (C) killing by the accused
    (D) intent

95. How does subrogation affect the courtroom preparation for trial?

    (A) In many cases, it requires additional seating and tables for attorneys and representatives for interested parties.
    (B) It affects the quality of attorneys the plaintiff can hire.
    (C) It allows television coverage of the trial.
    (D) It requires a judge from outside the local range of television to be assigned to try the case.

96. When criminal pretrial motions are scheduled, what are the court officer's duties?

    (A) ensure the prisoners are present
    (B) if doctors are involved, keep their beepers and inform them if they have a page
    (C) clear the courtroom of spectators and visiting attorneys not involved in the case
    (D) keep multiple sets of handcuffs nearby for dissatisfied parties

97. Evidence that the accused was voluntarily intoxicated at the time of committing the crime for which he or she is on trial is admissible evidence

    (A) as a defense based on excuse or lack of knowledge at time the crime was committed
    (B) whenever a specific intent is a necessary element to constitute a particular degree of the crime charged
    (C) only when total intoxication prevented the forming of a specific criminal intent
    (D) solely for the purpose of mitigating the punishment upon conviction of the crime charged

98. An appeal from which of the following courts is not taken directly to the Appellate Division of the Supreme Court?

    (A) Surrogate's Court
    (B) Civil Court
    (C) Appellate Term of the Supreme Court
    (D) Supreme Court

99. To control bleeding from a cut artery, pressure may be applied at some point where the main artery to the injured part lies close to the bone. The one of the following that is not a recognized "pressure point" where hand or finger pressure against a bone may stop bleeding is
    (A) the body side of the upper arm halfway between the shoulder and elbow
    (B) just in front of the ear
    (C) behind the inner end of the collar bone
    (D) about 1 inch below the kneecap

100. The degree of the crime of larceny is never affected by the
    (A) intent of the perpetrator
    (B) kind of property stolen
    (C) place from which the property is stolen
    (D) time when the property is taken

101. Every injured person is potentially a patient in shock and should be regarded and treated as such. The one of the following that is not a common symptom of shock is
    (A) shallow, irregular breathing
    (B) nausea
    (C) weak pulse
    (D) hot, dry skin

102. It would be most incorrect to state that
    (A) an "alienist" is a physician or psychiatrist specializing in the mental disease or conditions of persons
    (B) a "bill of attainder" is a law that fixes the guilt of a person without the benefit of a trial
    (C) a "chattel" is an unoccupied house or other building
    (D) a "defalcation" is an embezzlement

103. For the purposes of the statute of limitations, criminal prosecution is deemed to have been commenced when
    (A) an information is laid before a magistrate
    (B) the defendant is lawfully arrested
    (C) an indictment, having been presented by the Grand Jury, is received and filed in court
    (D) the crime in question becomes or is made known to the police

104. Never administer a liquid to an unconscious person. The basic reason for this admonition is most probably the fact that
    (A) liquids will have a harmful effect on the heart under these circumstances
    (B) the body of the person may already be overheated
    (C) the liquids may cause the person to choke
    (D) alcohol is an excessive stimulant

105. A break in a bone should be classified as a compound fracture if
    (A) one or more parts of the bone protrude through the surface of the skin
    (B) any portion of the bone is splintered
    (C) the bone is broken in two or more places
    (D) the break in the bone is vertical rather than horizontal

106. The essential distinction between a felony and a misdemeanor under the criminal laws of New York State depends primarily on the
    (A) seriousness of the injury caused by the criminal act
    (B) actual penalty imposed on the perpetrator after conviction
    (C) inherent evil in the act itself that the community recognizes as socially and morally wrong
    (D) maximum penalty that the court may legally impose upon the perpetrator after conviction of the crime charged

107. During a jury trial, what role does the court officer play, other than calling the witnesses and giving the oath?

(A) observes the spectators for any unusual activity

(B) observes the jurors and alternate jurors for lack of attention, falling asleep, or behavior not considered normal

(C) is attentive to the judge's needs while trial is in session

(D) all the above

108. What is an instanter?

(A) an immediate recess for medical emergencies

(B) a ruling in favor of the plaintiff at the end of plaintiff's proof

(C) a stopping of a proceeding in progress to begin a new case

(D) an order given to a court officer to bring a named individual immediately before the judge signing the order

109. The jury that has been chosen for a criminal trial may visit the place in which the crime is alleged to have been committed provided the

(A) crime charged is a felony

(B) court believes that such visit is proper

(C) jury feels that such a visit might prove helpful

(D) crime charged is murder

110. The law will allow a compulsory disclosure of

(A) the deliberations of a grand jury

(B) the deliberations of a trial jury

(C) matters that transpired during a criminal trial

(D) the deliberations of the court

111. When a judge orders a defendant placed in custody, what does the court officer do?

(A) call for a uniformed officer

(B) handcuff the defendant immediately and remove him from the courtroom, pat for weapons and wait until a uniformed deputy arrives

(C) search adjoining courtrooms for police officers

(D) physically place the defendant against the courtroom wall and pat down, then handcuff and remove him from the courtroom

112. Lie-detector machines are operated on the principle that

(A) most people are unable to tell a consistent story

(B) emotional stress causes physiological changes in a person

(C) many individuals are not afraid to lie

(D) a guilty person will unconsciously associate ideas in an indicative manner

113. A single action that is divided into two or more separate actions, each of which terminates in a separate judgment, is known as

(A) consolidation

(B) severance

(C) joinder

(D) election of remedies

114. Of the following instances, the one in which the Court of Appeals has the power to review the questions of *fact,* is

(A) contested divorce actions

(B) any felony committed by a minor

(C) death penalty case

(D) personal injury case based on negligence

115. That a court is a court of record means that
  (A) its process is valid anywhere in the state
  (B) the justices are elected rather than appointed
  (C) it was created by the State Constitution
  (D) its records are perpetuated

116. Where a complaint is dismissed "without prejudice," it means that
  (A) it is a final determination of the merits
  (B) no costs will be charged against the plaintiff
  (C) the cause of action may be brought again
  (D) the defendant will hold no prejudice against the plaintiff

117. The best definition of a motion is
  (A) an application for an order
  (B) an application for a dismissal
  (C) the right to introduce evidence
  (D) an application to start a suit

118. Most jury trials have a plaintiff table and defense table. When a trial involves cross complaints, where do the litigants sit?
  (A) The court officer flips a coin and the winner sits at the plaintiff table closest to the jury box.
  (B) Pretrial conference with the presiding judge and attorneys determines seating.
  (C) The litigant who files first sits at the plaintiff's table.
  (D) After reading the pleadings from both sides, the clerk of the court determines seating.

119. During domestic cases, especially those involving child custody, what are the court officer's duties?
  (A) make sure that the children are not seated in the courtroom
  (B) visually look for any weapons and do not hesitate to ask the parties' attorneys if they think there is a possibility of trouble
  (C) if prior domestic assault has occurred, order a uniformed officer to attend the hearing to prevent a sudden outburst
  (D) all of the above

120. When a criminal trial concludes with a verdict for the defense, what should you do?
  (A) have the defendant returned to the jail until the District Attorney decides what to do
  (B) do not let the defendant visit with family until the jail has processed the order
  (C) tell the defendant to retrieve his belongings from the jail whenever he wishes
  (D) if in custody at the time of the hearing, have the defendant returned to the jail for processing

121. A person accused of a crime may be permitted to testify before a grand jury provided
  (A) he or she has not been arrested
  (B) it is a capital crime
  (C) he or she is a citizen
  (D) he or she files a request to be heard

122. If the court deems the evidence insufficient to warrant a conviction of one or more of the crimes in the indictment, it may advise the jury to acquit the defendant thereof. In this instance, the jury
- **(A)** need not follow the recommendation until evidence on both sides has been introduced
- **(B)** must follow the advice
- **(C)** may disregard the advice if it believes otherwise
- **(D)** may accept the advice on condition that a new trial be ordered

123. Legal proceedings concerning the property of a deceased person are ordinarily held in the
- **(A)** Supreme Court
- **(B)** Surrogate's Court
- **(C)** County Court
- **(D)** Court of Claims

124. "A wrong is not presumed" means most nearly
- **(A)** one cannot presume that a person has done wrong just because he or she has committed a crime
- **(B)** hard cases make bad law
- **(C)** one wrong does not excuse another
- **(D)** a person is innocent until proven guilty

125. Generally, the plaintiff furnishes the court with copies of the summons and pleadings, noting in the margin which allegations are admitted and which are denied. These papers are known as
- **(A)** supplemental pleadings
- **(B)** marked pleadings
- **(C)** alternative pleadings
- **(D)** amended pleadings

ANSWER KEY AND EXPLANATIONS

1. A	26. A	51. C	76. C	101. D
2. C	27. B	52. A	77. C	102. C
3. D	28. A	53. C	78. C	103. C
4. B	29. B	54. B	79. D	104. C
5. B	30. D	55. A	80. C	105. A
6. B	31. B	56. C	81. A	106. D
7. D	32. B	57. D	82. B	107. D
8. C	33. B	58. C	83. A	108. D
9. C	34. D	59. A	84. D	109. B
10. B	35. B	60. B	85. C	110. C
11. A	36. D	61. B	86. D	111. B
12. C	37. D	62. B	87. D	112. B
13. A	38. B	63. B	88. D	113. B
14. B	39. A	64. A	89. B	114. C
15. D	40. C	65. B	90. B	115. D
16. A	41. C	66. D	91. B	116. C
17. C	42. C	67. D	92. D	117. A
18. D	43. C	68. A	93. C	118. C
19. A	44. C	69. A	94. B	119. D
20. B	45. A	70. C	95. A	120. D
21. C	46. B	71. C	96. C	121. D
22. D	47. B	72. A	97. B	122. B
23. C	48. C	73. C	98. B	123. B
24. B	49. A	74. D	99. D	124. D
25. D	50. B	75. D	100. A	125. B

1. **The correct answer is (A).** The plaintiff is the person bringing the lawsuit.

2. **The correct answer is (C).** *Et al* means "and others." Therefore, et al indicates that there are two or more defendants in addition to Jones.

3. **The correct answer is (D).** Estate and trust law deals with wills, financial planning, etc.

4. **The correct answer is (B).** An *authentication* is an attestation by a proper officer that a record is in due form of law. A *verification* is a confirmation by affidavit of the truth of a statement. An *oath* is an attestation of the truth of a statement. The *jurat* is a certification by an officer that a writing was sworn to by the signer. *Attestation* is the act of witnessing the signing of a writing and subscribing it as such witness.

5. **The correct answer is (B).** Felonies are 1 year or more, while misdemeanors are crimes with sentences less than 1 year.

6. **The correct answer is (B).** McKinney's Consolidated Laws of New York State includes all state laws with citations, notes, commentaries, and annotations from state and federal courts.

7. **The correct answer is (D).** The United States Supreme Court has decided this issue.

8. **The correct answer is (C).** A *Statute of Limitations* states the time after which an action may not be commenced. The Statute of Limitations varies with the nature of the matter; action on a contract, for instance, must be instituted within 6 years. The *Statute of Frauds* states that certain agreements, such as agreements for sale of real property, must be in writing.

9. **The correct answer is (C).** A person found in contempt has violated a court order.

10. **The correct answer is (B).** Both are sworn, signed statements, but a *deposition* is specifically the testimony of the deponent, usually in the form of questions and answers, while an *affidavit* is any sworn statement.

11. **The correct answer is (A).** B and D apply to various civil matters.

12. **The correct answer is (C).** The Latin word *res* means "thing." The subject matter or property is the thing with which an action is concerned. *Fee simple* is full, unencumbered ownership of real property. A *freehold* is a fee simple absolute, ownership without time limitation. *Abstract of title* is a document prepared by a title company presenting its findings after search of title records for liens, taxes, judgments, and so forth.

13. **The correct answer is (A).** Venue is the area that has jurisdiction over a lawsuit.

14. **The correct answer is (B).** An exception is an attorney's formal objection to the action of the court in denying a request or overruling an objection. Objections are taken to adverse rulings and to the court's instructions to a jury.

15. **The correct answer is (D).** An ex parte only has one party represented at the time of the order.

16. **The correct answer is (A).** A person can be charged for a crime and be sued for the tort.

17. **The correct answer is (C).** Real property deals with land and land transactions.

18. **The correct answer is (D).** Prosecution of all felonies is by *indictment*. Misdemeanors may be prosecuted on the basis of an *information*.

19. **The correct answer is (A).** The other three answers are guaranteed rights found in other amendments.

20. **The correct answer is (B).** "Polling the jury" is done by the attorney for the losing party. The attorney calls each juror by name and asks each whether or not the verdict is a true verdict. If so, the verdict is recorded.

21. **The correct answer is (C).** The legislature and administrative agencies create statutory law.

22. **The correct answer is (D).** A child under 12 may testify without oath if, in the opinion of the court, the child does not understand the nature of an oath but that child is sufficiently intelligent to justify reception of the child's evidence. Such testimony must be corroborated.

23. **The correct answer is (C).** *Civil contempt* is remedial and coercive in nature. It involves a neglect or violation of duty or other misconduct by which a right or a remedy of a party to a civil action or proceeding pending in the court may be defeated, impaired, or prejudiced. *Criminal contempt* may occur in any court. It is punitive in nature. The State and the People are interested in its prosecution. It does not involve any personal right or injury.

24. **The correct answer is (B).** "No person shall be rendered incompetent to be a witness on account of his opinions on matters of religious belief." (New York Constitution) The person may affirm to tell the truth, instead of taking an oath.

25. **The correct answer is (D).** Bail is not solely contingent on the crime with which a person is charged. Bail can also be set so high that not everyone can make bail.

26. **The correct answer is (A).** A *statute* is a legislative enactment. *Adjective law* is law governing procedures, such as the CPLR.

27. **The correct answer is (B).**

28. **The correct answer is (A).** Everyone, except those physically unable, is directed to rise. This is a symbol of respect and dignity, which attaches to the court.

29. **The correct answer is (B).** The *statute of limitations* prescribes the time periods within which various actions should be commenced. Felonies, for instance, must be prosecuted within five years.

30. **The correct answer is (D).** Article 2.10 of the Criminal Procedure Law enumerates who is designated a peace officer.

31. **The correct answer is (B).** Criminal defendants are allowed to be present in the courtroom during the proceedings.

32. **The correct answer is (B).** *Adjournment* means postponement.

33. **The correct answer is (B).** A *peremptory* challenge of a juror is a challenge for which no reason is given. A limited number of peremptory challenges is allowed. A challenge *for cause* is a challenge for a reason, such as bias. A challenge *to the favor* is a challenge for a reason such as that the juror is an interested party, perhaps an employee of one of the parties. An *exception* is an attorney's objection to a court ruling.

34. **The correct answer is (D).** A *petit jury* is a trial jury of 12 persons. A *struck jury* is a special or Blue Ribbon panel. A *grand jury* consisting of 16 to 23 persons is not a trial jury.

35. **The correct answer is (B).** An *alias* is a fictitious name. An *alibi* is a claim of being at another place at the time in question. A *facsimile* is an exact copy. An *alienist* is a psychiatrist.

36. **The correct answer is (D).** A *recidivist* is a backslider, a repeater, or a habitual offender.

37. **The correct answer is (D).** *Pro se* describes someone who is representing himself or herself in a case.

38. **The correct answer is (B).** Some cases can only be brought in certain state or federal courts.

39. **The correct answer is (A).** Family law deals with divorce, child support, custody, orders of protection, adoptions, etc.

40. **The correct answer is (C).** After all testimony has been given and after summation by both parties in the case, the court makes its charge to the jury. The *charge to the jury* states to the jury all matters of law that the judge considers necessary for their information as they consider and reach their verdict. The charge may also inform the jury that they are the exclusive judges of all questions of fact but that punishment should not enter their deliberations. Punishment rests with the judge.

41. **The correct answer is (C).** An *alienist* is a psychiatrist. An *alien* is a foreigner; an illegal alien has entered the country illegally. An *alias* is an assumed name. A *criminologist* studies causes of crime.

42. **The correct answer is (C).** *Polling of the jury* may occur after announcement but before recording of the verdict. The purpose is to ensure that the jurors concur.

43. **The correct answer is (C).** During the adjourned period, the jurors may not converse among themselves or with others on any subject connected with the trial, nor may they form or express any opinion on the matter before them until the cause is finally submitted by the court. Separation of the jury and communication on other topics are permitted.

44. **The correct answer is (C).** In a criminal case, *impeaching a witness* is attacking the credibility of the witness by demonstrating bad character, bias, or criminal record. A witness may also be impeached by his own actions in making contradictory statements.

45. **The correct answer is (A).** Tort law would cover issues such as assault and battery. If the parties were married or related, there might be issues of family law, but that necessary information was not provided here.

46. **The correct answer is (B).** Supreme Court decisions can be 5-4 decisions.

47. **The correct answer is (B).** There are unlimited challenges for cause (there is a specific prejudicial reason the juror cannot be impartial).

48. **The correct answer is (C).** A plaintiff files a complaint; a defendant files an answer to a complaint. *Complaint* is a plaintiff's pleading; *answer* is a defendant's pleading. *Demurrage* is the compensation payable to owners of a vessel for delays in loading or unloading.

49. **The correct answer is (A).** A *tortfeasor* is a wrongdoer or trespasser. A *decedent* is one who has died. A *testator* is one who has made a will. A *demurrer* is a legal objection by a defendant based on some irregularity.

50. **The correct answer is (B).** An *injunction* is a restraining order. It prohibits one party from committing any acts in violation of the other's rights. A *subpoena* is a request for the appearance of a witness in court. *Mandamus* is a court order to a public official demanding performance of a specified act. *Rescission* is the annulling of a contract by mutual agreement, by one of the parties, or by a court.

51. **The correct answer is (C).** Appeals from murder convictions go directly to the Court of Appeals. Appeals from other convictions ordinarily go to the Appellate Division of the Supreme Court.

52. **The correct answer is (A).** The legislature makes law applicable to both criminal and civil settings. Judge-made law is common or case law.

53. **The correct answer is (C).** Leading questions usually suggest the answer the attorney wants from the witness and are normally allowed only on cross-examination.

54. **The correct answer is (B).** In the case of an armed assailant, the first consideration on the part of the court officer is the safety of the persons in the courtroom. The officer should make every effort to subdue the armed person in order to prevent injury to others.

55. **The correct answer is (A).** The court officer must be ready to assist and must be friendly. He or she must never argue with parties to litigations nor with anyone else in the courtroom. The court officer must be firm in enforcement of courtroom rules.

56. **The correct answer is (C).** *Evidence* is the means used to prove or disprove a fact. *Proof* is the result of the evidence. An *exhibit* is a document or object introduced as evidence. *Testimony* is spoken or written evidence.

57. **The correct answer is (D).** An attorney usually asks open-ended questions when he or she is examining his own witness. The open-ended question allows for the witness to give detailed information regarding the subject.

58. **The correct answer is (C).** *Perjury* is lying under oath. *Slander* is making false statements about another so as to defame that person's character. *Forgery* is counterfeiting of documents or signature. *Barratry* is habitual bringing of groundless lawsuits.

59. **The correct answer is (A).** The court officer serves the bidding of the court. As long as the argument is verbal, the court officer should do nothing but await instructions from the bench. If the witness becomes physically violent, the court officer as peace officer must restrain the witness.

60. **The correct answer is (B).** In *fainting*, an inadequate flow of blood to the brain causes pallor and weakness. The person who has fainted should be laid flat with the head slightly lower than the trunk so that blood may flow to the head.

61. **The correct answer is (B).** Health and safety are first considerations. The court officer must render first aid and send for professional assistance, then consider arrest according to proper procedures.

62. **The correct answer is (B).** Defendants do not have a right to have free legal representation in civil cases, but they do in criminal cases.

63. **The correct answer is (B).** The order of appeals proceeds as follows: U.S. District Court to the Court of Appeals to the U.S. Supreme Court.

64. **The correct answer is (A).** Contract law deals with warranties, misrepresentations, agreements, etc.

65. **The correct answer is (B).** A *true bill* is an indictment on the concurrence of at least twelve grand jurors and signed by the foreman. A *presentment* is the report of a grand jury on an investigation conducted by them. A *commission* is an authority granted by a court to a person named to perform certain acts or to exercise certain jurisdiction.

66. **The correct answer is (D).** An *information* is a formal allegation before a magistrate, charging a named person with a specific crime and serving the same function as an indictment in a felony charge.

67. **The correct answer is (D).** Writs must be executed on federal prisoners for the "body" to testify in a state court or vice versa. If the prisoner refuses to sign the writ, then the court officer must write "served by hand" and give a copy to the prisoner. In these cases, writs of habeas corpus become "tools" for the courts.

68. **The correct answer is (A).** *Pornography* constitutes obscene art or literature. *Amercement* is punishment by assessing and collecting a fine. *Didacticism* is boring instruction. *Masochism* is the gaining of sexual pleasure from self-inflicted physical pain.

69. **The correct answer is (A).** Taking a reward (in effect, accepting a bribe) to withhold evidence or to refrain from prosecuting a crime (in effect, to obstruct justice) is *compounding a crime*. *Compromising a crime* is adjusting of misdemeanors by mutual concession without resort to the law, a settling out of court in the criminal sphere. Compromise is legal if done according to law. *Misprision* is failure to reveal a crime.

70. **The correct answer is (C).** A *tortfeasor* is a wrongdoer. A *litigant* is one of the parties to a lawsuit.

71. **The correct answer is (C).** Witnesses are removed from the courtroom until called by the court officer.

72. **The correct answer is (A).** The court officer checks out televisions, VCRs, recorders, etc., prior to the commencement of the trial.

73. **The correct answer is (C).** An *information* is the basis of jurisdiction over a misdemeanor as an indictment is the basis of jurisdiction over a felony.

74. **The correct answer is (D).** The *counterclaim* is, in effect, the defendant's "complaint" or "counter-complaint," just as the complaint is the plaintiff's claim.

75. **The correct answer is (D).** A *default judgment* is rendered in favor of the party that appears when the opposing party fails to appear on the trial date. A default judgment may be reopened if the court later deems that the default was excusable. An *interlocutory judgment* is a provisional, not final, judgment. A *declaratory judgment* declares the rights of the parties or expresses the opinion of the court on a question of law without ordering anything to be done. *Nonsuit* is the name of a judgment given against a plaintiff who is unable to prove a case.

76. **The correct answer is (C).** *Ballots* are the pieces of paper containing the names of the prospective jurors. *Canons* are laws or rules.

77. **The correct answer is (C).** *Concurrent sentences* are sentences for more than one crime all being served at the same time. For instance, a defendant serving 5 years for burglary and 2 years for breaking and entering need serve only the 5-year sentence, since the 2-year sentence is being served at the same time. *Consecutive* and *cumulative* sentences (the same thing) are served one after another.

78. **The correct answer is (C).** *Dactylography* is the science of fingerprinting. *Ballistics* is the science of projectiles that come from firearms. *Semantics* is the study of linguistics and deals with the meanings of words. *Anthropometry* is the measurement of body bones.

79. **The correct answer is (D).** An *infamous* crime is a felony punishable by imprisonment in a state prison. Infamous crime is a legal term. Malicious crimes, lascivious crimes, and crimes of moral turpitude (vileness) may all be felonies, but they are not legal terms.

80. **The correct answer is (C).** Each judge has a bailiff or court officer who is permanently assigned to oversee additional court officers.

81. **The correct answer is (A).** A *subpoena* is a writ requiring appearance in court to give testimony.

82. **The correct answer is (B).** A *subpoena duces tecum* is a writ requiring testimony and all records pertaining to a case.

83. **The correct answer is (A).** A *guardian ad litem* is a guardian appointed by the court to represent the rights of a minor or incompetent in a particular civil suit. The guardianship is for this single purpose.

84. **The correct answer is (D).** The reason for allowing people to be free before trial is to avoid punishment without proof of guilt. The purpose of bail is to guarantee the appearance of the accused at the trial.

85. **The correct answer is (C).** The *common law*, the great body of unwritten law, is founded in precedent or on the decisions of courts in previous cases decided on the same or similar facts and circumstances. *Statutory law* is the written law, the laws passed by a legislature.

86. **The correct answer is (D).** The court officer guarding the door has the authority to refuse admittance. Noticing the revolver, but not knowing whether the person has a pistol permit, the court officer must not act hastily or belligerently, but must be wary and cautious. Since the answer choice has placed a detective nearby, the stage is set to call in the detective to do the questioning.

87. **The correct answer is (D).** Accused persons tend to be ingenious in devising escape methods. Poisoning of a prisoner in a holding pen seems unlikely, but it is possible that the man is truly ill. On the other hand, this may be a calculated ploy to have the gate opened and to create confusion, during which prisoners may escape. There should be a sufficient number of officers on hand before the door is opened.

88. **The correct answer is (D).** This behavior constitutes contempt of court and, as such, should be reported to the judge presiding in the case.

89. **The correct answer is (B).** The deliberation should be stopped and the court clerk notified. If there are alternate jurors, the judge may select an alternate to take the place of the ailing juror. Deliberations may then resume.

90. **The correct answer is (B).** Soliciting business in this way is a violation of the Code of Ethics. This is not an emergency situation as in jury tampering or contempt of court, but the behavior should be reported to the judge for action.

91. **The correct answer is (B).** Your instructions are to admit no one, so admit no one. If the case has reached sentencing, the detective who made the arrest has had plenty of time to be heard.

92. **The correct answer is (D).** Judges are human beings, and undoubtedly the judge will act with compassion, suspend deliberation, and release the juror to go to his wife. However, only the judge has the power to suspend the deliberations. Get the message to the judge at once, so that he or she may grant this permission.

93. **The correct answer is (C).** In a civil case, the *execution* describes the judgment and directs the sheriff to enforce or satisfy the judgment. The judgment specifies if specific property is to be recovered, money is to be paid or performance is mandated. The decree appointing an executor of a decedent's estate is called *Letters Testamentary*.

94. **The correct answer is (B).** The death of the victim cannot be established by circumstantial evidence; there must be direct evidence.

95. **The correct answer is (A).** Subrogation can result in additional defense tables and chairs for numerous attorneys.

96. **The correct answer is (C).** Pretrial motions involving the judge, court reporter, and attorneys are generally heard after the court officer has cleared the courtroom of spectators and attorneys not involved in the case at hand.

97. **The correct answer is (B).** Evidence of intoxication cannot be used as a defense to the crime. However, should it be necessary to prove motive or intent as a necessary element of a crime, the jury may take into consideration the fact that the accused was intoxicated at the time.

98. **The correct answer is (B).** Appeals from the Civil Court go first to the Appellate Term of the Supreme Court and only from there to the Appellate Division.

99. **The correct answer is (D).** In the portion of the leg just below the kneecap, the artery is not sufficiently close to the bone for application of pressure to stop the flow of blood.

100. **The correct answer is (A).** The intent of the perpetrator is important for the purpose of determining whether a larceny was committed but it has no role in affecting the degree of the larceny. The kind of property stolen, the dollar value of the property, the place from which the property was stolen, and the time of day all help determine the degree of larceny.

101. **The correct answer is (D).** The symptoms of shock are pale, cold, clammy skin; weak pulse; and shallow breathing.

102. **The correct answer is (C).** *Chattel* is property that is not realty.

103. **The correct answer is (C).** Action in a criminal prosecution has commenced when an indictment has been rendered, received, and filed in the proper court or when an information has been laid before a magistrate and a warrant has been issued. Either stops the running of the statute of limitations.

104. **The correct answer is (C).** An unconscious person is unable to swallow, so administering of a liquid may cause choking.

105. **The correct answer is (A).** The word "compound" in *compound fracture* means that more than one thing has happened. The bone has broken and the skin has been punctured by the bone. If the skin is not broken, the fracture is a simple fracture, no matter how many breaks there are or how serious a fracture it may be.

106. **The correct answer is (D).** The fundamental distinction between "felony" and "misdemeanor" rests on the maximum penalty that may be imposed. The character of the crime is not determined by the extent of the injuries caused nor by the vile nature of the crime itself. A felony is a crime punishable by death or by imprisonment in a state prison; any other crime is a misdemeanor.

107. **The correct answer is (D).** The court officer has to observe the spectators, jurors, and judge.

108. **The correct answer is (D).** Instanters are seldom used, but once issued, and given to the court officer, all sworn personnel within the jurisdiction of the court may take the defendant into custody for immediate transfer to the courtroom.

109. **The correct answer is (B).** The matter of a jury's visit to the scene of a crime is left to the discretion of the court. The nature or degree of the crime is irrelevant.

110. **The correct answer is (C).** Any person who comes within the category of being a party properly interested in a trial or its outcome may compel the disclosure of what occurred during such trial. However, a combination of statutory law and court decisions makes the deliberations of judges, grand jurors, and trial jurors privileged.

111. **The correct answer is (B).** Handcuffing the defendant immediately will keep the situation under control and not allow the person time to react.

112. **The correct answer is (B).** A person who knows that he or she is guilty of lying will suffer fear and emotional stress. Emotional stress or apprehension leads to physiological changes in blood pressure, pulse, respiration, and perspiration. The lie-detector technique, the polygraph (literally, "many measures"), is designed to measure and record these changes.

113. **The correct answer is (B).** *Severance* means cutting apart or separating. It is the opposite of consolidation. An action may be severed if the court deems it desirable in the interests of justice and if it can be done without prejudice to a substantial right of any of the parties.

114. **The correct answer is (C).** The essential function of the Court of Appeals is to review questions of law. However, the Court of Appeals can review questions of fact in cases involving the death penalty and in civil cases where the Appellate Division has made new findings of fact and has rendered a final judgment or order.

115. **The correct answer is (D).** A court of record is a court in which the acts and judicial proceedings are recorded as a permanent record, thereby serving as precedent for future decisions.

116. **The correct answer is (C).** Dismissal of a case *without prejudice* is not a final determination on the merits of the case, but rather a dismissal because of some technicality that can be cured. Dismissal without prejudice means that the plaintiff has not lost the right to reinstitute the action.

117. **The correct answer is (A).** A *motion* is an application for an order. During the pendency of an action, numerous applications may be made to the court for various orders, such as an order to set aside service of a summons or an order to amend the complaint. The papers on which these applications are brought to the attention of the court are commonly called *motion papers*.

118. **The correct answer is (C).** The party who files first sits at the plaintiff's table, although the jury could award damages to either party, regardless of where they are sitting.

119. **The correct answer is (D).** The court officer should shield children from the court proceedings whenever possible and try to prevent any violent incidents during the trial.

120. **The correct answer is (D).** The defendant is free, based on the decision, but the jail needs to process the order and return belongings before the defendant leaves.

121. **The correct answer is (D).** The accused may file a request to appear in person before a grand jury. Such request must be filed with the foreman of the grand jury and with the District Attorney. The accused must also file a waiver of immunity with the county clerk in order to be heard.

122. **The correct answer is (B).** This is a directed verdict. If the court deems evidence insufficient to warrant a conviction on one or more of the counts of an indictment or information, it may advise the jury to acquit the defendant and the jury must follow the advice. The court cannot advise the jury to convict, only to acquit.

123. **The correct answer is (B).** The Surrogate's Court handles matters concerning decedents' estates, probate of wills, and such. The Court of Claims handles suits against the state of New York.

124. **The correct answer is (D).** The basic principle of all criminal prosecutions in the United States is the presumption under the law that the defendant is innocent until proven guilty.

125. **The correct answer is (B).** *Marked pleadings* enable the court to determine the nature of the action, which facts are at issue, and the questions of law that will be presented. *Supplemental pleadings*, filed later, show additional causes of action and new facts that occurred after the commencement of the action. *Amended pleadings* are corrections to the original pleadings. *Alternative pleadings* are usually not permitted. All pleadings should be clear and unequivocal from the outset.

APPENDIXES

APPENDIX A   Civil Practice Law and Rules

APPENDIX B   Criminal Procedure Law

APPENDIX C   Judiciary Court Acts

APPENDIX D   Penal Law

APPENDIX E   Glossary of Legal Terms

Civil Practice Law and Rules

Article		Section
1.	Short title, applicability and definitions....................	101-107
2.	Limitations of time	201-218
3.	Jurisdiction and service, appearance, and choice of court	301-318, 320-322, 325-326
4.	Special proceedings.....................................	401-411
5.	Venue	501-512
6.	Joinder of claims, consolidation and severance	601-604
10.	Parties generally	1001-1025
11.	Poor persons..	1101-1103
12.	Infants and incompetents	1201-1211
13.	Actions by the state....................................	1301-1303
14.	Actions between joint tortfeasors	1401, 1402
15.	Actions against persons jointly liable	1501-1502
20.	Mistakes, defects, irregularities and extensions of time........	2001-2004
21.	Papers	2101-2106
22.	Stay, motions, orders and mandates	2201, 2211-2223
23.	Subpoenas, oaths and affirmations	2301-2310
24.	Publication	2401-2402
25.	Undertakings	2501-2513
26.	Property paid into court................................	2601-2609
27.	Disposition of property in litigation	2701-2703
30.	Remedies and pleading	3001-3005, 3011-3026, 3031-3037, 3041-3044
31.	Disclosure	3101-3118, 3120-3126, 3130-3134, 3140
32.	Accelerated judgment	3201, 3211-3222
34.	Calendar practice; trial preferences.....................	3401-3404
40.	Trial generally	4001, 4011-4018
41.	Trial by a jury..	4101-4113
42.	Trial by the court	4201, 4211-4213
43.	Trial by a referee.....................................	4301, 4311-4321
44.	Trial motions	4401-4406
45.	Evidence	4501-4508, 4511-4543
50.	Judgments generally	5001-5004, 5011-5021
51.	Enforcement of judgments and orders generally.............	5101-5107
52.	Enforcement of money judgments	5201-5211, 5221-5240, 5250-5252
53.	Recognition of foreign country money judgments	5301-5309
54.	Enforcement of judgments entitled to full faith and credit.......	5401-5408
55.	Appeals generally	5501, 5511-5532
56.	Appeals to the court of appeals.........................	5601-5602, 5611-5615

appendix a

Article		Section
57.	Appeals to the appellate division	5701-5704, 5711-5713
60.	Provisional remedies generally.	6001
61.	Arrest.	6101, 6102, 6111-6119
62.	Attachment.	6201-6204, 6211-6226
63.	Injunction.	6301, 6311-6315
64.	Receivership.	6401-6405
65.	Notice of pendency	6501, 6511-6515
70.	Habeas corpus	7001-7012
71.	Recovery of chattel	7101-7112
72.	Recovery of penalty or forfeiture	7201-7205
75.	Arbitration	7501-7514
76.	Proceeding to enforce agreement for determination of issue	7601
77.	Proceeding relating to express trust.	7701-7705
78.	Proceeding against body or officer	7801-7806
80.	Fees.	8001-8021
81.	Costs generally	8101-8110
82.	Amount of costs	8201-8204
83.	Disbursements and additional allowances	8301-8303
84.	Taxation of costs.	8401-8404
85.	Security for costs	8501-8503
90.	Failure or adjournment of term of court	9001-9003
94.	Admission to practice	9401-9407
97.	Records of clerks of the courts	9701-9703
100.	Repeal; saving clauses; effective date	10001-10005

SELECTED ARTICLES AND SECTIONS OF THE CIVIL PRACTICE LAW AND RULES

(Full text of the CPLR, along with notes, commentaries, and amendments, may be found in Volume 7B of McKinney's *Consolidated Laws of New York State*)

105. DEFINITIONS

(a) Applicability. Unless the context requires otherwise, the definitions in this section apply to the civil practice law and rules.

(b) Action and special proceeding. The word "action" includes a special proceeding; the words "plaintiff" and "defendant" include the petitioner and the respondent, respectively, in a special proceeding; and the words "summons" and "complaint" include the notice of petition and the petition, respectively, in a special proceeding.

(c) Attorney. The word "attorney" includes a party prosecuting or defending an action in person.

(d) Civil judicial proceeding. A "civil judicial proceeding" is a prosecution, other than a criminal action, of an independent application to a court for relief.

(e) Clerk. The word "clerk," as used in any provision respecting an action or any proceedings therein, means the clerk of the court in which the action is friable.

(f) Court and judge. The word "court,'" as used in any provision concerning a motion, order or special proceeding, includes a judge thereof authorized to act out of court with respect to such motion, order, or special proceeding.

(g) Domestic and foreign corporation. A "domestic corporation" is a corporation created by or under the laws of the state, or a corporation located in the state and created by or under the laws of the United States, or a corporation created by or pursuant to the laws in force in the colony of New York before April nineteenth, seventeen hundred seventy-five. Every other corporation is a "foreign corporation."

(h) Garnishee. A "garnishee" is a person who owes a debt to a judgment debtor, or a person other than the judgment debtor who has property in his possession or custody in which a judgment debtor has an interest.

(i) Judgment. The word "judgment" means a final or interlocutory judgment.

(j) Judgment creditor. A "judgment creditor" is a person in whose favor a money judgment is entered or a person who becomes entitled to enforce it.

(k) Judgment debtor. A "judgment debtor" is a person, other than a defendant not summoned in the action, against whom a money judgment is entered.

(l) Law. The word "law" means any statute or any civil practice rule.

(m) Matrimonial action. The term "matrimonial action" includes actions for a separation, for an annulment or dissolution of a marriage, for a divorce, for a declaration of the nullity of a void marriage, for a declaration of the validity or nullity of a foreign judgment of divorce and for a declaration of the validity or nullity of a marriage.

(n) Money judgment. A "money judgment" is a judgment, or any part thereof, for a sum of money or directing the payment of a sum of money.

(o) Place where action is friable. The place where an action is "friable" means the place where the action is pending; or, if no action has been commenced, any proper place of trial or any proper place to commence the action; or, after entry of judgment, the place where the judgment was entered.

(p) Real property. "Real property" includes chattels real.

(q) Verified pleading. A "verified pleading" may be utilized as an affidavit whenever the latter is required.

106. CIVIL AND CRIMINAL PROSECUTIONS NOT MERGED

Where the violation of a right admits of both a civil and criminal prosecution, the one is not merged in the other.

308. PERSONAL SERVICE UPON A NATURAL PERSON

Personal service upon a natural person shall be made by any of the following methods:

1. by delivering the summons within the state to the person to be served; or

2. except in matrimonial actions, by delivering the summons within the state to a person of suitable age and discretion at the actual place of business, dwelling place or usual place of abode of the person to be served and by mailing the summons to the person to be served at his last known residence; proof of such service shall be filed within twenty days thereafter with the clerk of the court designated in the summons; service shall be complete ten days after such filing; proof of service shall identify such person of suitable age and discretion and state the date, time and place of service; or

3. except in matrimonial actions, by delivering the summons within the state to the agent for service of the person to be served as designated under rule 318;

4. except in matrimonial actions, where service under paragraphs one and two cannot be made with due diligence, by affixing the summons to the door of either the actual place of business, dwelling place or usual place of abode within the state of the person to be served and by mailing the summons to such person at his last known residence; proof of such service shall be filed within twenty days thereafter with the clerk of the court designated in the summons; service shall be complete ten days after such filing;

5. in such manner as the court, upon motion without notice, directs, if service is impracticable under paragraphs one, two, and four of this section.

321. ATTORNEYS

(a) Appearance in person or by attorney. A party, other than one specified in section 1201, may prosecute or defend a civil action in person or by attorney, except that a corporation or voluntary association shall appear by attorney. If a party appears by attorney he may not act in person in the action except by consent of the court.

(b) Change of attorney. An attorney of record may be changed by court order or, unless the party is a person specified in section 1201, by filing with the clerk a consent to the change signed by the retiring attorney and signed and acknowledged by the party. Notice of such change of attorney shall be given to the attorneys for all parties in the action or, if a party appears without an attorney, to the party.

(c) Death, removal or disability of attorney. If an attorney dies, becomes physically or mentally incapacitated, or is removed, suspended or otherwise becomes disabled at any time before judgment, no further proceeding shall be taken in the action against the party for whom he appeared, without leave of the court, until thirty days after notice to appoint another attorney has been served upon that party either personally or in such manner as the court directs.

RULE 3402. NOTE OF ISSUE

(a) Placing case on calendar. At any time after issue is first joined, or at least forty days after service of a summons has been completed irrespective of joinder of issue, any party may place a case upon the calendar by filing, within five days after service, with proof of such service, two copies of a note of issue with the clerk and such other data as may be required by the applicable rules of the court in which the note is filed. The clerk shall enter the case on the calendar as of the date of the filing of the note of issue.

(b) New parties. A party who brings in a new party shall within five days thereafter serve him with the note of issue and file a statement with the clerk advising him of the bringing in of such new party and of any change in the title of the action, with proof of service of the note of issue upon the new party, and of such statement upon all parties who have appeared in the action. The case shall retain its place upon the calendar unless the court otherwise directs.

RULE 3403. TRIAL PREFERENCES

(a) Preferred cases. Civil cases shall be tried in the order in which notes of issue have been filed, but the following shall be entitled to a preference:

1. fan action brought by or against the state, or a political subdivision of the state, or an officer or board of officers of the state or a political subdivision of the state, in his or its official capacity, on the application of the state, the political subdivision, or the officer or board of officers;

2. fan action where a preference is provided for by statute; and

3. fan action in which the interests of justice will be served by an early trial.

(b) Obtaining preference. Unless the court otherwise orders, notice of a motion for preference shall be served with the note of issue by the party serving the note of issue, or ten days after such service by any other party.

RULE 4011. SEQUENCE OF TRIAL

The court may determine the sequence in which the issues shall be tried and otherwise regulate the conduct of the trial in order to achieve a speedy and unprejudiced disposition of the matters at issue in a setting of proper decorum.

RULE 4016. OPENING AND CLOSING STATEMENTS

Before any evidence is offered, an attorney for each plaintiff having a separate right and an attorney for each defendant having a separate right may make an opening statement. At the close of all the evidence on the issues tried, an attorney for each such party may make a closing statement in inverse order to opening statements.

4103. ISSUES TRIABLE BY A JURY REVEALED AT TRIAL; DEMAND AND WAIVER OF TRIAL BY JURY

When it appears in the course of a trial by the court that the relief required, although not originally demanded by a party, entitles the adverse party to a trial by jury of certain issues of fact, the court shall give the adverse party an opportunity to demand a jury trial of such issues. Failure to make such demand within the time limited by the court shall be deemed a waiver of the right to trial by jury. Upon such demand, the court shall order a jury trial of any issues of fact that are required to be tried by a jury.

4104. NUMBER OF JURORS

(a) Specification of number of jurors. A party demanding a jury trial under sections 2218, 4102 or 4103 shall specify in the demand whether he demands trial by a jury composed of twelve persons or six persons. Where a party has not specified the number of jurors, he shall be deemed to have demanded a trial by a jury composed of twelve persons.

(b) Increased number of jurors. If, under this section, a party demands a jury of six, any other party may, within ten days after service of the demand, serve upon all other parties and file a demand for a jury of twelve. If, under sections 2218 or 4103, a party demands a jury of six, the court shall give the other parties an opportunity to demand a jury of twelve.

4105. PERSONS WHO CONSTITUTE THE JURY

The first twelve or, if a jury of six is demanded, the first six, persons who appear as their names are drawn and called and are approved as indifferent between the parties, and not discharged or excused, must be sworn and constitute the jury to try the issue.

4106. ALTERNATE JURORS

The court, in its discretion, may direct the calling of one or two additional jurors, to be known as "alternate jurors." Such jurors shall be drawn at the same time, from the same source, in the same manner, and have the same qualifications as the regular jurors, and be subject to the same examinations and challenges. They shall be seated with, take the oath with, and be treated in the same manner as the regular jurors, except that after final submission of the case, the court shall discharge the alternate jurors. If, before the final submission of the case, a regular juror dies, or becomes ill, or for any other reason is unable to perform his duty, the court may order him to be discharged and draw the name of an alternate, who shall replace the discharged juror in the jury box, and be treated as if he had been selected as one of the regular jurors.

RULE 4111. GENERAL AND SPECIAL VERDICTS AND WRITTEN INTERROGATORIES

(a) General and special verdict defined. The court may direct the jury to find either a general verdict or a special verdict. A general verdict is one in which the jury finds in favor of one or more parties. A special verdict is one in which the jury finds the facts only, leaving the court to determine which party is entitled to judgment thereon.

(b) Special verdict. When the court requires a jury to return a special verdict, the court shall submit to the jury written questions susceptible of brief answer or written forms of the several findings which might properly be made or it shall use any other appropriate method of submitting the issues and requiring written findings thereon. The court shall give sufficient instruction to enable the jury to make its findings upon each issue. If the court omits any issue of fact raised by the pleadings or evidence, each party waives his right to a trial by jury of the issue so omitted unless before the jury retires he demands its submission to the jury. As to an issue omitted without demand, the court may make an express finding or shall be deemed to have made a finding in accordance with the judgment.

(c) General verdict accompanied by answers to interrogatories. When the court requires the jury to return a general verdict, it may also require written answers to written interrogatories submitted to the jury upon one or more issues of fact. The court shall give sufficient instruction to enable the jury to render a general verdict and to answer the interrogatories. When the answers are consistent with each other but one or more is inconsistent with the general verdict, the court shall direct the entry of judgment in accordance with the answers, notwithstanding the general verdict, or it shall require the jury to further consider its answers and verdict or it shall order a new trial. When the answers are inconsistent with each other and one or more is inconsistent with the general verdict, the court shall require the jury to further consider its answers and verdict or it shall order a new trial.

RULE 4112. ENTRY OF VERDICT

When the jury renders a verdict, the clerk shall make an entry in his minutes specifying the time and place of the trial, the names of the jurors and witnesses, the general verdict and any answers to written interrogatories, or the questions and answers or other written findings constituting the special verdict and the direction, if any, which the court gives with respect to subsequent proceedings.

4113. DISAGREEMENT BY JURY

(a) Unanimous verdict not required. A verdict may be rendered by not less than five-sixths of the jurors constituting a jury.

(b) Procedure where jurors disagree. Where five-sixths of the jurors constituting a jury cannot agree after being kept together for as long as is deemed reasonable by the court, the court shall discharge the jury and direct a new trial before another jury.

Criminal Procedure Law

PART ONE—GENERAL PROVISIONS

Title A—Short Title, Applicability and Definitions

Article		Section
1.	Short Title, Applicability and Definitions................	1.00-1.20
2.	Peace Officers	2.10-2.30

Title B—The Criminal Courts

10.	The Criminal Courts................................	10.10-10.30

Title C—General Principles to Requirements for and Exemptions from Criminal Prosecution

20.	Geographical Jurisdiction of Offenses	20.10-20.60
30.	Timeliness of Prosecutions and Speedy Trial	30.10-30.30
40.	Exemption from Prosecution by Reason of Previous Prosecution.	40.10-40.40
50.	Compulsion of Evidence by Offer of Immunity	50.10-50.30

Title D—Rules of Evidence, Standards of Proof and Related Matters

60.	Rules of Evidence and Related Matters	60.10-60.70
70.	Standards of Proof	70.10-70.20

PART TWO—THE PRINCIPAL PROCEEDINGS

Title H—Preliminary Proceedings in Local Criminal Court

100.	Commencement of Action in Local Criminal Court—Local Criminal Court Accusatory Instruments	100.05-100.55
110.	Requiring Defendant's Appearance in Local Criminal Court for Arraignment......................................	110.10-110.20
120.	Warrant of Arrest...................................	120.10-120.90
130.	The Summons	130.10-130.60
140.	Arrest Without a Warrant	140.05-140.55
150.	The Appearance Ticket...............................	150.10-150.75
160.	Fingerprinting and Photographing of Defendant After Arrest—Criminal Identification Records and Statistics..............	160.10-160.60
170.	Proceedings upon Information, Simplified Traffic Information, Prosecutor's Information, and Misdemeanor Complaint from Arraignment to Plea	170.10-170.70
180.	Proceedings upon Felony Complaint from Arraignment Thereon Through Disposition Thereof.........................	180.10-180.80
185.	Alternate Method of Arraignment	185.10-185.40

Title I—Preliminary Proceedings in Superior Court

190.	The Grand Jury and Its Proceedings	190.05-190.90
195.	Waiver of Indictment	195.10-195.40
200.	Indictment and Related Instruments.....................	200.10-200.90
210.	Proceedings in Superior Court from Filing of Indictment to Plea.	210.05-210.50

Title J—Prosecution of Indictments in Superior Court—Plea to Sentence

220.	The Plea.	220.10-220.60
230.	Removal of Action	230.10-230.40
240.	Discovery.	240.10-240.90
250.	Pretrial Notices of Defenses	250.10-250.20
255.	Pretrial Motions	255.10-255.20
260.	Jury Trial—Generally	260.10-260.30
270.	Jury Trial—Formation and Conduct of Jury	270.05-270.50
280.	Jury Trial—Motion for a Mistrial	280.10-280.20
290.	Jury Trial—Trial Order of Dismissal	290.10
300.	Jury Trial—Court's Charge and Instructions to Jury	300.10-300.50
310.	Jury Trial—Deliberation and Verdict of Jury	310.10-310.85
320.	Waiver of Jury Trial and Conduct of Nonjury Trial	320.10-320.20
330.	Proceedings from Verdict to Sentence	330.10-330.50

Title K—Prosecution of Information in Local Criminal Courts—Plea to Sentence

340.	Pretrial Proceedings	340.10-340.50
350.	Nonjury Trials	350.10-350.20
360.	Jury Trial	360.05-360.55
370.	Proceedings from Verdict to Sentence	370.10

Title L—Sentence

380.	Sentencing in General	380.10-380.70
390.	Presentence Reports	390.10-390.60
400.	Presentence Proceedings	400.10-400.40
410.	Sentences of Probation and of Conditional Discharge	410.10-410.90
420.	Fines, Restitution and Reparation.	420.10-420.30
430.	Sentences of Imprisonment	430.10-430.30

Title M—Proceedings After Judgment

440.	Postjudgment Motions.	440.10-440.50
450.	Appeals—In What Cases Authorized and to What Courts Taken.	450.10-450.90
460.	Appeals—Taking and Perfection Thereof and Stays During Pendency Thereof.	460.10-460.80
470.	Appeals—Determination Thereof.	470.05-470.60

PART THREE—SPECIAL PROCEEDINGS AND MISCELLANEOUS PROCEDURES

Title P—Procedures for Securing Attendance at Criminal Actions and Proceedings of Defendants and Witnesses Under Control of Court—Recognizance, Bail, and Commitment

500.	Recognizance, Bail and Commitment—Definitions of Terms	500.10
510.	Recognizance, Bail and Commitment—Determination of Application for Recognizance or Bail, Issuance of Securing Orders, and Related Matters	510.10-510.50
520.	Bail and Bail Bonds	520.10-520.40
530.	Orders of Recognizance or Bail with Respect to Defendants in Criminal Actions and Proceedings—When and by What Courts Authorized	530.10-530.80
540.	Forfeiture of Bail and Remission Thereof	540.10-540.30

Title Q—Procedures for Securing Attendance at Criminal Actions and Proceedings of Defendants Not Securable by Conventional Means

550.	Securing Attendance of Defendants—In General	550.10
560.	Securing Attendance of Defendants Confined in Institutions Within the State	560.10
570.	Securing Attendance of Defendants Who are Outside the State, but Within the United States—Rendition to Other Jurisdictions of Defendants Within the State—Uniform Criminal Extradition Act	570.02-570.66

580. Securing Attendance of Defendants Confined as Prisoners in Institutions of Other Jurisdictions of the United States— Rendition to Other Jurisdictions of Persons Confined as Prisoners in this State—Agreement on Detainers 580.10-580.30

590. Securing Attendance of Defendants Who Are Outside the United States. 590.10

600. Securing Attendance of Corporate Defendants and Related Matters. 600.10-600.20

Title R—Procedures for Securing Attendance of Witnesses in Criminal Actions

610. Securing Attendance of Witnesses by Subpoena. 610.10-610.50

620. Securing Attendance of Witnesses by Material Witness Order. . . 620.10-620.80

630. Securing Attendance as Witnesses of Persons Confined in Institutions Within the State 630.10-630.20

640. Securing Attendance as Witnesses of Persons at Liberty Outside the State—Rendition to Other Jurisdictions of Witnesses at Liberty Within the State—Uniform Act to Secure Attendance of Witnesses from Without the State in Criminal Cases 640.10

650. Securing Attendance as Witnesses of Prisoners Confined in Institutions of Other Jurisdictions of the United States— Rendition to Other Jurisdictions of Prisoners Confined in Institutions Within the State 650.10-650.30

Title S—Procedures for Securing Testimony for Future Use and for Using Testimony Given in a Prior Proceeding

660. Securing Testimony for Use in a Subsequent Proceeding— Examination of Witnesses Conditionally 660.10-660.60

670. Use in a Criminal Proceeding of Testimony Given in a Previous Proceeding. 670.10-670.20

680. Securing Testimony Outside State for Use in Proceeding Within the State—Examination of Witnesses on Commission 680.10-680.80

Title T—Procedures for Securing Evidence by Means of Court Order and for Suppressing Evidence Unlawfully or Improperly Obtained

690. Search Warrants 690.05-690.55

700. Eavesdropping Warrants 700.05-700.70

710. Motion to Suppress Evidence 710.10-710.70

715. Destruction of Dangerous Drugs 715.10-715.50

Title U—Special Proceedings Which Replace, Suspend, or Abate Criminal Actions

720. Youthful Offender Procedure. 720.10-720.35

725. Removal of Proceeding Against Juvenile Offender to Family Court 725.00-725.20

730. Mental Disease or Defect Excluding Fitness to Proceed 730.10-730.70

SELECTED ARTICLES AND SECTIONS OF THE CRIMINAL PROCEDURE LAW

(Full text of the CPL along with notes, commentaries and amendments may be found in Volume 11A of McKinney's *Consolidated Laws of New York State*)

1.20 DEFINITIONS OF TERMS OF GENERAL USE IN THIS CHAPTER

Except where different meanings are expressly specified in subsequent provisions of this chapter, the term definitions contained in section 10.00 of the penal law are applicable to this chapter, and, in addition, the following terms have the following meanings:

1. "Accusatory instrument" means an indictment, information, a simplified information, a prosecutor's information, a superior court information, a misdemeanor complaint or a felony complaint. Every accusatory instrument, regardless of the person designated therein as accuser, constitutes an accusation on behalf of the state as plaintiff and must be entitled "the people of the state of New York" against a designated person, known as the defendant.

2. "Local criminal court accusatory instrument" means any accusatory instrument other than an indictment or a superior court information.

3. "Indictment" means a written accusation by a grand jury, more fully defined and described in article two hundred, filed with a superior court, which charges one or more defendants with the commission of one or more offenses, at least one of which is a crime, and which serves as a basis for prosecution thereof.

3-a. "Superior court information" means a written accusation by a district attorney more fully defined and described in articles one hundred ninety-five and two hundred, filed with a superior court pursuant to article one hundred ninety-five, which charges one or more defendants with the commission of one or more offenses, at least one of which is a crime, and which serves as a basis for prosecution thereof.

4. "Information" means a verified written accusation by a person, more fully defined and described in article one hundred, filed with a local criminal court, which charges one or more defendants with the commission of one or more offenses, none of which is a felony, and which may serve both to commence a criminal action and as a basis for prosecution thereof.

5. (a) "Simplified information" means a simplified traffic information, a simplified parks information, or a simplified environmental conservation information.

(b) "Simplified traffic information" means a written accusation by a police officer, or other public servant authorized by law to issue same, more fully defined and described in article one hundred, filed with a local criminal court, which, being in a brief or simplified form prescribed by the commissioner of motor vehicles, charges a person with one or more traffic infractions or misdemeanors relating to traffic, and which may serve both to commence a criminal action for such offense and as a basis for prosecution thereof.

(c) "Simplified parks information" means a written accusation by a police officer, or other public servant authorized by law to issue same, filed with a local criminal court, which, being in a brief or simplified form prescribed by the commissioner of parks and recreation, charges a person with one or more offenses, other than a felony, for which a uniform simplified parks information may be issued pursuant to the parks and recreation law and the navigation law, and which may serve both to commence a criminal action for such offense and as a basis for prosecution thereof.

(d) "Simplified environmental conservation information" means a written accusation by a police officer, or other public servant authorized by law to issue same, filed with a local criminal court, which being in a brief or simplified form prescribed by the commissioner of environmental conservation, charges a person with one or more offenses, other than a felony, for which a uniform simplified environmental conservation information may be issued pursuant to the environmental conservation law, and which may serve both to commence a criminal action for such offense and as a basis for prosecution thereof.

6. "Prosecutor's information" means a written accusation by a district attorney, more fully defined and described in article one hundred, filed with a local criminal court, which charges one or more defendants with the commission of one or more offenses, none of which is a felony, and which serves as a basis for prosecution thereof.

7. "Misdemeanor complaint" means a verified written accusation by a person, more fully defined and described in article one hundred, filed with a local criminal court, which charges one or more defendants with the commission of one or more offenses, at least one of which is a misdemeanor and none of which is a felony, and which serves to commence a criminal action but which may not, except upon the defendant's consent, serve as a basis for prosecution of the offenses charged therein.

8. "Felony complaint" means a verified written accusation by a person, more fully defined and described in article one hundred, filed with a local criminal court, which charges one or more defendants with the commission of one or more felonies and which serves to commence a criminal action but not as a basis for prosecution thereof.

9. "Arraignment" means the occasion upon which a defendant against whom an accusatory instrument has been filed appears before the court in which the criminal action is pending for the purpose of having such court acquire and exercise control over his person with respect to such accusatory instrument and of setting the course of further proceedings in the action.

10. "Plea," in addition to its ordinary meaning as prescribed in sections 220.10 and 340.20, means, where appropriate, the occasion upon which a defendant enters such a plea to an accusatory instrument.

11. "Trial." A jury trial commences with the selection of the jury and includes all further proceedings through the rendition of a verdict. A nonjury trial commences with the first opening address, if there be any, and, if not, when the first witness is sworn, and includes all further proceedings through the rendition of a verdict.

12. "Verdict" means the announcement by a jury in the case of a jury trial, or by the court in the case of a nonjury trial, of its decision upon the defendant's guilt or innocence of the charges submitted to or considered by it.

13. "Conviction" means the entry of a plea of guilty to, or a verdict of guilty upon, an accusatory instrument other than a felony complaint, or to one or more counts of such instrument.

14. "Sentence" means the imposition and entry of sentence upon a conviction.

15. "Judgment." A judgment is comprised of a conviction and the sentence imposed thereon and is completed by imposition and entry of the sentence.

16. "Criminal action." A criminal action (a) commences with the filing of an accusatory instrument against a defendant in a criminal court, as specified in subdivision seventeen; (b) includes the filing of all further accusatory instruments directly derived from the initial one, and all proceedings, orders and motions conducted or made by a criminal court in the course of disposing of any such accusatory instrument, or which, regardless of the court in which they occurred or were made, could properly be considered as a part of the record of the case by an appellate court upon an appeal from a judgment of conviction; and (c) terminates with the imposition of sentence or some other final disposition in a criminal court of the last accusatory instrument filed in the case.

17. "Commencement of criminal action." A criminal action is commenced by the filing of an accusatory instrument against a defendant in a criminal court, and, if more than one accusatory instrument is filed in the course of the action, it commences when the first of such instruments is filed.

18. "Criminal proceeding" means any proceeding which (a) constitutes a part of a criminal action or (b) occurs in a criminal court and is related to a prospective, pending or completed criminal action, either of this state or of any other jurisdiction, or involves a criminal investigation.

19. "Criminal court" means any court defined as such by section 10.10.

20. "Superior court" means any court defined as such by subdivision two of section 10.10.

21. "Local criminal court" means any court defined as such by subdivision three of section 10.10.

22. "Intermediate appellate court" means any court possessing appellate jurisdiction, other than the court of appeals.

23. "Judge" means any judicial officer who is a member of or constitutes a court, whether referred to in another provision of law as a justice or by any other title.

24. "Trial jurisdiction." A criminal court has "trial jurisdiction" of an offense when an indictment or an information charging such offense may properly be filed with such court, and when such court has authority to accept a plea to, to try or otherwise finally to dispose of such accusatory instrument.

25. "Preliminary jurisdiction." A criminal court has "preliminary jurisdiction" of an offense when, regardless of whether it has trial jurisdiction thereof, a criminal action for such offense may be commenced therein, and when such court may conduct proceedings with respect thereto which lead or may lead to prosecution and final disposition of the action in a court having trial jurisdiction thereof.

26. "Appearance ticket" means a written notice issued by a public servant, more fully defined in section 150.10, requiring a person to appear before a local criminal court in connection with an accusatory instrument to be filed against him therein.

27. "Summons" means a process of a local criminal court, more fully defined in section 130.10, requiring a defendant to appear before such court for the purpose of arraignment upon an accusatory instrument filed therewith by which a criminal action against him has been commenced.

28. "Warrant of arrest" means a process of a local criminal court, more fully defined in section 120.10, directing a police officer to arrest a defendant and to bring him before such court for the purpose of arraignment upon an accusatory instrument filed therewith by which a criminal action against him has been commenced.

29. "Superior court warrant of arrest" means a process of a superior court directing a police officer to arrest a defendant and to bring him before such court for the purpose of arraignment upon an indictment filed therewith by which a criminal action against him has been commenced.

30. "Bench warrant" means a process of a criminal court in which a criminal action is pending, directing a police officer, or a uniformed court officer, pursuant to paragraph b of subdivision two of section 530.70 of this section, to take into custody a defendant in such action who has previously been arraigned upon the accusatory instrument by which the action was commenced, and to bring him before such court. The function of a bench warrant is to achieve the court appearance of a defendant in a pending criminal action for some purpose other than his initial arraignment in the action.

31. "Prosecutor" means a district attorney or any other public servant who represents the people in a criminal action.

32. "District attorney" means a district attorney, an assistant district attorney or a special district attorney, and, where appropriate, the attorney general, an assistant attorney general, a deputy attorney general or a special deputy attorney general.

33. "Peace officer" means a person listed in section 2.10 of this section.

34. "Police officer." The following persons are police officers:

(a) A sworn officer of the division of state police;

(b) Sheriffs, under-sheriffs and deputy sheriffs of counties outside of New York City;

(c) A sworn officer of an authorized county or county parkway police department;

(d) A sworn officer of an authorized police department or force of a city, town, village or police district;

(e) A sworn officer of an authorized police department of an authority or a sworn officer of the state regional park police in the office of parks and recreation;

(f) A sworn officer of the capital police force of the office of general services;

(g) An investigator employed in the office of a district attorney;

(h) An investigator employed by a commission created by an interstate compact who is, to a substantial extent, engaged in the enforcement of the criminal laws of this state;

(i) The chief and deputy fire marshals, the supervising fire marshals and the fire marshals of the bureau of fire investigation of the New York City fire department;

(j) A sworn officer of the division of law enforcement in the department of environmental conservation;

(k) A sworn officer of a police force of a public authority created by an interstate compact;

(l) Long Island railroad police;

(m) An employee of the department of taxation and finance assigned to enforcement of the tax on cigarettes imposed by article twenty of the tax law by the commissioner of taxation and finance for the purpose of applying for and executing search warrants under article 690 of this chapter in connection with the enforcement of such tax on cigarettes.

(n) A special investigator employed in the statewide organized crime task force, while performing his assigned duties pursuant to section 70-a of the executive law.

34. "Geographical area of employment." The "geographical area of employment" of certain police officers is as follows:

(a) New York State constitutes the "geographical area of employment" of any police officer employed as such by an agency of the state or by an authority that functions throughout the state;

(b) A county, city, town or village, as the case may be, constitutes the "geographical area of employment" of any police officer employed as such by an agency of such political subdivision or by an authority which functions only in such political subdivision; and

(c) Where an authority functions in more than one county, the "geographical area of employment" of a police officer employed thereby extends through all of such counties.

35. "Commitment to the custody of the sheriff," when referring to an order of a court located in a county or city that has established a department of correction, means commitment to the commissioner of correction of such county or city.

36. "County" ordinarily means (a) any county outside of New York City or (b) New York City in its entirety. Unless the context requires a different construction, New York City, despite its five counties, is deemed a single county within the meaning of the provisions of this chapter in which that term appears.

37. "Lesser included offense." When it is impossible to commit a particular crime without concomitantly committing, by the same conduct, another offense of lesser grade or degree, the latter is, with respect to the former, a "lesser

included offense." In any case in which it is legally possible to attempt to commit a crime, an attempt to commit such crime constitutes a lesser included offense with respect thereto.

38. "Oath" includes an affirmation and every other mode authorized by law of attesting to the truth of that which is stated.

39. "Petty offense" means a violation or a traffic infraction.

40. "Evidence in chief" means evidence, received at a trial or other criminal proceeding in which a defendant's guilt or innocence of an offense is in issue, which may be considered as a part of the quantum of substantive proof establishing or tending to establish the commission of such offense or an element thereof or the defendant's connection therewith.

41. "Armed felony" means any violent felony offense defined in section 70.02 of the penal law that includes as an element either:

(a) possession, being armed with or causing serious physical injury by means of a deadly weapon, if the weapon is a loaded weapon from which a shot, readily capable of producing death or other serious physical injury may be discharged; or

(b) display of what appears to be a pistol, revolver, rifle, shotgun, machine gun or other firearm.

42. "Juvenile offender" means (1) a person, 13 years old, who is criminally responsible for acts constituting murder in the second degree as defined in subdivisions one and two of section 125.25 of the penal law and, (2) a person fourteen or fifteen years old who is criminally responsible for acts constituting the crimes defined in subdivisions one and two of section 125.25 (murder in the second degree) and in subdivision three of such section provided that the underlying crime for the murder charge is one for which such person is criminally responsible; section 135.25 (kidnapping in the first degree); 150.20 (arson in the first degree); subdivisions one and two of section 120.10 (assault in the first degree); 125.20 (manslaughter in the first degree); subdivisions one and two of section 130.35 (rape in the first degree); subdivisions one and two of section 130.50 (sodomy in the first degree); 130.70 (aggravated sexual abuse); 140.30 (burglary in the first degree); subdivision one of section 140.25 (burglary in the second degree); 150.15 (arson in the second degree); 160.15 (robbery in the first degree) or subdivision two of section 160.10 (robbery in the second degree) of the penal law; or defined in the penal law as an attempt to commit murder in the second degree or kidnapping in the first degree.

2.10 PERSONS DESIGNATED AS PEACE OFFICERS

Notwithstanding the provisions of any general, special or local law or charter to the contrary, only the following persons shall have the powers of, and shall be peace officers:

1. Constables or police constables of a town or village, provided such designation is not inconsistent with local law.

2. The sheriff, undersheriff and deputy sheriffs of New York City.

3. Investigators of the office of the state commission of investigation.

4. Employees of the department of taxation and finance assigned to enforcement of the tax on cigarettes imposed by article twenty of the tax law by the commissioner of taxation and finance.

5. Employees of the New York City department of finance assigned to enforcement of the tax on cigarettes imposed by title D of chapter forty-six of the administrative code of the city of New York by the commissioner of finance.

6. Confidential investigators and inspectors, as designated by the commissioner of the department of agriculture and markets, pursuant to rules of the department.

7. Officers or agents of a duly incorporated society for the prevention of cruelty to animals or children.

8. Inspectors and officers of the New York City department of health when acting pursuant to their special duties as set forth in section 564-11.0 of the administrative code of the city of New York; provided, however, that nothing in this subdivision shall be deemed to authorize such officer to carry, possess, repair or dispose of a firearm unless the appropriate license therefore has been issued pursuant to section 400.00 of the penal law.

9. Park rangers in Suffolk County who shall be authorized to issue simplified traffic information, simplified parks information and simplified environmental conservation information.

10. Broome County park rangers who shall be authorized to issue appearance tickets, simplified traffic information, simplified parks information, and simplified environmental conservation information; provided, however, that nothing in this subdivision shall be deemed to authorize such officer to carry, possess, repair or dispose of a firearm unless the appropriate license therefore has been issued pursuant to section 400.00 of the penal law.

11. Park rangers in Onondaga County who shall be authorized to issue appearance tickets, simplified traffic information, simplified parks information and simplified environmental conservation information within the county of Onondaga.

12. Special policemen designated by the commissioner and the directors of in-patient facilities in the office of mental health pursuant to section 7.25 of the mental hygiene law, and special policemen designated by the commissioner and

the directors of facilities under his jurisdiction in the office of mental retardation and developmental disabilities pursuant to section 13.25 of the mental hygiene law; provided, however, that nothing in this subdivision shall be deemed to authorize such officers to carry, possess, repair or dispose of a firearm unless the appropriate license therefore has been issued pursuant to section 400.00 of the penal law.

13. Persons designated as special policemen by the director of a hospital in the department of health pursuant to section four hundred fifty-five of the public health law; provided, however, that nothing in this subdivision shall be deemed to authorize such officer to carry, possess, repair or dispose of a firearm unless the appropriate license therefore has been issued pursuant to section 400.00 of the penal law.

14. Peace officers appointed by the state university pursuant to paragraph m of subdivision two of section three hundred fifty-five of the education law; provided, however, that nothing in this subdivision shall be deemed to authorize such officer to carry, possess, repair or dispose of a firearm unless the appropriate license therefore has been issued pursuant to section 400.00 of the penal law.

15. Uniformed enforcement forces of the New York State Thruway Authority, when acting pursuant to subdivision two of section three hundred sixty-one of the public authorities law; provided, however, that nothing in this subdivision shall be deemed to authorize such officer to carry, possess, repair or dispose of a firearm unless the appropriate license therefore has been issued pursuant to section 400.00 of the penal law.

16. Employees of the department of health designated pursuant to section thirty-three hundred eighty-five of the public health law; provided, however, that nothing in this subdivision shall be deemed to authorize such officer to carry, possess, repair or dispose of a firearm unless the appropriate license therefore has been issued pursuant to section 400.00 of the penal law.

17. Uniformed housing guards of the Buffalo municipal housing authority.

18. Bay constable of the city of Rye and bay constables of the towns of East Hampton, Hempstead, Oyster Bay, Southampton, Southold, Islip, Shelter Island, Brookhaven, Babylon and North Hempstead; provided, however, that nothing in this subdivision shall be deemed to authorize the bay constables in the city of Rye or the towns of Brookhaven, Babylon, East Hampton, Southold, Islip and Shelter Island to carry, possess, repair or dispose of a firearm unless the appropriate license therefore has been issued pursuant to section 400.00 of the penal law.

19. Harbor masters appointed by a county, city, town or village.

20. Bridge and tunnel officers, sergeants and lieutenants of the Triborough Bridge and Tunnel Authority.

21. (a) Uniformed court officers of the unified court system.

(b) Court clerks of the unified court system in the first and second departments.

(c) Marshal, deputy marshal, clerk or uniformed court officer of a district court.

(d) Marshals or deputy marshals of a city court, provided, however, that nothing in this subdivision shall be deemed to authorize such officer to carry, possess, repair or dispose of a firearm unless the appropriate license therefore has been issued pursuant to section 400.00 of the penal law.

22. Persons appointed as railroad policemen pursuant to section eighty-eight of the railroad law.

23. Parole officers or warrant officers in the division of parole.

24. Probation officers.

25. Officials, as designated by the commissioner of the department of correctional services pursuant to rules of the department, and correction officers of any state correctional facility or of any penal correctional institution.

26. Peace officers designated pursuant to the provisions of the New York State defense emergency act, as set forth in chapter 784 of the laws of 1951 as amended when acting pursuant to their special duties during a period of attack by enemy forces, or during official drills in preparation for an attack by enemy forces; provided, however, that nothing in this subdivision shall be deemed to authorize such officer to carry, possess, repair or dispose of a firearm unless the appropriate license therefore has been issued pursuant to section 400.00 of the penal law; and provided further, that such officer shall have the powers set forth in section 2.20 of this article only during a period of attack by enemy forces.

27. New York City special patrolmen appointed by the police commissioner pursuant to subdivision (c) or (e) of section 434a-7.0 of the administrative code of the city of New York; provided, however, that nothing in this subdivision shall be deemed to authorize such officer to carry, possess, repair or dispose of a firearm unless the appropriate license therefore has been issued pursuant to section 400.00 of the penal law and the employer has authorized such officer to possess a firearm during any phase of the officer's on-duty employment. Special patrolmen shall have the powers set forth in section 2.20 of this article only when they are acting pursuant to their special duties.

28. All officers and members of the uniformed force of the New York City fire department as set forth and subject to the limitations contained in section 487a-15.0 of the administrative code of the city of New York; provided, however,

that nothing in this subdivision shall be deemed to authorize such officer to carry, possess, repair, or dispose of a firearm unless the appropriate license therefore has been issued pursuant to section 400.00 of the penal law.

29. Special policemen for horse racing, appointed pursuant to the provisions of the pari-mutuel revenue law as set forth in chapter 254 of the laws of 1940, as amended; provided, however, that nothing in this subdivision shall be deemed to authorize such officer to carry, possess, repair or dispose of a firearm unless the appropriate license therefore leas been issued pursuant to section 400.00 of the penal Law.

30. Supervising fire inspectors, fire inspectors, the fire marshal and assistant fire marshals, all full-time employees of the county of Nassau fire marshal's office, when acting pursuant to their special duties in matters arising under the laws relating to fires, the extinguishment thereof and fire perils.

31. A district ranger, assistant district ranger or a forest ranger employed by the state department of environmental conservation.

32. Investigators of the department of motor vehicles, pursuant to 392-b of the vehicle and traffic law; provided, however, that nothing in this subdivision shall be deemed to authorize such officer to carry, possess, repair or dispose of a firearm unless the appropriate license therefore has been issued pursuant to section 400.00 of the penal law.

33. A city marshal of the city of New York who has received training in firearms handling from the Federal Bureau of Investigation or in the New York City police academy, or in the absence of the available training programs from the Federal Bureau of Investigation and the New York City police academy, from another law enforcement agency located in the state of New York, and who has received a firearms permit from the license division of the New York city police department.

34. Waterfront and airport investigators, pursuant to subdivision four of section ninety-nine hundred six of the unconsolidated laws; provided, however, that nothing in this subdivision shall be deemed to authorize such officer to carry, possess, repair or dispose of a firearm unless the appropriate license therefore has been issued pursuant to section 400.00 of the penal law.

35. Special investigators appointed by the state board of elections, pursuant to section 3-107 of the election law.

36. Investigators appointed by the state liquor authority, pursuant to section fifteen of the alcoholic beverage control law; provided, however, that nothing in this subdivision shall be deemed to authorize such officer to carry, possess, repair or dispose of a firearm unless the appropriate license therefore has been issued pursuant to section 400.00 of the penal law.

37. Special patrolmen of a political subdivision, appointed pursuant to 209-v of the general municipal law; provided, however, that nothing in this subdivision shall be deemed to authorize such officer to carry, possess, repair or dispose of a firearm unless the appropriate license therefore has been issued pursuant to section 400.00 of the penal law.

38. A special investigator of the New York City department of investigation who has received training in firearms handling in the New York police academy and has received a firearms permit from the license division of the New York City police department.

39. Broome County special patrolmen, appointed by the Broome County attorney; provided, however, that nothing in this subdivision shall be deemed to authorize such officer to carry, possess, repair or dispose of a firearm unless the appropriate license therefore has been issued pursuant to section 400.00 of the penal law.

40. Special officers employed by the city of New York or by the New York City Health and Hospitals Corporation; provided, however, that nothing in this subdivision shall be deemed to authorize such officer to carry, possess, repair or dispose of a firearm unless the appropriate license therefore has been issued pursuant to section 400.00 of the penal law.

41. Fire police squads organized pursuant to section 209-c of the general municipal law, at such times as the fire department, fire company or an emergency rescue and first aid squad of the fire department or fire company are on duty, or when, on orders of the chief of the fire department or fire company of which they are members, they are separately engaged in response to a call for assistance pursuant to the provisions of section 209 of the general municipal law; provided, however, that nothing in this subdivision shall be deemed to authorize such officer to carry, possess, repair or dispose of a firearm unless the appropriate license therefore has been issued pursuant to section 400.00 of the penal law.

42. Special deputy sheriffs appointed by the sheriff of a county within which any part of the grounds of Cornell University or the grounds of any state institution constituting a part of the educational and research plants owned or under the supervision, administration or control of said university are located pursuant to section 5709 of the education law; provided, however, that nothing in this subdivision shall be deemed to authorize such officer to carry, possess, repair or dispose of a firearm unless the appropriate license therefore has been issued pursuant to section 400.00 of the penal law.

43. Housing patrolmen of the Mount Vernon housing authority, acting pursuant to rules of the Mount Vernon housing authority; provided, however, that nothing in this subdivision shall be deemed to authorize such officer to carry,

possess, repair or dispose of a firearm unless the appropriate license therefore has been issued pursuant to section 400.00 of the penal law.

44. The officers, employees and members of the New York City division of fire prevention, in the bureau of fire, as set forth and subject to the limitations contained in subdivision one of section 487a-1.0 of the administrative code of the city of New York; provided, however, that nothing in this subdivision shall be deemed to authorize such officer to carry, possess, repair or dispose of a firearm unless the appropriate license therefore has been issued pursuant to section 400.00 of the penal law.

45. Persons appointed and designated as peace officers by the Niagara frontier transportation authority, pursuant to subdivision thirteen of section twelve hundred ninety nine-a of the public authorities law.

46. Persons appointed as peace officers by the Sea Gate Association pursuant to the provisions of chapter 391 of the laws of 1940, provided, however, that nothing in this subdivision shall be deemed to authorize such officer to carry, possess, repair or dispose of a firearm unless the appropriate license therefore has been issued pursuant to section 400.00 of the penal law.

47. Employees of the insurance frauds bureau of the state department of insurance when designated as peace officers by the superintendent of insurance and acting pursuant to their special duties; provided, however, that nothing in this subdivision shall be deemed to authorize such officer to carry, possess, repair or dispose of a firearm unless the appropriate license therefore has been issued pursuant to section 400.00 of the penal law.

10.10 THE CRIMINAL COURTS; ENUMERATION AND DEFINITIONS

1. The "criminal courts" of this state are comprised of the superior courts and the local criminal courts.

2. "Superior court" means:

(a) The supreme court; or

(b) A county court.

3. "Local criminal court" means:

(a) A district court; or

(b) The New York City criminal court; or

(c) A city court; or

(d) A town court; or

(e) A village court; or

(f) A supreme court justice sitting as a local criminal court; or

(g) A county judge sitting as a local criminal court.

4. "City court" means any court for a city, other than New York City, having trial jurisdiction of offenses of less than felony grade only committed within such city, whether such court is entitled a city court, a municipal court, a police court, a recorder's court or is known by any other name or title.

5. "Town court." A "town court" is comprised of all the town justices of a town.

6. "Village court." A "village court" is comprised of the justice of a village, or all the justices thereof if there be more than one, or, at a time when he or they are absent, an acting justice of a village who is authorized to perform the functions of a village justice during his absence.

7. Notwithstanding any other provision of this section, a court specified herein which possesses civil as well as criminal jurisdiction does not act as a criminal court when acting solely in the exercise of its civil jurisdiction, and an order or determination made by such court in its civil capacity is not an order or determination of a criminal court even though it may terminate or otherwise control or affect a criminal action or proceeding.

10.20 SUPERIOR COURTS; JURISDICTION

1. Superior courts have trial jurisdiction of all offenses. They have:

(a) Exclusive trial jurisdiction of felonies; and

(b) Trial jurisdiction of misdemeanors concurrent with that of the local criminal courts; and

(c) Trial jurisdiction of petty offenses, but only when such an offense is charged in an indictment which also charges a crime.

2. Superior courts have preliminary jurisdiction of all offenses, but they exercise such jurisdiction only by reason of and through the agency of their grand juries.

10.30 LOCAL CRIMINAL COURTS; JURISDICTION

1. Local criminal courts have trial jurisdiction of all offenses other than felonies. They have:

(a) Exclusive trial jurisdiction of petty offenses except for the superior court jurisdiction thereof prescribed in paragraph (c) of subdivision one of section 10.20; and

(b) Trial jurisdiction of misdemeanors concurrent with that of the superior courts but subject to divestiture thereof by the latter in any particular case.

2. Local criminal courts have preliminary jurisdiction of all offenses subject to divestiture thereof in any particular case by the superior courts and their grand juries.

3. Notwithstanding the provisions of subdivision one, a superior court judge sitting as a local criminal court does not have trial jurisdiction of any offense, but has preliminary jurisdiction only, as provided in subdivision two.

30.10 TIMELINESS OF PROSECUTIONS; PERIODS OF LIMITATION

1. A criminal action must be commenced within the period of limitation prescribed in the ensuing subdivisions of this section.

2. Except as otherwise provided in subdivision three:

(a) A prosecution for a class A felony may be commenced at any time;

(b) A prosecution for any other felony must be commenced within five years after the commission thereof;

(c) A prosecution for a misdemeanor must be commenced within two years after the commission thereof;

(d) A prosecution for a petty offense must be commenced within one year after the commission thereof.

3. Notwithstanding the provisions of subdivision two, the periods of limitation for the commencement of criminal actions are extended as follows in the indicated circumstances:

(a) A prosecution for larceny committed by a person in violation of a fiduciary duty may be commenced within one year after the facts constituting such offense are discovered or, in the exercise of reasonable diligence, should have been discovered by the aggrieved party or by a person under a legal duty to represent him who is not himself implicated in the commission of the offense.

(b) A prosecution for any offense involving misconduct in public office by a public servant may be commenced at any time during the defendant's service in such office or within five years after the termination of such service; provided however, that in no event shall the period of limitation be extended by more than five years beyond the period otherwise applicable under subdivision two.

(c) A prosecution for any crime set forth in section 27-0914 of the environmental conservation law may be commenced within two years after the facts constituting such crime are discovered or, in the exercise of reasonable diligence, should have been discovered by a public servant who has the responsibility to enforce the provisions of said section.

4. In calculating the time limitation applicable to commencement of a criminal action, the following periods shall not be included:

(a) Any period following the commission of the offense during which (i) the defendant was continuously outside this state, or (ii) the whereabouts of the defendant were continuously unknown and continuously unascertainable by the exercise of reasonable diligence. However, in no event shall the period of limitation be extended by more than five years beyond the period otherwise applicable under subdivision two.

(b) When a prosecution for an offense is lawfully commenced within the prescribed period of limitation therefore, and when an accusatory instrument upon which such prosecution is based is subsequently dismissed by an authorized court under directions or circumstances permitting the lodging of another charge for the same offense or an offense based on the same conduct, the period extending from the commencement of the thus defeated prosecution to the dismissal of the accusatory instrument does not constitute a part of the period of limitation applicable to commencement of prosecution by a new charge.

30.30 SPEEDY TRIAL; TIME LIMITATIONS

1. Except as otherwise provided in subdivision three, a motion made pursuant to paragraph (e) of subdivision one of section 170.30 or paragraph (g) of subdivision one of section 210.20 must be granted where the people are not ready for trial within:

(a) six months of the commencement of a criminal action wherein a defendant is accused of one or more offenses, at least one of which is a felony;

(b) ninety days of the commencement of a criminal action wherein a defendant is accused of one or more offenses, at least one of which is a misdemeanor punishable by a sentence of imprisonment of more than three months and none of which is a felony;

(c) sixty days of the commencement of a criminal action wherein the defendant is accused of one or more offenses, at least one of which is a misdemeanor punishable by a sentence of imprisonment of not more than three months and none of which is a crime punishable by a sentence of imprisonment of more than three months;

(d) thirty days of the commencement of a criminal action wherein the defendant is accused of one or more offenses, at least one of which is a violation and none of which is a crime.

2. Except as provided in subdivision three, where a defendant has been committed to the custody of the sheriff in a criminal action he must be released on bail or on his own recognizance, upon such conditions as may be just and reasonable, if the people are not ready for trial in that criminal action within:

(a) ninety days from the commencement of his commitment to the custody of the sheriff in a criminal action wherein the defendant is accused of one or more offenses, at least one of which is a felony;

(b) thirty days from the commencement of his commitment to the custody of the sheriff in a criminal action wherein the defendant is accused of one or more offenses, at least one of which is a misdemeanor punishable by a sentence of imprisonment of more than three months and none of which is a felony;

(c) fifteen days from the commencement of his commitment to the custody of the sheriff in a criminal action wherein the defendant is accused of one or more offenses, at least one of which is a misdemeanor punishable by a sentence of imprisonment of not more than three months and none of which is a crime punishable by a sentence of imprisonment of more than three months;

(d) five days from the commencement of his commitment to the custody of the sheriff in a criminal action wherein the defendant is accused of one or more offenses, at least one of which is a violation and none of which is a crime.

3. (a) Subdivisions one and two do not apply to a criminal action wherein the defendant is accused of an offense defined in sections 125.10, 125.15, 125.20, 125.25 and 125.27 of the penal law.

(b) A motion made pursuant to subdivisions one or two upon expiration of the specified period may be denied where the people are not ready for trial if the people were ready for trial prior to the expiration of the specified period and their present unreadiness is due to some exceptional fact or circumstance, including, but not limited to, the sudden unavailability of evidence material to the people's case, when the district attorney has exercised due diligence to obtain such evidence and there are reasonable grounds to believe that such evidence will become available in a reasonable period.

(c) A motion made pursuant to subdivision two shall not:

(i) apply to any defendant who is serving a term of imprisonment for another offense;

(ii) require the release from custody of any defendant who is also being held in custody pending trial of another criminal charge as to which the applicable period has not yet elapsed;

(iii) prevent the re-detention of or otherwise apply to any defendant who, after being released from custody pursuant to this section or otherwise, is charged with another crime or violates the conditions on which he has been released, by failing to appear at a judicial proceeding at which his presence is required or otherwise.

4. In computing the time within which the people must be ready for trial pursuant to subdivisions one and two, the following periods must be excluded:

(a) reasonable period of delay resulting from other proceedings concerning the defendant, including but not limited to proceedings for the determination of competency and the period during which defendant is incompetent to stand trial; demand to produce; pre-trial motions; appeals; trial of other charges; and the period during which such matters are under consideration by the court; or

(b) the period of delay resulting from a continuance granted by the court at the request of, or with the consent of, the defendant or his counsel. The court must grant such a continuance only if it is satisfied that postponement is in the interest of justice, taking into account the public interest in the prompt dispositions of criminal charges. A defendant without counsel must not be deemed to have consented to a continuance unless he has been advised by the court of his rights under these rules and the effect of his consent; or

(c) the period of delay resulting from the absence or unavailability of the defendant. A defendant must be considered absent whenever his location is unknown and he is attempting to avoid apprehension or prosecution, or his location cannot be determined by due diligence. A defendant must be considered unavailable whenever his location is known but his presence for trial cannot be obtained by due diligence; or

(d) a reasonable period of delay when the defendant is joined for trial with a codefendant as to whom the time for trial pursuant to this section has not run and good cause is not shown for granting a severance; or

(e) the period of delay resulting from detention of the defendant in another jurisdiction provided the district attorney is aware of such detention and has been diligent and has made reasonable efforts to obtain the presence of the defendant for trial; or

(f) the period during which the defendant is without counsel through no fault of the court; except when the defendant is proceeding as his own attorney with the permission of the court; or

(g) other periods of delay occasioned by exceptional circumstances, including but not limited to, the period of delay resulting from a continuance granted at the request of a district attorney if

(i) the continuance is granted because of the unavailability of evidence material to the people's case, when the district attorney has exercised due diligence to obtain such evidence and there are reasonable grounds to believe that such evidence will become available in a reasonable period; or

(ii) the continuance is granted to allow the district attorney additional time to prepare the people's case and additional time is justified by the exceptional circumstances of the case.

5. For purposes of this section,

(a) where the defendant is to be tried following the withdrawal of the plea of guilty or is to be retried following a mistrial, an order for a new trial or an appeal or collateral attack, the criminal action and the commitment to the custody of the sheriff, if any, must be deemed to have commenced on the date the withdrawal of the plea of guilty or the date the order occasioning a retrial becomes final;

(b) where a defendant has been served with an appearance ticket, the criminal action must be deemed to have commenced on the date such appearance ticket is returnable in a local criminal court;

(c) where a criminal action is commenced by the filing of a felony complaint, and thereafter, in the course of the same criminal action either the felony complaint is replaced with or converted to an information, prosecutor's information or misdemeanor complaint pursuant to article 180 or a prosecutor's information is filed pursuant to section 190.70, the period applicable for the purposes of subdivision one must be the period applicable to the charges in the new accusatory instrument, calculated from the date of the filing of such new accusatory instrument; provided, however, that when the aggregate of such period and the period of time, excluding the periods provided in subdivision four, already elapsed from the date of the filing of the felony complaint to the date of the filing of the new accusatory instrument exceeds six months, the period applicable to the charges in the felony complaint must remain applicable and continue as if the new accusatory instrument had not been filed;

(d) where a criminal action is commenced by the filing of a felony complaint, and thereafter, in the course of the same criminal action either the felony complaint is replaced with or converted to an information, prosecutor's information or misdemeanor complaint pursuant to article 180 or a prosecutor's information is filed pursuant to section 190.70, the period applicable for the purposes of subdivision two must be the period applicable to the charges in the new accusatory instrument, calculated from the date of the filing of such new accusatory instrument; provided, however, that when the aggregate of such period and the period of time, excluding the periods provided in subdivision four, already elapsed from the date of the filing of the felony complaint to the date of the filing of the new accusatory instrument exceeds ninety days, the period applicable to the charges in the felony complaint must remain applicable and continue as if the new accusatory instrument had not been filed.

6. The procedural rules prescribed in subdivisions one through seven of section 210.45 with respect to a motion to dismiss an indictment are also applicable to a motion made pursuant to subdivision two.

190.05 GRAND JURY; DEFINITION AND GENERAL FUNCTIONS

1. A grand jury is a body consisting of not less than sixteen nor more than twenty-three persons, impaneled by a superior court and constituting a part of such court, the functions of which are to hear and examine evidence concerning offenses and concerning misconduct, nonfeasance and neglect in public office, whether criminal or otherwise, and to take action with respect to such evidence as provided in section 190.60.

190.10 GRAND JURY; FOR WHAT COURTS DRAWN

1. The appellate division of each judicial department shall adopt rules governing the number and the terms for which grand juries shall be drawn and impaneled by the superior courts within its department; provided, however, that a grand jury may be drawn and impaneled for any extraordinary term of the supreme court upon the order of a justice assigned to hold such term.

190.15 GRAND JURY; DURATION OF TERM AND DISCHARGE

1. A term of a superior court for which a grand jury has been impaneled remains in existence at least until and including the opening date of the next term of such court for which a grand jury has been designated. Upon such date, or within five days preceding it, the court may, upon declaration of both the grand jury and the district attorney that such grand jury has not yet completed or will be unable to complete certain business before it, extend the term of court and the existence of such grand jury to a specified future date, and may subsequently order further extensions for such purpose.

2. At any time when a grand jury is in recess and no other appropriate grand jury is in existence in the county, the court may, upon application of the district attorney or of a defendant held by a local criminal court for the action of a grand jury, order such grand jury reconvened for the purpose of dealing with a matter requiring grand jury action.

190.20 GRAND JURY; FORMATION, ORGANIZATION AND OTHER MATTERS PRELIMINARY TO ASSUMPTION OF DUTIES

1. The mode of selecting grand jurors and of drawing and impaneling grand juries is governed by the judiciary law.

2. Neither the grand jury panel nor any individual grand juror may be challenged, but the court may:

(a) At any time before a grand jury is sworn, discharge the panel and summon another panel if it finds that the original panel does not substantially conform to the requirements of the judiciary law; or

(b) At any time after a grand juror is drawn, refuse to swear him, or discharge him after he has been sworn, upon a finding that he is disqualified from service pursuant to the judiciary law, or incapable of performing his duties because of bias or prejudice, or guilty of misconduct in the performance of his duties such as to impair the proper functioning of the grand jury.

3. After a grand jury has been impaneled, the court must appoint one of the grand jurors as foreman and another to act as foreman during any absence or disability of the foreman. At some time before commencement of their duties, the grand jurors must appoint one of their number as secretary to keep records material to the conduct of the grand jury's business.

4. The grand jurors must be sworn by the court. The oath may be in any form or language that requires the grand jurors to perform their duties faithfully.

5. After a grand jury has been sworn, the court must deliver or cause to be delivered to each grand juror a printed copy of all the provisions of this article, and the court may, in addition, give the grand jurors any oral instructions relating to the proper performance of their duties as it deems necessary or appropriate.

6. If two or more grand juries are impaneled at the same court term, the court may thereafter, for good cause, transfer grand jurors from one panel to another, and any grand juror so transferred is deemed to have been sworn as a member of the panel to which he has been transferred.

190.25 GRAND JURY; PROCEEDINGS AND OPERATION IN GENERAL

1. Proceedings of a grand jury are not valid unless at least sixteen of its members are present. The finding of an indictment, a direction to file a prosecutor's information, a decision to submit a grand jury report and every other affirmative official action or decision requires the concurrence of at least twelve members thereof.

2. The foreman or any other grand juror may administer an oath to any witness appearing before the grand jury.

3. During the deliberations and voting of a grand jury, only the grand jurors may be present in the grand jury room. During its other proceedings, the following persons, in addition to witnesses, may, as the occasion requires, also be present:

(a) The district attorney;

(b) A clerk or other public servant authorized to assist the grand jury in the administrative conduct of its proceedings;

(c) A stenographer authorized to record the proceedings of the grand jury;

(d) An interpreter. Upon request of the grand jury, the prosecutor must provide an interpreter to interpret the testimony of any witness who does not speak the English language well enough to be readily understood. Such interpreter must, if he has not previously taken the constitutional oath of office, first take an oath before the grand jury that he will faithfully interpret the testimony of the witness and that he will keep secret all matters before such grand jury within his knowledge;

(e) A public servant holding a witness in custody. When a person held in official custody is a witness before a grand jury, a public servant assigned to guard him during his grand jury appearance may accompany him in the grand jury room. Such public servant must, if he has not previously taken the constitutional oath of office, first take an oath before the grand jury that he will keep secret all matters before it within his knowledge.

(f) An attorney representing a witness pursuant to section 190.52 of this chapter while that witness is present.

4. (a) Grand jury proceedings are secret, and no grand juror, or other person specified in subdivision three of this section or section 215.70 of the penal law, may, except in the lawful discharge of his duties or upon written order of the court, disclose the nature or substance of any grand jury testimony, evidence, or any decision, result or other matter attending a grand jury proceeding. For the purpose of assisting the grand jury in conducting its investigation, evidence obtained by a grand jury may be independently examined by the district attorney, members of his staff, police officers specifically assigned to the investigation, and such other persons as the court may specifically authorize. Such evidence may not be disclosed to other persons without a court order. Nothing contained herein shall prohibit a witness from disclosing his own testimony.

(b) When a district attorney obtains evidence during a grand jury proceeding which provides reasonable cause to suspect that a child has been abused or maltreated, as those terms are defined by section ten hundred twelve of the family court act, he must apply to the court supervising the grand jury for an order permitting disclosure of such evidence to the state central register of child abuse and maltreatment. A district attorney need not apply to the court for such order if he has previously made or caused a report to be made to the state central register of child abuse and maltreatment pursuant to section four hundred thirteen of the social services law and the evidence obtained during the grand jury proceeding, or substantially similar information, was included in such report. The district attorney's application to the court shall be made ex parte and in camera. The court must grant the application and permit the district attorney to disclose the evidence to the state central register of child abuse and maltreatment unless the court finds that such disclosure would jeopardize the life or safety of any person or interfere with a continuing grand jury proceeding.

5. The grand jury is the exclusive judge of the facts with respect to any matter before it.

6. The legal advisors of the grand jury are the court and the district attorney, and the grand jury may not seek or receive legal advice from any other source. Where necessary or appropriate, the court or the district attorney, or both, must instruct the grand jury concerning the law with respect to its duties or any matter before it, and such instructions must be recorded in the minutes.

190.71 GRAND JURY; DIRECTION TO FILE REQUEST FOR REMOVAL TO FAMILY COURT

(a) Except as provided in subdivision six of section 200.20 of this chapter, a grand jury may not indict (i) a person thirteen years of age for any conduct or crime other than conduct constituting a crime defined in subdivisions one and two of section 125.25 (murder in the second degree); (ii) a person fourteen or fifteen years of age for any conduct or crime other than conduct constituting a crime defined in subdivisions one and two of section 125.25 (murder in the second degree) and in subdivision three of such section provided that the underlying crime for the murder charge is one for which such person is criminally responsible; 135.25 (kidnapping in the first degree); 150.20 (arson in the first degree); subdivisions one and two of section 120.10 (assault in the first degree); 125.20 (manslaughter in the first degree); subdivisions one and two of section 130.35 (rape in the first degree); subdivisions one and two of section 130.50 (sodomy in the first degree); 130.70 (aggravated sexual abuse); 140.30 (burglary in the first degree); subdivision one of section 140.25 (burglary in the second degree); 150.15 (arson in the second degree); 160.15 (robbery in the first degree); or subdivision two of section 160.10 (robbery in the second degree) of the penal law; or defined in the penal law as an attempt to commit murder in the second degree or kidnapping in the first degree.

(b) A grand jury may vote to file a request to remove a charge to the family court if it finds that a person thirteen, fourteen or fifteen years of age did an act which, if done by a person over the age of sixteen, would constitute a crime provided (1) such act is one for which it may not indict; (2) it does not indict such person for a crime; and (3) the evidence before it is legally sufficient to establish that such person did such act and competent and admissible evidence before it provides reasonable cause to believe that such person did such act.

(c) Upon voting to remove a charge to the family court pursuant to subdivision (b) of this section, the grand jury must through its foreman or acting foreman, file a request to transfer such charge to the family court. Such request shall be filed with the court by which it was impaneled. It must (1) allege that a person named therein did any act which, if done by a person over the age of sixteen, would constitute a crime; (2) specify the act and the time and place of its commission; and (3) be signed by the foreman or the acting foreman.

(d) Upon the filing of such grand jury request, the court must, unless such request is improper or insufficient on its face, issue an order approving such request and direct that the charge be removed to the family court in accordance with the provisions of article seven hundred twenty-five of this chapter.

190.95 GRAND JURY; GRAND JURY REPORTS

1. The grand jury may submit to the court by which it was impaneled, a report:

(a) Concerning misconduct, nonfeasance or neglect in public office by a public servant as the basis for a recommendation of removal or disciplinary action; or

(b) Stating that after investigation of a public servant it finds no misconduct, nonfeasance or neglect in office by him provided that such public servant has requested the submission of such report; or

(c) Proposing recommendations for legislative, executive or administrative action in the public interest based upon stated findings.

2. The court to which such report is submitted shall examine it and the minutes of the grand jury and, except as otherwise provided in subdivision four, shall make an order accepting and filing such report as a public record only if the court is satisfied that it complies with the provisions of subdivision one and that:

(a) The report is based upon facts revealed in the course of an investigation authorized by section 190.55 and is supported by the preponderance of the credible and legally admissible evidence; and

(b) When the report is submitted pursuant to paragraph (a) of subdivision one, that each person named therein was afforded an opportunity to testify before the grand jury prior to the filing of such report, and when the report is submitted pursuant to paragraph (b) or (c) of subdivision one, it is not critical of an identified or identifiable person.

3. The order accepting a report pursuant to paragraph (a) of subdivision one, and the report itself, must be sealed by the court and may not be filed as a public record, or be subject to subpoena or otherwise be made public until at least thirty-one days after a copy of the order and the report are served upon each public servant named therein, or if an appeal is taken pursuant to section 190.90, until the affirmance of the order accepting the report, or until reversal of the order sealing the report, or until dismissal of the appeal of the named public servant by the appellate division, whichever occurs later. Such public servant may file with the clerk of the court an answer to such report not later than twenty days after service of the order and report upon him. Such an answer shall plainly and concisely state the facts and law constituting the defense of the public servant to the charges in said report, and, except for those parts of the answer which the court may determine to be scandalously or prejudicially and unnecessarily inserted therein, shall become an appendix to the report. Upon the expiration of the time set forth in this subdivision, the district attorney shall deliver a true copy of such report, and the appendix if any, for appropriate action, to each public servant or body having removal or disciplinary authority over each public servant named therein.

4. Upon the submission of a report pursuant to subdivision one, if the court finds that the filing of such report as a public record may prejudice fair consideration of a pending criminal matter, it must order such report sealed and such report may not be subject to subpoena or public inspection during the pendency of such criminal matter, except upon order of the court.

5. Whenever the court to which a report is submitted pursuant to paragraph (a) of subdivision one is not satisfied that the report complies with the provisions of subdivision two, it may direct that additional testimony be taken before the same grand jury, or it must make an order sealing such report, and the report may not be filed as a public record, or be subject to subpoena or otherwise be made public.

PROSECUTION OF INDICTMENTS

260.10 JURY TRIAL; REQUIREMENT THEREOF

Except as otherwise provided in section 320.10, every trial of an indictment must be a jury trial.

260.20 JURY TRIAL; DEFENDANT'S PRESENCE AT TRIAL

A defendant must be personally present during the trial of an indictment; provided, however, that a defendant who conducts himself in so disorderly and disruptive a manner that his trial cannot be carried on with him in the courtroom may be removed from the courtroom if, after he has been warned by the court that he will be removed if he continues such conduct, he continues to engage in such conduct.

260.30 JURY TRIAL; IN WHAT ORDER TO PROCEED

The order of a jury trial, in general, is as follows:

1. The jury must be selected and sworn.

2. The court must deliver preliminary instructions to the jury.

3. The people must deliver an opening address to the jury.

4. The defendant may deliver an opening address to the jury.

5. The people must offer evidence in support of the indictment.

6. The defendant may offer evidence in his defense.

7. The people may offer evidence in rebuttal of the defense evidence, and the defendant may then offer evidence in rebuttal of the people's rebuttal evidence. The court may in its discretion permit the parties to offer further rebuttal or surrebuttal evidence in this pattern. In the interest of justice, the court may permit either party to offer evidence upon rebuttal which is not technically of a rebuttal nature but more properly a part of the offering party's original case.

8. At the conclusion of the evidence, the defendant may deliver a summation to the jury.

9. The people may then deliver a summation to the jury.

10. The court must then deliver a charge to the jury.

11. The jury must then retire to deliberate and, if possible, render a verdict.

270.05 TRIAL JURY; FORMATION IN GENERAL

1. A trial jury consists of twelve jurors, but "alternate jurors" may be selected and sworn pursuant to section 270.30.

2. The panel from which the jury is drawn is formed and selected as prescribed in the judiciary law. The first twelve members of the panel returned for the term who appear as their names are drawn and called, and who are not excluded as prescribed by this article, must be sworn and thereupon constitute the trial jury.

270.50 TRIAL JURY; VIEWING OF PREMISES

1. When the court is of the opinion that a viewing or observation by the jury of the premises or place where an offense on trial was allegedly committed, or of any other premises or place involved in the case, will be helpful to the jury in determining any material factual issue, it may in its discretion, at any time before the commencement of the summations, order that the jury be conducted to such premises or place for such purpose in accordance with the provisions of this section.

2. In such case, the jury must be kept together throughout under the supervision of an appropriate public servant or servants appointed by the court, and the court itself must be present throughout. The prosecutor, the defendant and counsel for the defendant may, as a matter of right, be present throughout, but such right may be waived.

3. The purpose of such an inspection is solely to permit visual observation by the jury of the premises or place in question, and neither the court, the parties, counsel nor the jurors may engage in discussion or argumentation concerning the significance or implications of anything under observation or concerning any issue in the case.

310.10 JURY DELIBERATION; REQUIREMENT OF; WHERE CONDUCTED

Following the court's charge, the jury must retire to deliberate upon its verdict in a place outside the courtroom. It must be provided with suitable accommodations therefore and must be continuously kept together under the supervision of a court officer or court officers. In the event such court officer or court officers are not available, the jury shall be under the supervision of an appropriate public servant or public servants. Except when so authorized by the court or when performing administerial duties with respect to the jurors, such court officers or public servants, as the case may be, may not speak to or communicate with them or permit any other person to do so.

310.20 JURY DELIBERATION; USE OF EXHIBITS AND OTHER MATERIAL

Upon retiring to deliberate, the jurors may take with them:

1. Any exhibits received in evidence at the trial which the court, after according the parties an opportunity to be heard upon the matter, in its discretion permits them to take; and

2. A written list prepared by the court containing the offenses submitted to the jury by the court in its charge and the possible verdicts thereon.

310.30 JURY DELIBERATION; REQUEST FOR INFORMATION

At any time during its deliberation, the jury may request the court for further instruction or information with respect to the law, with respect to the content or substance of any trial evidence, or with respect to any other matter pertinent to the jury's consideration of the case. Upon such a request, the court must direct that the jury be returned to the courtroom and, after notice to both the people and counsel for the defendant, and in the presence of the defendant, must give such requested information or instruction as the court deems proper. With the consent of the parties and upon the request of the jury for further instruction with respect to a statute, the court may also give to the jury copies of the text of any statute which, in its discretion, the court deems proper.

PROSECUTION OF INFORMATION

ARTICLE 350—NONJURY TRIALS

350.10 CONDUCT OF SINGLE JUDGE TRIAL

1. A single judge trial of an information in a local criminal court must be conducted pursuant to this section.

2. The court, in addition to determining all questions of law, is the exclusive trier of all issues of fact and must render a verdict.

3. The order of the trial must be as follows:

(a) The court may in its discretion permit the parties to deliver opening addresses. If the court grants such permission to one party, it must grant it to the other also. If both parties deliver opening addresses, the people's address must be delivered first.

(b) The order in which evidence must or may be offered by the respective parties is the same as that applicable to a jury trial of an indictment as prescribed in subdivisions five, six and seven of section 260.30.

(c) The court may in its discretion permit the parties to deliver summations. If the court grants such permission to one party, it must grant permission to the other also. If both parties deliver summations, the defendant's summation must be delivered first.

(d) The court must then consider the case and render a verdict.

4. The provisions governing motion practice and general procedure with respect to a jury trial of an indictment are, wherever appropriate, applicable to a non-jury trial of an information.

5. If the information contains more than one count, the court must render a verdict upon each count not previously dismissed or must otherwise state upon the record its disposition of each such count. A verdict which does not so dispose of each count constitutes a verdict of not guilty with respect to each count that is undisposed.

6. In rendering a verdict of guilty upon a count charging a misdemeanor, the court may find the defendant guilty of such misdemeanor, if it is established by legally sufficient trial evidence, or guilty of any lesser included offense which is established by legally sufficient trial evidence.

350.20 TRIAL BY JUDICIAL HEARING OFFICER

1. Notwithstanding any provision of section 350.10 of this article, in any case where a single judge trial of an information in a local criminal court is authorized or required, the court may, upon agreement of the parties, assign a judicial hearing officer to conduct the trial. Where such assignment is made, the judicial hearing officer shall entertain the case in the same manner as a court and shall:

(a) determine all questions of law;

(b) act as the exclusive trier of all issues of fact; and

(c) render a verdict.

2. In the discharge of this responsibility, the judicial hearing officer shall have the same powers as a judge of the court in which the proceeding is pending. The rules of evidence shall be applicable at a trial conducted by a judicial hearing officer.

3. Any action taken by a judicial hearing officer in the conduct of a trial shall be deemed the action of the court in which the proceeding is pending.

4. This section shall not apply where the single judge trial is of an information at least one count of which charges a class A misdemeanor.

360.10 TRIAL JURY; FORMATION IN GENERAL

1. A trial jury consists of six jurors, but "alternate jurors" may be selected and sworn pursuant to section 360.35.

2. The panel from which the jury is drawn is formed and selected as prescribed in the uniform district court act, uniform city court act, and uniform justice court act. In the New York City criminal court, the panel from which the jury is drawn is formed and selected in the same manner as is prescribed for the formation and selection of a panel in the supreme court in counties within cities having a population of one million or more.

360.40 TRIAL JURY; CONDUCT OF JURY TRIAL IN GENERAL

A jury trial of an information must be conducted generally in the same manner as a jury trial of an indictment, and the rules governing preliminary instructions by the court, supervision of the jury, motion practice and other procedural matters involved in the conduct of a jury trial of an indictment are, where appropriate, applicable to the conduct of a jury trial of an information.

360.55 DELIBERATION AND VERDICT OF JURY

The provisions of article three hundred ten, governing the deliberation and verdict of a jury upon a jury trial of an indictment in a superior court, are applicable to a jury trial of an information in a local criminal court.

380.20 SENTENCE REQUIRED

The court must pronounce sentence in every case where a conviction is entered. If an accusatory instrument contains multiple counts and a conviction is entered on more than one count the court must pronounce sentence on each count.

380.30 TIME FOR PRONOUNCING SENTENCE

1. In general, sentence must be pronounced without unreasonable delay.

2. Court to fix time. Upon entering a conviction the court must:

(a) Fix a date for pronouncing sentence; or

(b) Fix a date for one of the pre-sentence proceedings specified in article four hundred; or

(c) Pronounce sentence on the date the conviction is entered in accordance with the provisions of subdivision three.

3. Sentence on date of conviction. The court may sentence the defendant at the time the conviction is entered if:

(a) A pre-sentence report or a fingerprint report is not required; or

(b) Where any such report is required, the report has been received.

Provided, however, that the court may not pronounce sentence at such time without inquiring as to whether an adjournment is desired by the defendant. Where an adjournment is requested, the defendant must state the purpose thereof and the court may, in its discretion, allow a reasonable time.

4. Time for pre-sentence proceedings. The court may conduct one or more of the pre-sentence proceedings specified in article four hundred at any time before sentence is pronounced. Notice of any such proceeding issued after the date for pronouncing sentence has been fixed automatically adjourns the date for pronouncing sentence. In such case the court must fix a date for pronouncing sentence at the conclusion of such proceeding.

380.40 DEFENDANT'S PRESENCE AT SENTENCING

1. In general, the defendant must be personally present at the time sentence is pronounced.

2. Exception. Where sentence is to be pronounced for a misdemeanor or for a petty offense, the court may, on motion of the defendant, dispense with the requirement that the defendant be personally present. Any such motion must be accompanied by a waiver, signed and acknowledged by the defendant, reciting the maximum sentence that may be imposed for the offense and stating that the defendant waives the right to be personally present at the time sentence is pronounced.

3. Corporations. Sentence may be pronounced against a corporation in the absence of counsel if counsel fails to appear on the date of sentence after reasonable notice thereof.

380.50 STATEMENTS AT TIME OF SENTENCE

At the time of pronouncing sentence, the court must accord the prosecutor an opportunity to make a statement with respect to any matter relevant to the question of sentence. The court must then accord counsel for the defendant an opportunity to speak on behalf of the defendant. The defendant also has the right to make a statement personally in his own behalf, and before pronouncing sentence the court must ask him whether he wishes to make such a statement.

The court may, either before or after receiving such statements, summarize the factors it considers relevant for the purpose of sentence and afford an opportunity to the defendant or his counsel to comment thereon.

380.60 AUTHORITY FOR THE EXECUTION OF SENTENCE

Except where a sentence of death is pronounced, a certificate of conviction showing the sentence pronounced by the court, or a certified copy thereof, constitutes the authority for execution of the sentence and serves as the order of commitment, and no other warrant, order of commitment or authority is necessary to justify or to require execution of the sentence.

380.70 MINUTES OF SENTENCE

In any case where a person receives an indeterminate sentence of imprisonment or a reformatory or alternative local reformatory sentence of imprisonment, a certified copy of the stenographic minutes of the sentencing proceeding must be delivered to the person in charge of the institution to which the defendant has been delivered within thirty days from the date such sentence was imposed; provided, however, that a sentence or commitment is not defective by reason of a failure to comply with the provisions of this section.

Judiciary Court Acts

FAMILY COURT ACT

Article		Section
1.	Family court established	111
	Part	
	1. Applicability of act and creation of court	111
	2. Number, appointment, term and compensation of judges within the city of New York	121
	3. Number, election, term and compensation of judges not within the city of New York	131
	4. Family court judges	141
	5. General powers	151
	6. General provisions concerning hearings	161
	7. Proceeding in counties other than original county	171
2.	Administration, medical examinations, law guardians, auxiliary services	211
	Part	
	1. Administration	211
	2. Support bureau; duties to cooperate	221
	3. Medical examinations and treatment	231
	4. Law guardians	241
	5. Auxiliary services	251
	6. Counsel for indigent adults in family court proceedings	261
3.	Juvenile delinquency	301.1
	Part	
	1. Jurisdiction and preliminary procedures	301.1
	2. Initial appearance and probable cause hearing	320.1
	3. Discovery	330.1
	4. The fact-finding hearing	340.1
	5. The dispositional hearing	350.1
	6. Post-dispositional procedures	360.1
	7. Security testimony and records	370.1
	8. General provisions	380.1
4.	Support proceedings	411
	Part	
	1. Jurisdiction and duties of support	411
	2. Venue and preliminary procedure	421
	3. Hearing	431
	4. Orders	441
	5. Compliance with orders	451
	6. Effect of action for separation, divorce or annulment	461
	7. Undertaking	471
5.	Paternity proceedings	511
	Part	
	1. Jurisdiction and duties to support	511
	2. Venue and preliminary procedure	521
	3. Hearings	531

4.	Orders	541
5.	Related proceedings	561
5-A.	Special provisions relating to enforcement of support and establishment of paternity	571
6.	Permanent termination of parental rights, adoption, guardianship and custody	611

Part

1.	Permanent termination of parental custody by reason of permanent neglect	611
2.	Adoption	641
3.	Custody	651
4.	Guardianship	661
5.	Warrant	671
7.	Proceedings concerning whether a person is in need of supervision	711

Part

1.	Jurisdiction	711
2.	Custody and detention	721
3.	Preliminary procedure	731
4.	Hearings	741
5.	Orders	751
6.	New hearing and reconsideration of orders	761
7.	Compliance with orders	771
8.	Effect of proceedings	781
8.	Family offenses proceedings	811

Part

1.	Jurisdiction	811
2.	Preliminary procedure	821
3.	Hearing	831
4.	Orders	841
9.	Conciliation proceedings	911

Part

1.	Purpose and jurisdiction	911
2.	Procedure	921
10.	Child protective proceedings	1011

Part

1.	Jurisdiction	1011
2.	Temporary removal and preliminary orders	1021
3.	Preliminary procedure	1031
4.	Hearings	1041
5.	Orders	1051
6.	New hearing and reconsideration of orders	1061
7.	Compliance with orders	1071
11.	Appeals	1111
12.	Separability	1211

SELECTED ARTICLES AND SECTIONS OF THE FAMILY COURT ACT OF THE JUDICIARY COURT ACTS

(Full text of the Family Court Act along with notes, commentaries, and amendments may be found in Volume 29A-Part 1 of McKinney's *Consolidated Laws of New York State*)

117. PARTS OF COURT

(a) There is hereby established in the family court a "child abuse part." Such part shall be held separate from all other proceedings of the court, and shall have jurisdiction over all proceedings in the family court involving abused children, and shall be charged with the immediate protection of these children. All cases involving abuse shall be originated in or be transferred to this part from other parts as they are made known to the court unless there is or was before the court a proceeding involving any members of the same family or household, in which event the Judge who heard said proceeding may hear the case involving abuse. Consistent with its primary purpose, nothing in this section is intended to prevent the child abuse part from hearing other cases.

(b) For every juvenile delinquency proceeding under article three involving an allegation of an act committed by a person which, if done by an adult, would be a crime (i) defined in sections 125.27 (murder in the first degree); 125.25 (murder in the second degree); 135.25 (kidnapping in the first degree); or 150.20 (arson in the first degree) of the penal law committed by a person thirteen, fourteen or fifteen years of age; (ii) defined in sections 120.10 (assault in the first degree); 125.20 (manslaughter in the first degree); 130.25 (rape in the first degree); 130.50 (sodomy in the first degree); 135.20 (kidnapping in the second degree), but only where the abduction involved the use or threat of use of deadly physical force; 150.15 (arson in the second degree); or 160.15 (robbery in the first degree) of the penal law committed by a person thirteen, fourteen, or fifteen years of age; (iii) defined in the penal law as an attempt to commit murder in the first or second degree or kidnapping in the first degree committed by a person thirteen, fourteen or fifteen years of age; (iv) defined in section 140.30 (burglary in the first degree); subdivision one of section 140.25 (burglary in the second degree); or subdivision two of section 160.10 (robbery in the second degree) of the penal law committed by a person fourteen or fifteen years of age; (v) defined in section 120.05 (assault in the second degree) or 160.10 (robbery in the second degree) of the penal law committed by a person fourteen or fifteen years of age but only where there has been a prior finding by a court that such person has previously committed an act which, if committed by an adult, would be the crime of assault in the second degree, robbery in the second degree or any designated felony act specified in clause (i), (ii), or (iii) of this subdivision regardless of the age of such person at the time of the commission of the prior act; or (vi) other than a misdemeanor, committed by a person at least seven but less than sixteen years of age, but only where there have been two prior findings by the court that such person has committed a prior act which, if committed by an adult would be a felony:

> (i) There is hereby established in the family court in the city of New York at least one "designated felony act part." Such part or parts shall be held separate from all other proceedings of the court, and shall have jurisdiction over all proceedings involving such an allegation. All such proceedings shall be originated in or be transferred to this part from other parts as they are made known to the court.

> (ii) Outside the city of New York, all proceedings involving such an allegation shall have a hearing preference over every other proceeding in the court, except proceedings under article ten.

(c) The appellate division of the supreme court in each department may provide, in accordance with the standards and policies established by the administrative board of the judicial conference, that the family court in counties within its department shall or may be organized into such other parts, if any, as may be appropriate.

153. SUBPOENA, WARRANT AND OTHER PROCESS TO COMPEL ATTENDANCE

The family court may issue a subpoena or in a proper case a warrant or other process to secure or compel the attendance of an adult respondent or child or any other person whose testimony or presence at a hearing or proceeding is deemed by the court to be necessary, and to admit to, fix or accept bail, or parole him pending the completion of the hearing or proceeding. The court is also authorized to issue a subpoena *duces tecum* in accordance with the applicable provisions of the civil practice act and, upon its effective date, in accordance with the applicable provisions of the CPLR.

153-A. WARRANT OF ARREST; WHEN AND HOW EXECUTED

(a) A warrant of arrest may be executed on any day of the week and at any hour of the day or night.

(b) Unless encountering physical resistance, flight or other factors rendering normal procedure impractical, the arresting police officer must inform the subject named therein that a warrant for his arrest for attendance at the proceeding designated therein has been issued. Upon request of such subject, the police officer must show him the warrant if he has it in his possession. The officer need not have the warrant in his possession, and, if he does not, he must show it to the subject upon request as soon after the arrest as possible.

(c) In order to effect the arrest, the police officer may use such physical force as is justifiable pursuant to section 35.30 of the penal law.

(d) In order to effect the arrest, the police officer may enter any premises in which he reasonably believes the subject named therein to be present. Before such entry, he must give, or make reasonable effort to give, notice of his authority and purpose to an occupant thereof.

(e) If the officer, after giving such notice, is not admitted, he may enter such premises, and by a breaking if necessary.

153-B. SERVICE OF PROCESS REQUEST FOR ORDER OF PROTECTION

Whenever a petitioner requests an order of protection or temporary order of protection under any article of this act:

(a) the summons and the petition and, if one has been issued, the temporary order of protection, or a copy or copies thereof, may be served on any day of the week, and at any hour of the day or night;

(b) a peace officer, acting pursuant to his special duties, or a police officer may serve the summons and the petition and, if one has been issued, the temporary order of protection.

153-C. TEMPORARY ORDER OF PROTECTION

Any person appearing at family court when the court is open requesting a temporary order of protection under any article of this act shall be entitled to file a petition without delay on the same day such person first appears at the family court, and a hearing on that request shall be held on the same day or the next day that the family court is open following the filing of such petition.

154. STATE-WIDE PROCESS

(a) The family court may send process or other mandates in any matter in which it has jurisdiction into any county of the state for service or execution in like manner and with the same force and effect as similar process or mandates of county courts as provided by law.

(b) In a proceeding to establish paternity or to seek support, the court may send process without the state in the same manner and with the same effect as process sent within the state in the exercise of personal jurisdiction over any person, subject to the jurisdiction of the court under section three hundred one or three hundred two of the civil practice law and rule, notwithstanding that such person is not a resident or domiciliary of the state where:

> (1) the child was conceived in this state and the person over whom jurisdiction is sought is a parent or an alleged or probable parent of the child; or

> (2) the child resides in the state as a result of the acts or directives of the person over whom jurisdiction is sought; or

> (3) the person over whom jurisdiction is sought has resided with the child in this state; or

> (4) the person has acknowledged paternity, in writing, or has furnished support for the child while either such person or the child resided in the state; or

> (5) the person has filed with the putative father registry maintained by the state department of social services; or

> (6) there is any basis consistent with the constitutions of this state or the United States for the exercise of personal jurisdiction.

154-A. SERVICE OF PETITION

In every proceeding in family court, a copy of the petition filed therein shall be served upon the respondent at the time of service of process or, if that is not practicable, at the first court appearance by respondent.

155. ARRESTED ADULT

1. If an adult respondent is arrested under this act when the family court is not in session, he shall be taken to the most accessible magistrate and arraigned before him. The production of a warrant issued by the family court, a certificate of warrant, a copy or a certificate of order of protection or an order of protection or of temporary order of protection shall be evidence of the filing of a proper information or petition, and the magistrate shall thereupon hold such respondent, admit to, fix or accept bail, or parole him for hearing before the family court. Subject to the complainant's right of election under section 812 or 847 of this chapter to initiate a proceeding in criminal court, all subsequent proceedings shall be held in the family court.

2. If no warrant, order of protection or temporary order of protection has been issued by the family court, whether or not an information or petition has been filed, and an act alleged to be a family offense as defined in section 812 of this act is the basis of an arrest, the magistrate shall permit the complainant to file a petition, information or accusatory instrument and for good cause shown, shall thereupon hold such respondent, admit to, fix or accept bail, or parole such respondent for hearing before the family court or appropriate criminal court as the complainant shall choose in accordance with the provisions of section 812 of this act.

155-A. ADMISSION TO BAIL

A desk officer in charge at a police station, county jail or police headquarters, or any of his superior officers, may, in such place, take cash bail for his appearance before the family court the next morning from any person arrested pursuant to a warrant issued by the family court; provided that such arrest occurs between eleven o'clock in the morning and eight o'clock the next morning, except that in the city of New York bail shall be taken between two o'clock in the afternoon and eight o'clock the next morning. The amount of such cash bail shall be the amount fixed in the warrant of arrest.

Article 3—Juvenile Delinquency

301.2 DEFINITIONS

As used in this article, the following terms shall have the following meanings:

1. "Juvenile delinquent" means a person over seven and less than sixteen years of age, who, having committed an act that would constitute a crime if committed by an adult, (a) is not criminally responsible for such conduct by reason of infancy, or (b) is the defendant in an action ordered removed from a criminal court to the family court pursuant to article 725 of the criminal procedure law.

2. "Respondent" means the person against whom a juvenile delinquency petition is filed pursuant to section 310.1 provided, however, that any act of the respondent required or authorized under this article may be performed by his attorney or law guardian unless expressly provided otherwise.

3. "Detention" means the temporary care and maintenance away from their own homes of children held pursuant to this article, or held pending a hearing for alleged violation of the conditions of release from a school or center of the division for youth, or held pending return to a jurisdiction other than the one in which the child is held, or held pursuant to a securing order of a criminal court if the person named therein as principal is under sixteen years of age.

4. "Secure detention facility" means a facility characterized by physically restricting construction, hardware and procedures.

5. "Non-secure detention facility" means a facility characterized by the absence of physically restricting construction, hardware and procedures.

6. "Fact-finding hearing" means a hearing to determine whether the respondent or respondents committed the crime or crimes alleged in the petition or petitions.

7. "Dispositional hearing" means a hearing to determine whether the respondent requires supervision, treatment or confinement.

8. "Designated felony act" means an act which, if done by an adult, would be a crime: (i) defined in sections 125.27 (murder in the first degree); 125.25 (murder in the second degree); 135.25 (kidnapping in the first degree); or 150.20 (arson in the first degree) of the penal law committed by a person thirteen, fourteen, or fifteen years of age; (ii) defined in sections 120.10 (assault in the first degree); 125.20 (manslaughter in the first degree); 130.35 (rape in the first degree); 130.50 (sodomy in the first degree); 130.70 (aggregated sexual abuse); 135.20 (kidnapping in the second degree) but only where the abduction involved the use or threat of use of deadly physical force; 150.15 (arson in the second degree) or 160.15 (robbery in the first degree) of the penal law committed by a person thirteen, fourteen or fifteen years of age; (iii) defined in the penal law as an attempt to commit murder in the first or second degree or kidnapping in the first degree committed by a person thirteen, fourteen or fifteen years of age; (iv) defined in section 140.30 (burglary in the first degree); subdivision one of section 140.25 (burglary in the second degree); or subdivision two of section 160.10 (robbery in the second degree) of the penal law committed by a person fourteen or fifteen years of age: (v) defined in section 120.05 (assault in the second degree) or 160.10 (robbery in the second degree) of the penal law committed by a person fourteen or fifteen years of age but only where there has been a prior finding by a court that such person has previously committed an act which, if committed by an adult, would be the crime of assault in the second degree, robbery in the second degree or any designated felony act specified in paragraph (i), (ii), or (iii) of this subdivision regardless of the age of such person at the time of the commission of the prior act; or (vi) other than a misdemeanor committed by a person at least seven but less than sixteen years of age, but only where there have been two prior findings by the court that such person has committed a prior felony.

9. "Designated Class A felony act" means a designated felony act defined in paragraph (i) of subdivision eight.

10. "Secure facility" means a residential facility in which the respondent may be placed under this article, which is characterized by physically restricting construction, hardware and procedures, and is designated as a secure facility by the division for youth.

11. "Restrictive placement" means a placement pursuant to section 353.5.

12. "Presentment agency" means the agency or authority which, pursuant to section two hundred fifty-four or two hundred fifty-four-a, is responsible for presenting a juvenile delinquency petition.

13. "Incapacitated person" means a respondent who, as a result of mental illness, mental retardation or developmental disability as defined in subdivisions twenty, twenty-one and twenty-two of section 1.03 of the mental hygiene law, lacks capacity to understand the proceedings against him or to assist in his own defense.

14. Any reference in this article to the commission of a crime includes any act which, if done by an adult, would constitute a crime.

301.4. SEPARABILITY CLAUSE

If any clause, sentence, paragraph, section or part of this article shall be adjudged by any court of competent jurisdiction to be invalid, such judgment shall not affect, impair, or invalidate the remainder thereof, but shall be confined in its operation to the clause, sentence, paragraph, section or part thereof directly involved in the controversy in which such judgment shall have been rendered.

302.1. JURISDICTION

1. The family court has exclusive original jurisdiction over any proceeding to determine whether a person is a juvenile delinquent.

2. In determining the jurisdiction of the court, the age of such person at the time the delinquent act allegedly was committed is controlling.

302.2. STATUTE OF LIMITATIONS

A juvenile delinquency proceeding must be commenced within the period of limitation prescribed in section 30.10 of the criminal procedure law or, unless the alleged act is a designated felony as defined in subdivision eight of section 301.2, commenced before the respondent's eighteenth birthday, whichever occurs earlier. When the alleged act constitutes a designated felony as defined in subdivision eight of section 301.2 such proceeding must be commenced within such period of limitation or before the respondent's twentieth birthday, whichever occurs earlier.

302.3. VENUE

1. Juvenile delinquency proceedings shall be originated in the county in which the act or acts referred to in the petition allegedly occurred. For purposes of determining venue, article twenty of the criminal procedure law shall apply.

2. Upon motion of the respondent or the appropriate presentment agency, the family court in which the proceedings have been originated may order, for good cause shown, that the proceeding be transferred to another county. If the order is issued after motion by the presentment agency, the court may impose such conditions as it deems equitable and appropriate to ensure that the transfer does not subject the respondent to an unreasonable burden in making his defense.

3. Any motion made pursuant to subdivision two by the respondent shall be made within the time prescribed by section 332.2. Any such motion by a presentment agency must be based upon papers stating the ground therefor and must be made within thirty days from the date that the action was originated unless such time is extended for good cause shown.

4. In cases heard outside of the city of New York, and except for designated felony act petitions, after entering a finding pursuant to subdivision one of section 345.1, and prior to the commencement of the dispositional hearing, the court may, in its discretion and for good cause shown, order that the proceeding be transferred to the county in which the respondent resides. The court shall not order such a transfer, however, unless it grants the respondent and the presentment agency an opportunity to state on the record whether each approves or disapproves of such a transfer and the reasons therefor. The court shall take into consideration the provisions of subdivisions two and three of section 340.2 in determining such transfer.

305.2. CUSTODY BY A PEACE OFFICER OR A POLICE OFFICER WITHOUT A WARRANT

1. For purposes of this section, the word "officer" means a peace officer or a police officer.

2. An officer may take a child under the age of sixteen into custody without a warrant in cases in which he may arrest a person for a crime under article one hundred forty of the criminal procedure law.

3. If an officer takes such child into custody or if a child is delivered to him under section 305.1, he shall immediately notify the parent or other person legally responsible for the child's care, or if such legally responsible person is unavailable the person with whom the child resides, that the child has been taken into custody.

4. After making every reasonable effort to give notice under subdivision three, the officer shall:

(a) release the child to the custody of his parents or other person legally responsible for his care upon the issuance in accordance with section 307.1 of a family court appearance ticket to the child and the person to whose custody the child is released; or

(b) forthwith and with all reasonable speed take the child directly, and without his first being taken to the police station house, to the family court located in the county in which the act occasioning the taking into custody allegedly was committed, unless the officer determines that it is necessary to question the child, in which case he may take the child to a facility designated by the state court administrator as a suitable place for the questioning of children and there question him for a reasonable period of time; or

(c) take the child to a place certified by the state division for youth as a juvenile detention facility for the reception of children.

5. If such child has allegedly committed a designated felony act as defined in subdivision eight of section 301.2, and the family court in the county is in session, the officer shall forthwith take the child directly to such family court, unless the officer takes the child to a facility for questioning in accordance with paragraph (b) of subdivision four. If such child has not allegedly committed a designated felony act and such family court is in session, the officer shall either forthwith take the child directly to such family court, unless the officer takes the child to a facility for questioning in accordance with paragraph (b) of subdivision four or release the child in accordance with paragraph (a) of subdivision four.

6. In all other cases, and in the absence of special circumstances, the officer shall release the child in accordance with paragraph (a) of subdivision four.

7. A child shall not be questioned pursuant to this section unless he and a person required to be notified pursuant to subdivision three if present, have been advised:

(a) of the child's right to remain silent;

(b) that the statements made by the child may be used in a court of law;

(c) of the child's right to have an attorney present at such questioning; and

(d) of the child's right to have an attorney provided for him without charge if he is indigent.

8. In determining the suitability of questioning and determining the reasonable period of time for questioning such a child, the child's age, the presence or absence of his parents or other persons legally responsible for his care and notification pursuant to subdivision three shall be included among relevant considerations.

307.1. FAMILY COURT APPEARANCE TICKET

1. A family court appearance ticket is a written notice issued and subscribed by a peace officer or police officer, a probation service director or his designee or the administrator responsible for operating a detention facility or his designee, directing a child and his parent or other person legally responsible for his care to appear, without security, at a designated probation service on a specified return date in connection with the child's alleged commission of the crime or crimes specified on such appearance ticket. The form of a family court appearance ticket shall be prescribed by rules of the chief administrator of the courts.

2. If the crime alleged to have been committed by the child is a designated felony as defined by subdivision eight of section 301.2, the return date shall be no later than seventy-two hours excluding Saturdays, Sundays and public holidays after issuance of such family court appearance ticket. If the crime alleged to have been committed by such child is not a designated felony, the return date shall be no later than fourteen days after the issuance of such appearance ticket.

3. A copy of the family court appearance ticket shall be forwarded by the issuing person or agency to the complainant, respondent, respondent's parent, and the appropriate probation service within twenty-four hours after its issuance.

311.1. THE PETITION; DEFINITION AND CONTENTS

1. A petition originating a juvenile delinquency proceeding is a written accusation by an authorized presentment agency.

2. A petition shall charge at least one crime and may, in addition, charge in separate counts one or more other crimes, provided that all such crimes are joinable in accord with section 311.6.

3. A petition must contain:

(a) the name of the family court in which it is filed;

(b) the title of the action;

(c) the fact that the respondent is a person under sixteen years of age at the time of the alleged act or acts;

(d) a separate accusation or count addressed to each crime charged, if there be more than one;

(e) the precise crime or crimes charged;

(f) a statement in each count that the crime charged was committed in a designated county;

(g) a statement in each count that the crime charged therein was committed on, or on or about, a designated date, or during a designated period of time;

(h) a plain and concise factual statement in each count which, without allegations of an evidentiary nature, asserts facts supporting every element of the crime charged and the respondent's commission thereof with sufficient precision to clearly apprise the respondent of the conduct which is the subject of the accusation;

(i) the name or names, if known, of other persons who are charged as corespondents in the family court or as adults in a criminal court proceeding in the commission of the crime or crimes charged;

(j) a statement that the respondent requires supervision, treatment or confinement; and

(k) the signature of the appropriate presentment attorney.

4. A petition shall be verified in accordance with the civil practice law and rules and shall conform to the provisions of section 311.2.

5. If the petition alleges that the respondent committed a designated felony act, it shall so state, and the term "designated felony act petition" shall be prominently marked thereon. Certified copies of prior delinquency findings shall constitute sufficient proof of such findings for the purpose of filing a designated felony petition. If all the allegations of a designated felony act are dismissed or withdrawn or the respondent is found to have committed crimes which are not designated felony acts, the term "designated felony act petition" shall be stricken from the petition.

6. The form of petition shall be prescribed by the chief administrator of the courts. A petition shall be entitled "In the Matter of," followed by the name of the respondent.

When an order of removal pursuant to article seven hundred twenty-five of the criminal procedure law is filed with the clerk of the court, such order and those pleadings and proceedings, other than the minutes of any hearing inquiry or trial, grand jury proceeding, or of any plea accepted or entered, held in this action that has not yet been transcribed shall be transferred with it and shall be deemed to be a petition filed pursuant to subdivision one of section 310.1 containing all of the allegations required by this section notwithstanding that such allegations may not be set forth in the manner therein prescribed. Where the order or the grand jury request annexed to the order specifies an act that is a designated felony act, the clerk shall annex to the order a sufficient statement and marking to make it a designated felony act petition. The date such order is filed with the clerk of the court shall be deemed the date a petition was filed under this article. For purposes of service in accord with section 312.1, however, only the order of removal shall be deemed the petition. All minutes of any hearing inquiry or trial held in this action, the minutes of any grand jury proceeding and the minutes of any plea accepted and entered shall be transferred to the family court within thirty days.

311.6. JOINDER, SEVERANCE, AND CONSOLIDATION

1. Two crimes are joinable and maybe included as separate counts in the same petition when:

(a) they are based upon the same act or upon the same criminal transaction, as that term is defined in subdivision two; or

(b) even though based upon different criminal transactions, such crimes, or the criminal transactions underlying them, are of such nature that either proof of the first crime would be material and admissible as evidence in chief upon a fact-finding hearing of the second, or proof of the second would be material and admissible as evidence in chief upon a fact-finding hearing of the first; or

(c) even though based upon different criminal transactions, and even though not joinable pursuant to paragraph (b), such crimes are defined by the same or similar statutory provisions and consequently are the same or similar in law.

2. "Criminal transaction" means conduct which establishes at least one crime, and which is comprised of two or more or a group of acts either:

(a) so closely related and connected in point of time and circumstance of commission as to constitute a single criminal incident; or

(b) so closely related in criminal purpose or objective as to constitute elements or integral parts of a single criminal venture.

3. In any case where two or more crimes or groups of crimes charged in a petition are based upon different criminal transactions, and where their joinability rests solely upon the fact that such crimes, or as the case may be at least one offense of each group, are the same or similar in law, as prescribed in paragraph (c) of subdivision one, the court, in the interest of justice and for good cause shown, may upon application of either the respondent or the presentment agency order that any one of such crimes or groups of crimes be tried separately from the other or others, or that two or more thereof be tried together but separately from two or more others thereof. Such application must be made within the period prescribed in section 332.2.

4. When two or more petitions against the same respondent charge different crimes of a kind that are joinable in a single petition pursuant to subdivision one, the court may, upon application of either the presentment agency or respondent, order that such petitions be consolidated and treated as a single petition for trial purposes. Such application must be made within the period prescribed in section 332.2. If the respondent requests consolidation with respect to

crimes which are, pursuant to paragraph (a) of subdivision one, of a kind that are joinable in a single petition by reason of being based upon the same act or criminal transaction, the court must order such consolidation unless good cause to the contrary be shown.

341.2. PRESENCE OF RESPONDENT AND HIS PARENT

1. The respondent and his counsel or law guardian shall be personally present at any hearing under this article and at the initial appearance.

2. If a respondent conducts himself in so disorderly and disruptive a manner that the hearing cannot be carried on with him in the courtroom, the court may order a recess for the purpose of enabling his parent or other person responsible for his care and his law guardian or counsel to exercise full efforts to assist the respondent to conduct himself so as to permit the proceedings to resume in an orderly manner. If such efforts fail, the respondent may be removed from the courtroom if, after he is warned by the court that he will be removed, he continues such disorderly and disruptive conduct. Such time shall not extend beyond the minimum period necessary to restore order.

3. The respondent's parent or other person responsible for his care shall be present at any hearing under this article and at the initial appearance. However, the court shall not be prevented from proceeding by the absence of such parent or person if reasonable and substantial effort has been made to notify such parent or other person and if the respondent and his law guardian or counsel are present.

343.1. RULES OF EVIDENCE; TESTIMONY GIVEN BY CHILDREN

1. Any person may be a witness in a delinquency proceeding unless the court finds that, by reason of infancy or mental disease or defect, he does not possess sufficient intelligence or capacity to justify reception of his evidence.

2. Every witness more than twelve years old may testify only under oath unless the court is satisfied that such witness cannot, as a result of mental disease or defect, understand the nature of an oath. A child less than twelve years old may not testify under oath unless the court is satisfied that he understands the nature of an oath. If the court is not so satisfied, such child or such witness over twelve years old who cannot, as a result of mental disease or defect, understand the nature of an oath may nevertheless be permitted to give unsworn evidence if the court is satisfied that the witness possesses sufficient intelligence and capacity to justify the reception thereof.

3. A respondent may not be found to be delinquent solely upon the unsworn evidence given pursuant to subdivision two.

343.2. RULES OF EVIDENCE; CORROBORATION OF ACCOMPLICE TESTIMONY

1. A respondent may not be found to be delinquent upon the testimony of an accomplice unsupported by corroborative evidence tending to connect the respondent with the commission of the crime or crimes charged in the petition.

2. An "accomplice" means a witness in a juvenile delinquency proceeding who, according to evidence adduced in such proceeding, may reasonably be considered to have participated in:

(a) the crime charged; or

(b) a crime based on the same or some of the same facts or conduct which constitutes the crime charged in the petition.

3. A witness who is an accomplice as defined in subdivision two is no less such because a proceeding, conviction or finding of delinquency against him would be barred or precluded by some defense or exemption such as infancy, immunity or previous prosecution amounting to a collateral impediment to such proceeding, conviction or finding, not affecting the conclusion that such witness engaged in the conduct constituting the crime with the mental state required for the commission thereof.

343.3. RULES OF EVIDENCE; IDENTIFICATION BY MEANS OF PREVIOUS RECOGNITION IN ABSENCE OF PRESENT IDENTIFICATION

1. In any juvenile delinquency proceeding in which the respondent's commission of a crime is in issue, testimony as provided in subdivision two may be given by a witness when:

(a) such witness testifies that:

(i) he observed the person claimed by the presentment agency to be the respondent either at the time and place of the commission of the crime or upon some other occasion relevant to the case; and

(ii) on a subsequent occasion he observed, under circumstances consistent with such rights as an accused person may derive under the constitution of this state or of the United States, a person whom he recognized as the same person whom he had observed on the first incriminating occasion; and

(iii) he is unable at the proceeding to state, on the basis of present recollection, whether or not the respondent is the person in question; and

(b) it is established that the respondent is in fact the person whom the witness observed and recognized on the second occasion. Such fact may be established by testimony of another person or persons to whom the witness promptly declared his recognition on such occasion.

2. Under circumstances prescribed in subdivision one, such witness may testify at the proceeding that the person whom he observed and recognized on the second occasion is the same person whom he observed on the first or incriminating occasion. Such testimony, together with the evidence that the respondent is in fact the person whom the witness observed and recognized on the second occasion, constitutes evidence in chief.

343.4. RULES OF EVIDENCE; IDENTIFICATION BY MEANS OF PREVIOUS RECOGNITION, IN ADDITION TO PRESENT IDENTIFICATION

In any juvenile delinquency proceeding in which the respondent's commission of a crime is in issue, a witness who testifies that: (a) he observed the person claimed by the presentment agency to be the respondent either at the time and place of the commission of the crime or upon some other occasion relevant to the case, and (b) on the basis of present recollection, the respondent is the person in question, and (c) on a subsequent occasion he observed the respondent, under circumstances consistent with such rights as an accused person may derive under the constitution of this state or of the United States, and then also recognized him as the same person whom he had observed on the first or incriminating occasion, may, in addition to making an identification of the respondent at the delinquency proceeding on the basis of present recollection as the person whom he observed on the first or incriminating occasion, also describe his previous recognition of the respondent and testify that the person whom he observed on such second occasion is the same person whom he had observed on the first or incriminating occasion. Such testimony constitutes evidence in chief.

343.5. RULES OF EVIDENCE; IMPEACHMENT OF OWN WITNESS BY PROOF OF PRIOR CONTRADICTORY STATEMENT

1. When, upon examination by the party who called him, a witness in a delinquency proceeding gives testimony upon a material issue of the case which tends to disprove the position of such party, such party may introduce evidence that such witness has previously made either a written statement signed by him or an oral statement under oath contradictory to such testimony.

2. Evidence concerning a prior contradictory statement introduced pursuant to subdivision one may be received only for the purpose of impeaching the credibility of the witness with respect to his testimony upon the subject, and does not constitute evidence in chief.

3. When a witness has made a prior signed or sworn statement contradictory to his testimony in a delinquency proceeding upon a material issue of the case, but his testimony does not tend to disprove the position of the party who called him and elicited such testimony, evidence that the witness made such prior statement is not admissible, and such party may not use such prior statement for the purpose of refreshing the recollection of the witness in a manner that discloses its contents to the court.

344.2. RULES OF EVIDENCE; STATEMENTS OF RESPONDENT; CORROBORATION

1. Evidence of a written or oral confession, admission, or other statement made by a respondent with respect to his participation or lack of participation in the crime charged, may not be received in evidence against him in a juvenile delinquency proceeding if such statement was involuntarily made.

2. A confession, admission or other statement is "involuntarily made" by a respondent when it is obtained from him:

(a) by any person by the use or threatened use of physical force upon the respondent or another person, or by means of any other improper conduct or undue pressure which impaired the respondent's physical or mental condition to the extent of undermining his ability to make a choice whether or not to make a statement; or

(b) by a public servant engaged in law enforcement activity or by a person then acting under his direction or in cooperation with him:

(i) by means of any promise or statement of fact, which promise or statement creates a substantial risk that the respondent might falsely incriminate himself; or

(ii) in violation of such rights as the respondent may derive from the constitution of this state or of the United States; or

(iii) in violation of section 305.2.

3. A child may not be found to be delinquent based on the commission of any crime solely upon evidence of a confession or admission made by him without additional proof that the crime charged has been committed.

Penal Law

PART ONE—GENERAL PROVISIONS
Title A—General Purposes, Rules of Construction, and Definitions

Article	Section
1. General purposes	1.00–1.05
5. General rules of construction and application	5.00–5.10
10. Definitions	10.00

Title B—Principles of Criminal Liability

15. Culpability	15.00–15.25
20. Parties to offenses and liability through accessorial conduct	20.00–20.25

Title C—Defenses

25. Defenses in general	25.00
30. Defense of infancy	30.00
35. Defense of justification	35.00–35.45
40. Other defenses involving lack of culpability	40.00–40.15

PART TWO—SENTENCES
Title E—Sentences

55. Classification and designation of offenses	55.00–55.10
60. Authorized dispositions of offenders	60.00–60.35
65. Sentences of probation, conditional discharge and unconditional discharge	65.00–65.20
70. Sentences of imprisonment	70.00–70.40
80. Fines	80.00–80.15
85. Sentence of intermittent imprisonment	85.00–85.20

PART THREE—SPECIFIC OFFENSES
Title G—Anticipatory Offenses

100. Criminal solicitation	100.00–100.20
105. Conspiracy	105.00–105.35
110. Attempt	110.00–110.10
115. Criminal facilitation	115.00–115.15

Title H—Offenses Against the Person Involving Injury, Sexual Conduct, Restraint, and Intimidation

120. Assault and related offenses	120.00–120.35
125. Homicide, abortion and related offenses	125.00–125.60
130. Sex offenses	130.00–130.70
135. Kidnapping, coercion, and related offenses	135.00–135.75

Title I—Offenses Involving Damages To and Intrusion Upon Property

140. Burglary and related offenses	140.00–140.40
145. Criminal mischief and related offenses	145.00–145.45
150. Arson	150.00–150.20

Title J—Offenses Involving Theft

155. Larceny	155.00–155.45
156. Offenses involving computers; definition of terms	156.00–156.50

160. Robbery.. 160.00–160.15
165. Other offenses relating to theft 165.00–165.65

Title K—Offenses Involving Fraud

170. Forgery and related offenses................................ 170.00–170.71
175. Offenses involving false written statements 175.00–175.45
176. Insurance fraud 176.00–176.30
180. Bribery not involving public servants and related offenses 180.00–180.55
185. Frauds on creditors...................................... 185.00–185.15
190. Other frauds... 190.00–190.65

Title L—Offenses Against Public Administration

195. Official misconduct and obstruction of public servants generally 195.00–195.20
200. Bribery involving public servants and related offenses 200.00–200.50
205. Escape and other offenses relating to custody 205.00–205.65
210. Perjury and related offenses 210.00–210.50
215. Other offenses relating to judicial and other proceedings 215.00–215.80

Title M—Offenses Against Public Health and Morals

220. Controlled substances offenses 220.00–220.65
221. Offenses involving marijuana 221.00–221.55
225. Gambling offenses 225.00–225.40
230. Prostitution offenses..................................... 230.00–230.40
235. Obscenity and related offenses 235.00–235.22

Title N—Offenses Against Public Order, Public Sensibilities and the Right to Privacy

240. Offenses against public order 240.00–240.60
245. Offenses against public sensibilities......................... 245.00–245.11
250. Offenses against the right to privacy 250.00–250.35

Title O—Offenses Against Marriage, the Family and the Welfare of Children and Incompetents

255. Offenses affecting the marital relationship..................... 255.00–255.30
260. Offenses relating to children and incompetents 260.00–260.25
263. Sexual performance by a child 263.00–263.25

Title P—Offenses Against Public Safety

265. Firearms and other dangerous weapons 265.00–265.40
270. Other offenses relating to public safety 270.00–270.20
275. Offenses relating to unauthorized recording of sound.............. 275.00–275.25

PART FOUR—ADMINISTRATIVE PROVISIONS

Title W—Provisions Relating to Firearms, Fireworks, Pornography Equipment, and Vehicles Used in the Transportation of Gambling Records

400. Licensing and other provisions relating to firearms 400.00–400.10
405. Licensing and other provisions relating to fireworks.............. 405.00–405.05
410. Seizure and forfeiture of equipment used in promoting pornography... 410.00
415. Seizure and forfeiture of vehicles, vessels, and aircraft used to transport or conceal gambling records 415.00
450. Disposal of stolen property 450.10

TITLE X—ORGANIZED CRIME CONTROL ACT

460. Enterprise corruption 460.00–460.80

Title Z—Laws Repealed; Time of Taking Effect

500. Laws repealed; time of taking effect 500.05, 500.10

SELECTED ARTICLES AND SECTIONS OF THE PENAL LAW

(Full text of the Penal Law along with notes, commentaries, and amendments may be found in Volume 39 of McKinney's *Consolidated Laws of New York State*)

10.00 DEFINITIONS OF TERMS OF GENERAL USE IN THIS CHAPTER

Except where different meanings are expressly specified in subsequent provisions of this chapter, the following terms have the following meanings:

1. "Offense" means conduct for which a sentence to a term of imprisonment or to a fine is provided by any law of this state or by any law, local law or ordinance of a political subdivision of this state, or by any order, rule or regulation of any governmental instrumentality authorized by law to adopt the same.

2. "Traffic infraction" means any offense defined as "traffic infraction" by section one hundred fifty-five of the vehicle and traffic law.

3. "Violation" means an offense, other than a "traffic infraction," for which a sentence to a term of imprisonment in excess of fifteen days cannot be imposed.

4. "Misdemeanor" means an offense, other than a "traffic infraction," for which a sentence to a term of imprisonment in excess of fifteen days may be imposed, but for which a sentence to a term of imprisonment in excess of one year cannot be imposed.

5. "Felony" means an offense for which a sentence to a term of imprisonment in excess of one year may be imposed.

6. "Crime" means a misdemeanor or a felony.

7. "Person" means a human being, and where appropriate, a public or private corporation, an unincorporated association, a partnership, a government or a governmental instrumentality.

8. "Possess" means to have physical possession or otherwise to exercise dominion or control over tangible property.

9. "Physical injury" means impairment of physical condition or substantial pain.

10. "Serious physical injury" means physical injury which creates a substantial risk of death, or which causes death or serious and protracted disfigurement, protracted impairment of health or protracted loss or impairment of the function of any bodily organ.

11. "Deadly physical force" means physical force that, under the circumstances in which it is used, is readily capable of causing death or other serious physical injury.

12. "Deadly weapon" means any loaded weapon from which a shot, readily capable of producing death or other serious physical injury, may be discharged, or a switchblade knife, gravity knife, pilum ballistic knife, dagger, billy, blackjack, or metal knuckles.

13. "Dangerous instrument" means any instrument, article or substance, including a "vehicle" as that term is defined in this section, which, under the circumstances in which it is used, attempted to be used or threatened to be used, is readily capable of causing death or other serious physical injury.

14. "Vehicle" means a "motor vehicle," "trailer" or "semi-trailer," as defined in the vehicle and traffic law, any snowmobile as defined in the parks and recreation law, any aircraft, or any vessel equipped for propulsion by mechanical means or by sail.

15. "Public servant" means (a) any public officer or employee of the state or of any political subdivision thereof or of any governmental instrumentality within the state, or (b) any person exercising the functions of any such public officer or employee. The term public servant includes a person who has been elected or designated to become a public servant.

16. "Juror" means any person who is a member of any jury, including a grand jury, impaneled by any court in this state or by any public servant authorized by law to impanel a jury. The term juror also includes a person who has been drawn or summoned to attend as a prospective juror.

17. "Benefit" means any gain or advantage to the beneficiary and includes any gain or advantage to a third person pursuant to the desire or consent of the beneficiary.

18. "Juvenile offender" means (1) a person thirteen years old who is criminally responsible for acts constituting murder in the second degree as defined in subdivisions one and two of this section 125.25 of this chapter and (2) a person fourteen or fifteen years old who is criminally responsible for acts constituting the crimes defined in subdivisions one and two of section 125.25 (murder in the second degree) and in subdivision three of such section provided that the underlying crime for the murder charge is one for which such person is criminally responsible; section 135.25 (kidnapping in the first degree); 150.20 (arson in the first degree); subdivisions one and two of section 120.10 (assault in the first degree); 125.20 (manslaughter in the first degree); subdivisions one and two of section 130.35 (rape in the first degree); subdivisions one and two of section 130.50 (sodomy in the first degree); 130.70 (aggravated sexual abuse); 140.30 (burglary in the first degree); subdivision one of section 140.25 (burglary in the second degree); 150.15 (arson in the second degree); 160.15 (robbery in the first degree); or subdivision two of section 160.10 (robbery in the

second degree) of this chapter; or defined in this chapter as an attempt to commit murder in the second degree or kidnapping in the first degree.

15.00 CULPABILITY; DEFINITIONS OF TERMS

The following definitions are applicable to this chapter:

1. "Act" means a bodily movement.

2. "Voluntary act" means a bodily movement performed consciously as a result of effort or determination, and includes the possession of property if the actor was aware of his physical possession or control thereof for a sufficient period to have been able to terminate it.

3. "Omission" means a failure to perform an act as to which a duty of performance is imposed by law.

4. "Conduct" means an act or omission and its accompanying mental state.

5. "To act" means either to perform an act or to omit to perform an act.

6. "Culpable mental state" means "intentionally" or "knowingly" or "recklessly" or with "criminal negligence," as these terms are defined in section 15.05.

15.05 CULPABILITY; DEFINITIONS OF CULPABLE MENTAL STATES

The following definitions are applicable to this chapter:

1. "Intentionally." A person acts intentionally with respect to a result or to conduct described by a statute defining an offense when his conscious objective it to cause such result or to engage in such conduct.

2. "Knowingly." A person acts knowingly with respect to conduct or to a circumstance described by a statute defining an offense when he is aware that his conduct is of such nature or that such circumstance exists.

3. "Recklessly." A person acts recklessly with respect to a result or to a circumstance described by a statute defining an offense when he is aware of and consciously disregards a substantial and unjustifiable risk that such result will occur or that such circumstance exists. The risk must be of such nature and degree that disregard thereof constitutes a gross deviation from the standard of conduct that a reasonable person would observe in the situation. A person who creates such a risk but is unaware thereof solely by reason of voluntary intoxication also acts recklessly with respect thereto.

4. "Criminal negligence." A person acts with criminal negligence with respect to a result or to a circumstance described by a statute defining an offense when he fails to perceive a substantial and unjustifiable risk that such result will occur or that such circumstance exists. The risk must be of such nature and degree that the failure to perceive it constitutes a gross deviation from the standard of care that a reasonable person would observe in the situation.

15.10 REQUIREMENTS FOR CRIMINAL LIABILITY IN GENERAL AND FOR OFFENSES OF STRICT LIABILITY AND MENTAL CULPABILITY

The minimal requirement for criminal liability is the performance by a person of conduct that includes a voluntary act or the omission to perform an act which he is physically capable of performing. If such conduct is all that is required for commission of a particular offense, or if an offense or some material element thereof does not require a culpable mental state on the part of the actor, such offense is one of "strict liability." If a culpable mental state on the part of the actor is required with respect to every material element of an offense, such offense is one of "mental culpability."

15.20 EFFECT OF IGNORANCE OR MISTAKE UPON LIABILITY

1. A person is not relieved of criminal liability for conduct because he engages in such conduct under a mistaken belief of fact, unless:

(a) Such factual mistake negatives the culpable mental state required for the commission of an offense; or

(b) The statute defining the offense or a statute related thereto expressly provides that such factual mistake constitutes a defense or exception; or

(c) Such factual mistake is a kind that supports a defense of justification as defined in article thirty-five of this chapter.

2. A person is not relieved of criminal liability for conduct because he engages in such conduct under a mistaken belief that it does not, as a matter of law, constitute an offense, unless such mistaken belief is founded upon an official statement of the law contained in (a) a statute or other enactment, or (b) an administrative order or grant of permission, or (c) a judicial decision of a state or federal court, or (d) an interpretation of the statute or law relating to the offense, officially made or issued by a public servant, agency or body legally charged or empowered with the responsibility or privilege of administering, enforcing or interpreting such statute or law.

3. Notwithstanding the use of the term "knowingly" in any provision of this chapter defining an offense in which the age of a child is an element thereof, knowledge by the defendant of the age of such child is not an element of any such offense and it is not, unless expressly so provided, a defense to a prosecution therefor that the defendant did not know the age of the child or believed such age to be the same as or greater than that specified in the statute.

15.25 EFFECTS OF INTOXICATION UPON LIABILITY

Intoxication is not, as such, a defense to a criminal charge; but in any prosecution for an offense, evidence of intoxication of the defendant may be offered by the defendant whenever it is relevant to negative an element of the crime charged.

400.00 LICENSES TO CARRY, POSSESS, REPAIR, AND DISPOSE OF FIREARMS

1. Eligibility. No license shall be issued or renewed pursuant to this section except by the licensing officer, and then only after investigation and finding that all statements in a proper application for a license are true. No license shall be issued or renewed except for an applicant (a) of good moral character; (b) who has not been convicted anywhere of a felony or a serious offense; (c) who has stated whether he has ever suffered any mental illness or been confined to any hospital or institution, public or private, for mental illness; and (d) concerning whom no good cause exists for the denial of the license. No person shall engage in the business of gunsmith or dealer in firearms unless licensed pursuant to this section. An applicant to engage in such business shall also be a citizen of the United States, more than twenty-one years of age and maintain a place of business in the city or county where the license is issued. For such business, if the applicant is a firm or partnership, each member thereof shall comply with all of the requirements set forth in this subdivision and if the applicant is a corporation, each officer thereof shall so comply.

2. Types of licenses. A license for gunsmith or dealer in firearms shall be issued to engage in such business. A license for a pistol or revolver shall be issued to (a) have and possess in his dwelling by a householder; (b) have and possess in his place of business by a merchant or storekeeper; (c) have and carry concealed while so employed by a messenger employed by a banking institution or express company; (d) have and carry concealed while so employed by a regular employee of an institution of the state, or of any county, city, town or village, under control of a commissioner of correction of the city or any warden, superintendent or head keeper of any state prison, penitentiary, workhouse, county jail or other institution for the detention of persons convicted or accused of crime or held as witnesses in criminal cases, provided that application is made therefor by such commissioner, warden, superintendent or head keeper; (e) have and carry concealed, without regard to employment or place of possession, by any person when proper cause exists for the issuance thereof; and (f) have, possess, collect and carry antique pistols which are defined as follows: (i) any single shot, muzzle loading pistol with a matchlock, flint lock, percussion cap, or similar type of ignition system manufactured in or before 1898, which is not designed for using rimfire or conventional centerfire fixed ammunition; and (ii) any replica of any pistol described in clause (i) hereof if such replica—

(1) is not designed or redesigned for using rimfire or conventional centerfire fixed ammunition, or

(2) uses rimfire or conventional centerfire fixed ammunition which is no longer manufactured in the United States and which is not readily available in the ordinary channels of commercial trade.

3. Applications. Applications shall be made and renewed, in the case of a license to carry or possess a pistol or revolver, to the licensing officer in the city or county, as the case may be, where the applicant resides, is principally employed or has his principal place of business as merchant or storekeeper; and, in the case of a license as gunsmith or dealer in firearms, to the licensing officer where such place of business is located. Blank applications shall, except in the city of New York, be approved as to form by the superintendent of state police. An application shall state the full name, date of birth, residence, present occupation of each person or individual signing the same, whether or not he is a citizen of the United States, whether or not he complies with each requirement for eligibility specified in subdivision one of this section and such other facts as may be required to show the good character, competency and integrity of each person or individual signing the application. An application shall be signed and verified by the applicant. Each individual signing an application shall submit one photograph of himself and a duplicate for each required copy of the application. Such photographs shall have been taken within thirty days prior to filing the application. In case of a license as gunsmith or dealer in firearms, the photographs submitted shall be two inches square, and the application shall also state the previous occupation of each individual signing the same and the location of the place of such business, or of the bureau, agency, subagency, office or branch office for which the license is sought, specifying the name of the city, town or village, indicating the street and number and otherwise giving such apt description as to point out reasonably the location thereof. In such case, if the applicant is a firm, partnership or corporation, its name, date and place of formation, and principal place of business shall be stated. For such firm or partnership, the application shall be signed and verified by each individual composing or intending to compose the same and, for such corporation, by each officer thereof.

4. Investigation. Before a license is issued or renewed, there shall be an investigation of all statements required in the application by the duly constituted police authorities of the locality where such application is made. For that purpose, the records of the department of mental hygiene concerning previous or present mental illness of the applicant shall be available for inspection by the investigating officer of the police authority. In order to ascertain any previous criminal record, the investigating officer shall take the fingerprints and physical descriptive data in quadruplicate of each individual by whom the application is signed and verified. Two copies of such fingerprints shall be taken on standard fingerprint cards eight inches square, and one copy may be taken on a card supplied for that purpose by the Federal Bureau of Investigation. When completed, one standard card shall be forwarded to and retained by the division of

criminal identification, department of correction, at Albany. A search of the files of such division and written notification of the results of the search to the investigating officer shall be made without unnecessary delay. Thereafter, such division shall notify the licensing officer and the executive department, division of state police, Albany, of any criminal record of the applicant filed therein subsequent to the search of its files. A second standard card, or the one supplied by the Federal Bureau of Investigation, as the case may be, shall be forwarded to that bureau at Washington with a request that the files of the bureau be searched and notification of the results of the search be made to the investigating police authority. The failure or refusal of the Federal Bureau of Investigation to make the fingerprint check provided for in this section shall not constitute the sole basis for refusal to issue a permit pursuant to the provisions of this section. Of the remaining two fingerprint cards, one shall be filed with the executive department, division of state police, Albany, within ten days after issuance of the license, and the other remain on file with the investigating police authority. No such fingerprints may be inspected by any person other than a peace officer, except on order of a judge or justice of a court of record either upon notice to the licensee or without notice, as the judge or justice may deem appropriate. Upon completion of the investigation, the police authority shall report the results to the licensing officer without unnecessary delay.

4-a. Processing of license applications. Applications for licenses shall be accepted for processing by the licensing officer at the time of presentment. Except upon written notice to the applicant specifically stating the reasons for any delay, in each case the licensing officer shall act upon any application for a license pursuant to this section within six months of the date of presentment of such an application to the appropriate authority. Such delay may only be for good cause and with respect to the applicant. In acting upon an application, the licensing officer shall either deny the application for reasons specifically and concisely stated in writing or grant the application and issue the license applied for.

5. Filing of approved applications. The application for any license, if granted, shall be a public record. Such application shall be filed by the licensing officer with the clerk of the county of issuance, except that in the city of New York and, in the counties of Nassau and Suffolk, the licensing officer shall designate the place of filing in the appropriate division, bureau or unit of the police department thereof, and in the county of Suffolk the county clerk is hereby authorized to transfer all records or applications relating to firearms to the licensing authority of that county. Upon application by a licensee who has changed his place of residence, such records or applications shall be transferred to the appropriate officer at the licensee's new place of residence. A duplicate copy of such application shall be filed by the licensing officer in the executive department, division of state police, Albany, within ten days after issuance of the license. Nothing in this subdivision shall be constructed to change the expiration date or term of such licenses if otherwise provided for in law.

6. License: validity. Any license issued pursuant to this section shall be valid notwithstanding the provisions of any local law or ordinance. No license shall be transferable to any other person or premises. A license to carry or possess a pistol or revolver, not otherwise limited as to place or time of possession, shall be effective throughout the state, except that the same shall not be valid within the city of New York unless a special permit granting validity is issued by the police commissioner of that city. Such license to carry or possess shall be valid within the city of New York in the absence of a permit issued by the police commissioner of that city, provided that (a) the firearms covered by such license are being transported by the licensee in a locked container; and (b) the trip through the city of New York is continuous and uninterrupted. A license as gunsmith or dealer in firearms shall not be valid outside the city or county, as the case may be, where issued.

7. License: form. Any license issued pursuant to this section shall, except in the city of New York, be approved as to form by the superintendent of state police. A license to carry or possess a pistol or revolver shall have attached the licensee's photograph, and a coupon which shall be removed and retained by any person disposing of a firearm to the licensee. Such license shall specify the weapon covered by caliber, make, model, manufacturer's name and serial number, or if none, by any other distinguishing number or identification mark, and shall indicate whether issued to carry on the person or possess on the premises, and if on the premises shall also specify the place where the licensee shall possess the same. If such license is issued to an alien, or to a person not a citizen of and usually a resident in the state, the licensing officer shall state in the license the particular reason for the issuance and the names of the persons certifying to the good character of the applicant. Any license as gunsmith or dealer in firearms shall mention and describe the premises for which it is issued and shall be valid only for such premises.

8. License: exhibition and display. Every licensee while carrying a pistol or revolver shall have on his person a license to carry the same. Every person licensed to possess a pistol or revolver on particular premises shall have the license for the same on such premises. Upon demand, the license shall be exhibited for inspection to any peace officer. A license as gunsmith or dealer in firearms shall be prominently displayed on the licensed premises. Failure of any licensee to so exhibit or display his license, as the case may be, shall be presumptive evidence that he is not duly licensed.

9. License: amendment. Elsewhere than in the city of New York, a person licensed to carry or possess a pistol or revolver may apply at any time to his licensing officer for amendment of his license to include one or more such weapons or to cancel weapons held under license. If granted, a record of the amendment describing the weapons

involved shall be filed by the licensing officer in the executive department, division of state police, Albany. Notification of any change of residence shall be made in writing by any licensee within ten days after such change occurs, and a record of such change shall be inscribed by such licensee on the reverse side of his license. Elsewhere than in the city of New York, and in the counties of Nassau and Suffolk, such notification shall be made to the executive department, division of state police, Albany, and in the city of New York to the police commissioner of that city, and in the county of Nassau to the police commissioner of that county, and in the county of Suffolk to the licensing officer of that county, who shall, within ten days after such notification shall be received by him, give notice in writing of such change to the executive department, division of state police, at Albany.

10. License: expiration and renewal. Any license for gunsmith or dealer in firearms and, in the city of New York and the counties of Nassau and Suffolk, any license to carry or possess a pistol or revolver, issued at any time pursuant to this section or prior to the first day of July, 1963 and not limited to expire on an earlier date fixed in the license, shall expire not more than three years after the date of issuance. Elsewhere than in the city of New York and the counties of Nassau and Suffolk, any license to carry or possess a pistol or revolver, issued at any time pursuant to this section or prior to the first day of July, 1963 and not previously revoked or cancelled, shall be in force and effect until revoked as herein provided. Any application to renew a license that has not previously expired, been revoked or cancelled shall thereby extend the term of the license until disposition of the application by the licensing officer. In the case of a license for gunsmith or dealer in firearms, in counties having a population of less than two hundred thousand inhabitants, photographs and fingerprints shall be submitted on original applications and upon renewal thereafter only at six-year intervals. Upon satisfactory proof that a currently valid original license has been despoiled, lost or otherwise removed from the possession of the licensee and upon application containing an additional photograph of the licensee, the licensing officer shall issue a duplicate license.

11. License: revocation. The conviction of a licensee anywhere of a felony or serious offense shall operate as a revocation of the license.

A license may be revoked and cancelled at any time in the city of New York, and in the counties of Nassau and Suffolk, by the licensing officer, and elsewhere than in the city of New York by any judge or justice of a court of record. The official revoking a license shall give written notice thereof without unnecessary delay to the executive department, division of state police, Albany, and shall also notify immediately the duly constituted police authorities of the locality.

12. Records required of gunsmiths and dealers in firearms. Any person licensed as gunsmith or dealer in firearms shall keep a record book approved as to form, except in the city of New York, by the superintendent of state police. In the record book shall be entered at the time of every transaction involving a firearm the date, name, age, occupation and residence of any person from whom a firearm is received or to whom a firearm is delivered, and the caliber, make, model, manufacturer's name and serial number, or if none, any other distinguishing number or identification mark on such firearm. Before delivering a firearm to any person, the licensee shall require him to produce either a license valid under this section to carry or possess the same, or proof of lawful authority as a peace officer or other exempt person pursuant to section 265.20. In addition, before delivering a firearm to a peace officer, the licensee shall verify that person's status as a peace officer with the division of state police. After completing the foregoing, the licensee shall remove and retain the attached coupon and enter in the record book the date of such license, number, if any, and name of the licensing officer, in the case of the holder of a license to carry or possess, or the shield or other number, if any, assignment and department or unit, in the case of an exempt person. The original transaction report shall be forwarded to the division of state police within ten days of delivering a firearm to any peace officer, and a duplicate copy shall be kept by the licensee. The record book shall be maintained on the premise mentioned and described in the license and shall be open at all reasonable hours for inspection by any peace officer, acting pursuant to his special duties, or police officer. In the event of cancellation or revocation of the license for gunsmith or dealer in firearms, or discontinuance of business by a licensee, such record book shall be immediately surrendered to the licensing officer in the city of New York, and in the counties of Nassau and Suffolk, and elsewhere in the state to the executive department, division of state police.

12-a. State police regulations applicable to licensed gunsmiths engaged in the business of assembling or manufacturing firearms. The superintendent of state police is hereby authorized to issue such rules and regulations as he deems reasonably necessary to prevent the manufacture and assembly of unsafe firearms in the state. Such rules and regulations shall establish safety standards in regard to the manufacture and assembly of firearms in the state;, including specifications as to materials and parts used, the proper storage and shipment of firearms, and minimum standards of quality control. Regulations issued by the state police pursuant to this subdivision shall apply to any person licensed as a gunsmith under this section engaged in the business of manufacturing or assembling firearms, and any violation thereof shall subject the licensee to revocation of license pursuant to subdivision eleven of this section.

13. Expenses. The expense of providing a licensing officer with blank applications, licenses and record books for carrying out the provisions of this section shall be a charge against the county, and in the city of New York against the city.

14. Fees. In the city of New York and the county of Nassau, the annual license fee shall be twenty-five dollars for gunsmiths and fifty dollars for dealers in firearms. In such city, the city council and in the county of Nassau the Board

of Supervisors shall fix the fee to be charged for a license to carry or possess a pistol or revolver and provide for the disposition of such fees. Elsewhere in the state, the licensing officer shall collect and pay into the county treasury the following fees: for each license to carry or possess a pistol or revolver, not less than three dollars nor more than ten dollars as may be determined by the legislative body of the county; for each amendment thereto, three dollars, and five dollars in the county of Suffolk; and for each license issued to a gunsmith or dealer in firearms, ten dollars. The fee for a duplicate license shall be five dollars. The fee for processing a license transfer between counties shall be five dollars. The fee for processing a license for a qualified retired police officer as defined under subdivision thirty-four of section 1.20 of the criminal procedure law shall be waived in all counties throughout the state.

15. Any violation by any person of any provision of this section is a class A misdemeanor.

16. Unlawful disposal. No person shall except as otherwise authorized pursuant to law dispose of any firearm unless he is licensed as gunsmith or dealer in firearms.

Glossary of Legal Terms

A

abate: destroy, remove

abet: encourage, aid

ab initio: from the beginning

abjure: renounce

abridge: reduce, contract

abrogate: repeal, annul

abscond: hide, absent oneself

accident: unforeseen event

accomplice: associate in crime

acknowledgment: act of going before an authorized official to declare an act as one's own, thus giving it legal validity

acquit: release, absolve

act: something done voluntarily

ad litem: for the suit

adduce: offer, present

adjacent: near to, close

adjective law: rules of procedure

adjudicate: to determine judicially

admiralty: court having jurisdiction over maritime cases

adult: one who has attained the age of majority or legal maturity

affiant: one who makes an affidavit

affidavit: a sworn, written statement

affiliation: order stating one to be the father of a child

affinity: relationship between persons through marriage with the kindred of each other; distinguished from consanguinity, which is relationship by blood

affirm: ratify

affirmation: a solemn declaration made under penalty of perjury by a person who conscientiously declines to take an oath

agent: one who represents and acts for another

aggressor: one who begins a quarrel

aid and comfort: help, encourage.

alias: a name that is not one's true name

alibi: a claim of having been elsewhere at the time of a commission of an act

alienist: a doctor specializing in legal aspects of psychiatry

allegation: the assertion, declaration, or statement of a party to an action, made in a pleading, setting out what he expects to prove

ambiguous: not clear, having two meanings, equivocal

amentia: mental deficiency

amercement: a pecuniary penalty or a fine imposed as punishment on conviction; same as mulct

amicus curiae: a friend of the court who advises on some legal matter

animus: mind; intent

animus furandi: intent to steal

annul: cancel, void

annus: a year

ante: before

ante mortem: before death

aphasia: inability to speak, although vocal cords are normal

a posteriori: from effect to cause

appeal: to request a higher court to review a decision of a lower court

appearance: the coming into court as defendant, attorney, etc.

229

appellant: one who appeals
appellee: one who opposes an appellant, a respondent
apprehend: arrest
appurtenant: belonging to
a priori: from cause to effect
arbiter: one who decides a dispute; a referee
arbitrary: an act having no cause or reason, absolute, despotic, peremptory
arraign: to call a prisoner before the court to answer to a charge
artifice: trickery; deception
asportation: moving a thing from one place to another, as in larceny
assert: to state as true
asseveration: an affirmation; a solemn declaration
asylum: a place of refuge
at bar: before the court
at issue: the point of contention between parties in a legal action
attach: seize property by court order and sometimes arrest a person
attainder: forfeiture of property and corruption of honor of one sentenced to death (compare to bill of attainder)
attempt: an act done with intent to commit a crime but falling short of consummating it
attest: to witness a will, etc.
authentic: genuine; true
authenticate: to give authority to a law, writing, or record
axio: a self-evident truth.

B

bail: the security given to obtain the temporary release of a prisoner
bailee: one to whom property is bailed
bailment: the giving of property to a bailee
bailor: the one who gives his property to a bailee
barratry: the persistent incitement of groundless judicial proceedings
bill of attainder: a law pronouncing a person guilty without trial, which is illegal
bludgeon: a club heavier at one end than at the other
blue laws: rigid Sunday laws
blue-sky laws: laws regulating investment companies to protect investors from frauds
bona fide: in good faith
bondsman: one who bails another by putting up a bond
boycott: a joining together in refusal to deal with, so as to punish or to coerce a desired result without force
breach of the peace: disturbing the public peace by disorder, violence, force, noise
bucket shop: a place where people bet on the stock market under pretense of buying and selling stocks
bunco game: any trick or cunning calculated to win confidence and to deceive whether by conversation, conduct, or suggestion

C

cadaver: a dead human body
camera: a judge's chamber
canon: a law, rule
capias: an order to arrest
carnal: relating to the body
carnal abuse: a sex act not amounting to penetration
carnal knowledge: sexual intercourse
cartilage: ground adjacent to a dwelling and used in connection with it, usually fenced off
cause of action: matter for which an action may be brought
caveat: a warning
caveat emptor: let the buyer beware
certiorari: an order from a high court to a lower court calling up for review the minutes of a trial
challenge: an exception taken to a juror
change of venue: the removal of the place of trial from one county to another
character: the qualities or traits that make up or distinguish an individual
charge: a complaint, information, or indictment
chastity: abstention from unlawful sexual intercourse
chattel: personal property
chattel mortgage: a mortgage on personal property
child: one under 16 years in criminal law.
cite: to summon, command one's presence

civil rights: rights granted to citizens by the Constitution or by statute

codicil: an addition to a will

coercion: compulsion, duress

cognomen: a family name

cohabit: to live together as husband and wife

comity: courtesy, respect; agreement between states to recognize each other's laws

commitment: an order to take one to prison

common law: law as it developed in England based on customs, usage, decisions

commute: change punishment to one less severe

complainant: one who seeks legal redress

complaint: a sworn allegation to a magistrate charging one with crime; also called information

compos mends: sound of mind

compromise: an agreement between one charged with certain crimes and the complainant to withdraw charges on payment of money, with court's consent

concubinage: habitual cohabitation of persons not legally married

concurrent: occurring at the same time

condemnation: taking private property for public use on payment thereof

confess: to admit the truth of a charge

confession: voluntary statement of guilt of a crime

confidence game: a swindle

confrontation: the right of the defendant to have the witness stand face-to-face with the defendant when the accusation is made

connivance: secret or indirect consent by one to a criminal act by another

consanguinity: blood relationship

consecutive: successive

conspiracy: a plan by two or more to commit a crime

Constitution: the fundamental law of a state or nation

constructive intent: if one intends one act and in carrying it out does another, the intent to do the first is construed to apply to the second

contiguous: adjacent

contingency: an event that may or may not happen

contra: against

contraband: illegal or prohibited trade

controvert: to dispute or oppose by reasoning

conviction: judgment that one is guilty as charged

corporal: bodily

corpus delicti: the substantial and fundamental fact necessary to prove a crime was committed

corroborate: to strengthen

corrupt: spoiled, tainted, debased

counselor: a lawyer

counterfeit: to forge, copy, imitate

credible: worthy of belief

crimen falsi: crimes involving deceit or falsification

criminal action: the process by which one is accused of a crime and brought to trial

criminal information: same as complaint

criminal intent: intent to commit a crime

criminology: the scientific study of crime, criminals, and penal treatment

culpable: blamable

cumulative: tending to prove the same point in evidence; increasing severity with repetition of the offense

custody: control exercised by legal authority over a ward or suspect.

D

deadly weapon: an instrument likely to produce death or serious bodily injury

debauch: to corrupt by intemperance or sensuality

decision: a judgment rendered by a court

deed: a signed instrument containing a legal transfer, bargain, or contract

defalcation: the act or instance of embezzling

de facto: actually or really existing

defamation: injuring a reputation by false statements

defendant: the accused in a criminal action

defraud: to deprive of property by fraud or deceit

de jure: by right of law

deliberate: to weigh or ponder before forming a decision

delict: an offense against the law

demented: mad or insane

deponent: one who gives written testimony under oath

deposition: sworn written testimony

design: plan, scheme, intent

dictum: an opinion on a point in a case expressed by a judge

dipsomaniac: one who has an irresistible desire for alcohol

disenfranchise: to deprive of a legal right

dismiss: to discharge a court action

disorderly house: a place where people behave so badly as to become a nuisance to the neighborhood

document: a written instrument

domicile: one's permanent home

duress: compulsion by threat, unlawful constraint

E

ego: the self

eleemosynary: related to or supported by charity donations

embezzlement: appropriation of entrusted property fraudulently for one's own use

embracery: an attempt to improperly influence a juror

eminent domain: the right of a government to take private property for public use

empirical: based on experience

entice: to solicit, persuade, tempt

entrapment: the act of luring one into a compromising statement or act

essence: the ultimate nature of a thing

evidence: all means used to prove or disprove a fact at issue

ex officio: by virtue of office

ex parte: on one side only

ex post facto law: a law passed after an act was done that retroactively makes such an act a crime

examined copy: one compared with the original and sworn to as a correct copy

exception: a formal objection to the action of the court in denying a request or overruling an objection

executed: completed

extradition: surrender of a fugitive from one geographic jurisdiction to another

extrajudicial: outside judicial proceeding

extremis: near death, beyond hope of recovery

F

facsimile: an exact or accurate copy of an original instrument

false pretenses: intentionally untrue representations

felo de se: one who kills himself; suicide

felonious: criminal, malicious

fence: one who receives stolen goods

fiduciary: holding in trust

filiation, order of: a court order declaring one to be the father of a child

finding: the result of the deliberation of a court or jury

firearm: a weapon that propels bullets by explosion of gunpowder

forge: to counterfeit or make falsely

fornication: sexual intercourse between persons not married to each other

foundling: a deserted child

franchise: a special privilege granted to an individual or group; elective franchise refers to the voting privilege

fratricide: killing of one's brother or sister

freeholder: one who owns real property

fugitive from justice: one who commits a crime and escapes

G

gamble: to bet on an event of which the outcome is uncertain

general verdict: a verdict in which a jury finds a defendant guilty or not guilty

genocide: the deliberate systematic destruction of certain races, nationalities, or religious groups

gift enterprise: a scheme for distribution of property by chance among persons who have paid or agreed to pay a consideration; the common term is lottery

grand jury: not fewer than 16 but no more than 23 citizens of a county sworn to inquire into crimes committed or triable in that county

grantee: one to whom a grant is made

grantor: the one who makes the grant

gravamen: the substantial part of a complaint

guardian ad litem: a person designated by a court to represent a child in a civil action

H

habeas corpus: an order to produce a person before a court to determine the legality of detention

hearsay: evidence based on repeating the words of another and not based on the witness's own personal observation or knowledge of that to which he testifies

hung jury: one so divided they can't agree on a verdict

hypothecate: to pledge without delivery of title or possession

hypothetical question: a question asked of an expert witness based on supposition from which the witness is asked to state his opinion

I

illicit: unlawful

impeach: to accuse, charge

inalienable: those rights that cannot be lawfully transferred or surrendered

in loco parentis: in place of a parent

incommunicado: denial of the right of a prisoner to communicate with friends or relatives

indictment: a written accusation of a crime presented by a grand jury

inducement: cause or reason why a thing is done or that which incites the person to do the act or commit a crime; the motive for the criminal act

infamous crime: a felony

infant: in civil cases, one under 21 years of age

information: a formal accusation of a crime

injunction: legal process requiring a person to do or refrain from doing a certain action

intent: state of mind to do or omit an act

ipso facto: by the fact itself

issue: what is affirmed by one and denied by another in an action.

J

jeopardy: danger, peril

judicial notice: acceptance by a court or judge of some fact of common knowledge thereby dispensing with the need to offer evidence to prove it, i.e., 24 hours equal one day

judiciary: relating to a court of justice

jurat: the part of an affidavit stating where, when, and before whom it was signed and sworn

jurisdiction: power or authority to apply or interpret the law

jury: a group of citizens sworn to inquire into facts and deliver a verdict. A trial jury tries cases; a grand jury decides whether to indict

K

kleptomaniac: one who has an irresistible propensity to steal

L

laches: unreasonable delay in asserting a legal right or privilege

latent: hidden, concealed

leading question: one so put as to suggest the answer

lien: a claim a creditor has on property until a debt is paid

lis pendens: a pending civil or criminal action

litigant: a party to a lawsuit

locus delicti: place of the crime (see situs delicti)

lucri causa: for sake of gain

M

mala in se: bad in themselves; such crimes usually require a specific criminal intent

mala prohibita: bad because it is prohibited by legislation, not because it is evil in its nature

malfeasance: wrongdoing or misconduct, especially by a public official

malice, intentional: wrongdoing to injure, vex or annoy

malo ammo: evil mind

mandamus: a court order to a public official to perform a specified act

maritime: pertaining to the sea or to commerce thereon

masochism: sexual pleasure in being abused or dominated

mens rea: criminal intent

meretricious: relating to a prostitute; flashy

minor: one who has not attained majority

miscegenation: marriage or sexual intercourse between persons of different races

misfeasance: improper performance of a lawful act

mittimus: a warrant of commitment to prison

moral certainty: evidence that convinces the mind beyond a reasonable doubt, hence the degree of proof required to prove defendant's guilt in a criminal action

moral turpitude: base or vile behavior

motive: reason for doing an act

mulct: a pecuniary fine imposed as punishment upon conviction of a crime; same as amercement

N

natural child: a child born out of wedlock

non prosequitur: an entry of record signifying that the plaintiff or prosecutor will not press the complaint

nolo contendere: equal to a plea of guilty

nominal damages: award of a trifling sum where no substantial injury is proved to have been sustained

nonfeasance: neglect of duty

noscitur a sociis: meaning of doubtful words in a statute may be ascertained by referring to the meaning of other words associated with it in the definition; also called ejusdem generis (see sui generis)

novation: substitution of a new obligation for an old one

nunc pro tune: now for then; dated as if occurring on an earlier date

O

oath: an attestation of the truth

obiter dictum: opinion expressed by a court on a matter not essentially involved in a case and hence not a decision; also called dicta if plural

onus probandi: burden of proof

opinion evidence: inferences or conclusions stated by a witness in testimony as distinguished from facts known to him; generally inadmissible

overt: open, manifest

P

panel: a group of jurors selected to serve during a term of the court

pardon: to release an offender from punishment for his crime

parens patriae: sovereign power of a state to protect or be a guardian over children and incompetents

parol: oral, verbal

parole: to release one from prison conditionally before the expiration of a sentence

peculation: embezzlement

pent treason: common law crime in which a wife kills her husband, or a servant kills his master, or a subordinate kills his superior. (Abolished as such under N.Y. Statute law when all such killings were classified as criminal homicides.)

police power: inherent power of the state or its political subdivisions to enact laws within constitutional limits to promote the general welfare of society or the community

polling the jury: calling the names of persons on a jury and requiring each juror to declare what his verdict is before it is legally recorded

post mortem: after death

power of attorney: an instrument authorizing one to act for another

premeditate: to think or consider beforehand

presentment: a report by a grand jury of an offense from their own knowledge, without any bill of indictment

presumption: an inference as to the existence of some fact not known arising from its connection with facts that exist or are known to exist

prima facie: at first sight

prima facie case: a case in which the evidence is very strong against the defendant

primary evidence: term applied to originals of written documents when placed in evidence

pro and con: for and against

probation: release of one after conviction, conditionally, without confining him in prison

probative: tending to prove

Q

quasi crime: violations of law not constituting crimes but punishable as wrongs against the local or general public welfare; thus, minor offenses

quo warranto: a legal procedure to test an official's right to a public office or the right to hold a franchise, or to hold an office in a domestic corporation

R

reasonable: fit and appropriate

reasonable doubt: a doubt regarding the guilt of the accused person, which entitles him to an acquittal

rebuttal: evidence to the contrary

recidivist: habitual criminal

recognizance: a written statement before a court to do an act specified or to suffer a penalty

recrimination: accusation made by an accused person against his accuser

rehabilitate: to reform

remand: to send a prisoner back to jail after a hearing

removal: a federal procedure by which a fugitive from justice under U.S. laws is returned for trial to the federal district wherein he committed his crime. May also refer to removing the trial for a criminal action from one county to another county or to another court

replevin: an action to recover goods unlawfully taken or withheld

res adjudicate: doctrine that an issue or dispute litigated and determined in a case between opposing parties is deemed permanently decided between these parties

rescission: annulment of a contract

respondeat superior: general rule charging the master or employer with liability for his servant's or employee's negligence in an act causing injury to third persons

S

scienter: allegation that the defendant had knowledge or willfully committed the crime with which he is charged

situs delicti: the place where a crime originates (see locus delicti)

special verdict: a verdict written by the jury that finds the facts only, leaving the legal judgment to the judge

stare decisis: general rule that when an issue has been settled by a court decision, it forms a precedent which is not to be departed from in deciding similar future issues

struck jury: a special jury or a blue ribbon jury

suborn: to induce to commit perjury

subpoena: a court process requiring one to appear as a witness

subpoena duces tecum: a subpoena to produce records, books, and documents

subrogation: substitution of one person for another in respect to rights and claims, debts

sui generis: of the same kind (see noscitur a sociis)

summons: a court order requesting one to appear to answer a charge

surety: a bondsman

surname: a family name

suspend sentence: hold back a sentence pending a prisoner's good behavior

T

talesman: person summoned to fill a panel of jurors when the regular panel is exhausted

testimony: spoken or written evidence

tolling the statute: facts that remove the statute of limitations as a bar to a criminal prosecution

tort: a breach of legal duty caused by a wrongful act or neglect resulting in injury or loss for which the injured party may sue for damages

trespass: illegal entry into another's property

true bill: indictment

trustee: one who lawfully holds property in custody for the benefit of another

turpitude: anything done contrary to justice, honesty, morals; same as moral turpitude

U

undertaking: a written agreement to appear in court when released on bail

usury: unlawful interest on a loan

V

veniremen: persons ordered to appear to serve on a jury or composing a panel of jurors

venue: the place or location where the cause of legal action arises

verdict: the findings of jury or judge in a criminal proceeding

vi et armis: phrase used in indictments and information indicating the crime was committed with force, by violence, weapons

voir dire: preliminary examination of a witness or a juror to test competency, suitability

W

waive: to give up a right

warrant: a written court order given to a peace officer to arrest the one named in it

Z

zoning laws: laws specifying the use to which land in a city may be put; for example, residential, commercial, industrial, etc. May regulate height, width, and size of structures in a certain district; justified as a form of police power by the city or state